THE FEMALE ATHLETE

a coach's guide to conditioning and training

THE FEMALE
ATHLETE *a coach's guide*
to conditioning and training

CARL E. KLAFS, Ph.D., F.A.C.S.M.

Professor Emeritus, Physical Education,
California State University, Long Beach, California

M. JOAN LYON, Ph.D.

Professor of Physical Education,
California State University,
Long Beach, California

SECOND EDITION

with 218 *illustrations*

THE C. V. MOSBY COMPANY

Saint Louis 1978

SECOND EDITION

Copyright © 1978 by The C. V. Mosby Company

All rights reserved. No part of this book may be reproduced in any manner without written permission of the publisher.

Previous edition copyrighted 1973

Printed in the United States of America

The C. V. Mosby Company
11830 Westline Industrial Drive, St. Louis, Missouri 63141

Library of Congress Cataloging in Publication Data

Klafs, Carl E
  The female athlete.

  Includes bibliographical references and index.
  1. Physical education for women. 2. Athletes,
Women. 3. Coaching (Athletics). 4. Sports—
Accidents and injuries. 5. Sports for women.
I. Lyon, Muriel Joan, joint author. II. Title.
GV439.K47 1978   796'.019'4   77-27418
ISBN 0-8016-2681-1

C/CB/CB 9 8 7 6 5 4 3 2 1

To the young female athletes of today,
who through their pursuit of excellence in sports,
will become the women champions
of tomorrow.

C. E. K.

M. J. L.

Preface

   With the emergence of girls and women into full-fledged sports participation, a new set of values has been established. No longer is it necessary to "justify" performance in certain sports nor are restraints or barriers imposed because common opinion holds an activity as being unsuitable for females. Girls and women today compete in almost all of the sports in which males participate and in many instances with or against them in a variety of situations. With the fund of new knowledge regarding the female and her response to stressful sports performance, the focus of this book is toward assisting the sportswoman and the coach in applying sound fundamental principles in devising and carrying out a program of preparation that will allow the athlete to work toward achieving her maximum potential.

   The presentation is geared to students whose scientific background may be somewhat limited, and to this end technical terms and expressions are clarified within the body of the text. A glossary further enhances the student's understanding of the material presented. Suggested reading materials and technical reference sources are found at the conclusion of each chapter.

   The emphasis of the book is on conditioning as a means of injury prevention as well as performance improvement. A number of chapters deal with injury prevention, sequelae, treatment, and physical restoration. Although this text is in no way to be considered an athletic injury book, nonetheless, we believe that a knowledge of basic sports medicine should be within the purview of every athlete and coach. To this end, an introduction to the causes, care, and treatment of the more common injuries is presented.

   An unusual feature of this book is the chapter "The Conditioning Program in Action," which presents the achievements and the personal conditioning programs of a number of national and world-class women champions and coaches in a wide variety of sports.

   We wish to express appreciation and gratitude to Barbara Cummings and Helene Arnheim for their very fine artwork, to Wendy Soon, Women's Athletic Trainer, California State University at Long Beach, for her suggestions, and to the many photographers who contributed so graciously, especially Bill Stuart. Special thanks are in order to the athletes and coaches who gave so willingly and enthusiastically of their time and information.

Carl E. Klafs
M. Joan Lyon

Contents

PART ONE

Historical background

1 □ History and current trends

Members of the human race have engaged in competitive sports since the dawn of time. Competition is a natural, healthy concomitant of man's life. Unfortunately history indicates that until contemporary times such competition was almost without exception the sole prerogative of the male, ostensibly growing out of his need to ready himself for war while permitting him to release the pent-up energy of his competitive nature in activities that provided an opportunity not only to match his prowess with that of his contemporaries but also created situations wherein he could earn the esteem and approbation of the opposite sex—a phenomenon observed in most higher animals.

For thousands of years feats of athletic prowess have been commemorated by inscriptions upon monuments dedicated to the physical abilities of the male; such reminders, however, have been virtually nonexistent for the female. Woman's lot throughout history has been that of childbearing, housekeeping, and toil. Until relatively recent times the exhibition of physical prowess was considered the sole domain of the male. Only since 1900 has woman been viewed as capable of holding her own in physical competition. Participation in sports by the female has been largely governed by the times. In the higher civilizations of the past, prejudicial societal patterns of culture, ethics, and morals decreed that woman was not only physically incapable of strenuous activity but that woman's participation in such activities was sinful and degrading.

There are only scattered references in ancient history to organized athletic activities for women prior to the advent of the Spartan state. As ancient Egypt progressed from a relatively primitive state to an advanced civilization, provision was made for the inclusion of physical activities within the structure of formal education, particularly for the young. These activities included gymnastics, exercises, wrestling, lifting and swinging weights, swimming, ball games, and dancing for both sexes of various ages. It is interesting to note that the Egyptians also engaged in ball-and-racket type of games. The participation of girls and women in these activities was a common occurrence. In most of the ancient cultures—China, Babylon, Sumer, and Assyria—the physical activities of women were limited principally to dancing, particularly in religious festivals, although there was a considerable amount of folk dancing. In Persia, however, physical activities and dancing in particular were forbidden to women by religious edict.

Ancient Greece

In ancient Greece, especially during the Aegean period, the physical activities of girls and women were restricted principally to dancing, which played an important role in the cultural and social life of that era. During the Homeric period, however, both girls and boys participated in a number of games and sports activities, many of which resembled those of modern times. As boys grew older, however, they continued to participate in these activities, while

3

the girls were relegated to household tasks. Plato, in developing his concept of the ideal state, postulated that all men *and* women should engage in similar gymnastic training.[8]

The lot of Spartan girls and women was indeed a quite different one. They were not secluded as they became older and held an important place in the societal structure. They were urged to participate in vigorous activities. The girls were given physical training similar to the boys, but under the direction and supervision of women trainers. Girls exercised in the nude publicly in such activities as running, jumping, throwing the javelin and weights, and wrestling. The aim was to train the body so that a strong, healthy, vigorous, mature woman would evolve, capable of bearing healthy children who would be a credit and of service to the state. Training of girls began at the age of about 7 years and continued until the age of 20 years (unless there was an early marriage). The girls were not removed from their homes as were the boys (who were taken by the state at the age of 6 years). Instead, girls were permitted to remain at home to learn household arts.

In Athenian society the picture was very different. Boys began their formal education at an early age, but girls remained at home and participated in little or no physical sports with the exception of some dancing. Athenian women recognized and acknowledged the superiority of the Spartan women in beauty, strength, and social position.[2]

The Grecian games. In all probability, organized sporting events have been held since the year 1000 B.C. References to such events appear in numerous historical documents dealing with that period. It is conceivable that they may have been held prior to that time as well. However, organized sports, or athletics as we usually identify them, appear to have come into a structured existence with the advent of the Olympic Games in 776 B.C. They were held uninterruptedly at 4-year intervals, wars notwithstanding, for a thousand years.[3] A careful perusal of the descriptions of these religious games shows that, with a few noticeable exceptions, the games were strictly all-male affairs. On occasion limited participation of women in special events was permitted. Harris,[3] who has probably done the most exhaustive research on the history of Greek athletics of that era, states that even though the information on men's athletics is scanty, information on womens' participation in athletic events is even more scarce.

The sum of knowledge of such participation is based solely upon three substantiating pieces of epigraphic information. One, from Delphi, is a base or pedestal upon which at one time stood three statues raised in honor of the three daughters of Hermesianax, citizens of Caesarea Tralles, who distinguished themselves at various games. The first daughter won the stade (200-yard foot race) at both the Pythian and at the Isthmian Games, the first girl ever to achieve such a feat; the second won the war chariot race at the Isthmian Games and the stade at both the Nemean and Sicyon Games; and the third daughter achieved fame by winning the stade at Asclepeia and another event (event and festival not discernible). This inscription dates from the middle of the first century A.D. From this inscription, Harris says that it has been determined that early in the Christian era there were well-established contests for women athletes at the same locales as those for the men—Olympia, Sicyon, Epidaurus, Nemea, Isthmia, and Delphi.

These games appear to have been of considerable size and reputation since girls from Asia Minor crossed to the Greek mainland to participate. Another such inscription commemorating the victory in a girls' race has been recorded from Patrae on the Gulf of Corinth.[4]

Men's athletics were exceedingly diversified, although in terms of importance wrestling came first and then running. The term "gymnastic" meant literally to perform exercises while naked; only the Spartan women performed in this fashion. The women did not participate in the more brutal events such as boxing and the pankration, an event in which there was a mixture of boxing and wrestling. Spartan women, however, did engage in wrestling. Running and chariot driving appear to have been the main types of competition in which the women took part. Plato in *The Republic* proposed athletic training for women and favored fencing and running, suggesting a program of races for girls ranging from the stade, or stadium (approximately 200 yards), up to a race of approximately 1/2 mile (dolichos).[4] It would appear from the very limited evidence at hand that for some centuries Greek girls, lightly clothed, engaged in races at local meetings and school contests and then, in the period marking the beginning of the Christian era, were able to compete in organized games that were held at the various sites for men's athletics.

The Middle Ages

During the Dark Ages, which followed the fall of the Roman empire, and during the early part of the Renaissance, asceticism and later scholasticism virtually eliminated the participation of women, and to a considerable degree that of men, in sports. Asceticism branded anything pleasurable as "sinful," while scholasticism established the feudal concept of chivalry, which permitted little or nothing of a physical nature to be done by women of the higher social classes. During the Renaissance, women began to participate in games again, although such games as tennis, as it was played in that period, were a far cry from the vigorous activity that marks tennis games today. In the seventeenth and eighteenth centuries a number of sports were introduced—tennis, club ball, archery, and handball—all finding immediate favor with the distaff side. 1600's—1700's

The nineteenth century 1800's

With the rise of the turnverein movement in Germany in 1810 and the subsequent development of Swedish gymnastics, provision was made for female participation. Since that time, both in this country and abroad, there has been a steady increase in women's sports activities, with some periods evidencing a sharp increase and others some recession. During the first half of the nineteenth century, athletic activities involving women occurred principally in Germany and the countries immediately adjacent to it. The Revolution of 1849 in Germany caused an exodus of many intellectuals to the United States, where a number of them were engaged as teachers and educators. Their enlightened views concerning the emancipation of women were soon widely disseminated and began to make an impact upon the cultural mores of the day, with the result that sports activities for women began to appear shortly after the Civil War, albeit in a somewhat scattered pattern.

The United States

Women's sports and athletics in the United States, exclusive of gymnastics and gymnastic drills (which were conducted in the American turnvereins instituted in 1859), trace their beginning to the acceptance of tennis as a sport at Mount Holyoke Female Seminary in 1875. Five years later Wellesley instituted crew rowing for women and in the following decade a number of other sports were established (Fig. 1-1). In 1894 Smith began to schedule a modified type of basketball for girls; such was its popularity that by the following year it had spread to the West Coast, remaining strictly a girls' game until 1910.[6]

During the first decade of the twentieth century, women's sports caught on. Many women's colleges had sports programs involving bicycling, tennis, boating, hiking, and basketball; they also participated in intercollegiate competition. Mount Holyoke Female Seminary, upon being presented with an ice rink, not only instituted skating but formed a hockey club as well![4] In 1905 a team of United States women golfers won the English women's tournament in Scotland. In the year 1910 interscholastic basketball was introduced, a sport which virtually swept the Midwest and the South and persisted in popularity for many years. In the 10 years preceding World War I, basketball became the prime sport, involving competition between colleges, high schools, and independent clubs. According to Rice et al.,[6] 22% of the colleges in 1920 had some form of intercollegiate sports for women.

During the 1920s there was a gradual rising tide of opposition to interscholastic competitive sports and athletics. The trend moved toward intramural and playday type of competition. This kind of competition persisted until quite recently and is still practiced in some areas as being preferable to interscholastic competition. During the 1920s, governing associations grew extensively and formulated rules and regulations that severely limited any form of extramural com-

Fig. 1-1. The sports clothing of the 1890s hampered physical performance.

petition. In some parts of the country the philosophy arose that not only was extramural competition unladylike but also that indulging in strenuous activities and competition was physically and mentally harmful to girls and young women. By 1930 the percentage of higher institutions participating in some form of intercollegiate women's competition had dropped to 12%.

This particular philosophy continued well into the 1950s, when in the aftermath of World War II, greater emancipation for women and a changing social pattern, coupled with ever-increasing scientific knowledge, reversed the trend almost entirely. During the last decade there has been a strong movement toward interscholastic and intercollegiate competition for women. The tremendous influence of the Olympic Games has brought to the public an awareness of the values of such competition so that today it has become the "in" thing to be associated with athletics rather than to consider such activity as an anathema.

Olympic competition

The first Olympic competition for women took place in 1900 when they were permitted to compete in swimming and tennis. In 1920 and again in 1924 women competed in these sports and also in fencing in the latter games. Two years later a special Olympic committee was formed to deal with regulation of the sports for women. Although an attempt was made to offer track and field for women in the next games, the response was anything but overwhelming. As a result, during the Olympic Congress of 1930, President Baillet-Latour of the International Olympic Committee attempted to limit women's competition solely to gymnastics, swimming, tennis, and skating. Fortunately the proposal was defeated by a majority vote.[1] Since that day the gates to Olympic competition for women have opened wide. Not only has the program of competition been greatly expanded to include most of the same activities in which the men participate but the total number of female competitors now compares favorably with that of the opposite sex.

Changing attitudes toward female sports participation

Athletics for men developed entirely outside the pale of educational institutions, with the result that for many years the control of such activities at both high school and college levels was totally without administrative sanction, being vested in the hands of former graduates and outside athletic organizations. These organizations operated to control sports completely outside the jurisdiction of the various educational institutions. Professionalism began to make inroads upon amateur sports. A philosophy geared to winning at all costs was among the undesirable concomitants of these organizations.

With the formulation of women's sports programs under the aegis of the various women's physical education departments (or physical training departments as they were then known), an attempt was made to avoid the same pitfall as the men. But the result was that the interim from the mid-1920s until the mid-1950s was characterized by a trend away from strenuous all-out interscholastic and intercollegiate competition in an attempt to keep such activities "feminine" and well within what were then considered safe psychological and physiological limits for women. This was particularly true with regard to competition during the menstrual cycle, when women were supposed to be completely shielded from any kind of emotional or physical trauma. To compound the situation, numerous "scientific" articles sought to verify woman's biological inferiority to man and her supposed inability to engage in active sports competition.[8] Rousseau, writing in 1762 about the desirable attributes of his future wife "Sophie," stated that "woman is especially designed for pleasing men." Diem quotes the famous German gynecologist H. Martius as stating in 1960:

> It contradicts the dignity of women when they try to establish records with contorted faces and limbs, and when they try to imitate the records of men in the decimal fractions of meters and minutes. For this kind of competition, women should be too proud. This kind of competition reminds us of the official gazette of the German swimming sports in 1895: "We have not lost our nerves in such a manner that we take the bait and we absolutely do not want to know anything of female natation!"[*]

Coubertin, often called the Father of modern Olympics, was no friend of women's sports where the Olympic Games were concerned. Writing in his *Revue Olympique* in 1912, he stated that the Olympic Games should be the sole purview of men. "Women," he stated, "have but one task, that of the role of crowning the winner with garlands, as was their role in ancient Greece."[1] When one reads statements like this, it appears that there are still those who believe woman's place on the field of competition should not be that of an active participant but rather that of an accessory after the fact.

Over the years most objections to women's sports participation have been subjective in nature, often predicated upon the sentimental thesis that woman is fragile in nature and dainty in appearance. From an esthetic standpoint the appearance of a woman exhibiting physical prowess or indulging in activity to the point of active perspiration was revolting to those who had an idealistic concept of womanhood. Oddly enough, little thought or consideration was given to the plight of the common women who since the beginning of time have toiled in the fields and performed hard physical labor comparable to that performed by their male counterparts. Not too many years ago a well-known female educator was heard to correct a male observer who, with some temerity, had ventured to suggest while observing a class of young women who were engaging in moderately strenuous physical exercise that it appeared to him, upon seeing evidence of perspiration upon their brows (probably because of the high temperature), that it was good for them to sweat. With some asperity the teacher corrected him, stating, "Young man, young ladies never sweat, nor do they perspire. They merely glow!" Today sweating is no longer an unmentionable word but is regarded rather as a natural, healthy biological function, certainly one that the male has no exclusive claim on.

In the mid-1920s an ever-increasing amount of scientific evidence regarding women's sports participation was accumulated using carefully controlled research procedures, but it was not until the mid-1960s that the women educators who controlled the female sports picture began to accept such evidence. The result has been a diametric change in the philosophy governing girls' and womens' athletics and a consequent change in the field of physical education and athletics,

---

[*]Quoted by Diem, L.: Rev. Anal. Educ. Phys. Sport **8:**2, 1966. Although this statement has suffered somewhat by translation, its meaning is clear.

a change that is still going on, as evidenced by new programs reflecting a more liberal approach. Today we see unlimited participation of women in practically all sports, especially on the intercollegiate level, and an ever-growing tide of such competition at the secondary school level (Fig. 1-2).

Increased knowledge of the effects of strenuous activity upon the female, coupled with the emancipation of woman from the roles of homemaker and mother, have done much to dispel previous doubts. Live coverage by television of the Olympic Games and other national and international competitive events has permitted the public to see not only that woman is capable of such activity but also that she is undoubtedly benefited by it as well; this has certainly helped in establishing a more positive attitude. Such portrayals have done much to engender enthusiasm in younger girls for participation in athletics. The young woman of today is a far cry from her predecessor of some generations ago. No longer is she the pampered, often self-indulgent young woman given to the "vapors" of mid-Victorian literature and prone to swoon upon any pretext. She is a self-reliant individual, strong and capable of performing activities that call for the highest degree of skill and physical prowess. What is more, she enjoys doing them.

Current trends

Many of the reasons advanced in the past for keeping girls and women from all-out sports participation have been "legitimatized," so-called medical reasons

Fig. 1-2. Modern gymnast Shari Smith, nationally ranked gymnast and member of the 1977 United States Gymnastic Team, demonstrates that clothing styles and performance techniques have undergone radical changes.

that have not been substantiated by research. Such misinformation can be attributed to an interwoven complex of cultural, emotional, physical, psychological, and social factors that established the role and the mores of women in society. Today, with the clamor of modern woman for more freedom and equality, her maternal, political, sexual, and vocational roles are being constantly dissected and examined.[3] The net result has been the discarding of the old wives' tales of yesteryear.[5] A great deal of research has been done and is continually being carried on, helping to dispel most of these fallacious beliefs.[7] The present trend toward unlimited participation for women in wholesome competitive activities is gaining momentum.

Let it be stated here, unequivocally, that there is no reason, either psychological, physiological, or sociological, to preclude normal, healthy females from participating in strenuous physical activities; nor does such participation accentuate or develop male characteristics. Strenuous activity for the well-trained and well-conditioned female athlete results in good health and accentuates the very qualities that make her a woman. (See Fig. 1-3.)

Cultures and mores change; that which was totally unacceptable a generation ago is established social practice today. The picture is changing rapidly. Television, with its pictorial reports of the Olympic Games and national and international competition in a variety of sports, has established athletic activity as a desir-

Fig. 1-3. Competitive sport leagues are open to all ages.

able attribute of the female social culture and has popularized it to the extent that today we see young girls of preadolescent and early pubertal ages undergoing serious training in a variety of athletic activities. Records are continually being broken and a number of record performances are being posted by girls in their very early teens and younger, giving additional impetus to female sports. The awareness of the responsibilities associated with the changing sports picture is giving rise to more and more capably trained women coaches and trainers. It is our hope that this book will contribute to the knowledge of the field of female ath-

Fig. 1-4. Performers of the caliber of A. Nadia Comaneci, from Romania, and Svetlana Grozdova, from the U.S.S.R., have contributed greatly to the expanding sports horizon of the female.

letics and make available information that will be of assistance to participant, coach, and trainer.

Values of the competitive experience

Probably never before has the sphere of competitive sports been so available as a means of personal enrichment and satisfaction for girls and women. There is no doubt that competitive sports provide many females with an acceptable outlet or mode of control for aggressive behavior, formerly available only to males.

Meaning and satisfaction are also derived from the competitive situation by the opportunities afforded to assert oneself and to test oneself against others. The fact that women athletes have demonstrated a willingness and capability to train strenuously and practice for long hours is evidence of a high achievement need that is fulfilled through athletic competition. See Fig. 1-4.

Cultural pressure on individuals to conform to strict sex-role expectations is diminishing. With greater freedom from confining and arbitrary behavioral stereotypes, individuals are finding greater opportunities to realize their potentialities as humans, regardless of sex. More than ever before, athletically inclined girls and women have freedom to develop their interests and abilities, within the framework of competitive sports.

REFERENCES

1. Diem, L.: The olympic sport for women, evaluation of declarations, Rev. Anal. Educ. Phys. Sport **8:**2, 1966.
2. Durant, W.: The life of Greece, New York, 1939, Simon & Schuster, Inc.
3. Gendel, E.: Women and the medical aspects of sports, New York, 1960, Harper & Row, Publishers.
4. Harris, H. A.: Greek athletes and athletics, London, 1964, Hutchinson & Co.
5. Klafs, C. E., and Arnheim, D. D.: Modern principles of athletic training, ed. 4, St. Louis, 1977, The C. V. Mosby Co.
6. Rice, E. A., Hutchinson, J. L., and Lee, M.: A brief history of physical education, New York, 1958, The Ronald Press Co.
7. Thomas, C. L.: Effect of vigorous athletic activity on women. In American Academy of Orthopaedic Surgeons symposium on sports medicine, St. Louis, 1969, The C. V. Mosby Co.
8. Ulrich, C.: Women and sport. In Johnson, W. R.: editor: Science and medicine of exercise and sports, New York, 1960, Harper & Row, Publishers.

PART TWO

Anthropometric and physiological factors in sports performance

2 □ Anthropometric characteristics

ANATOMIC SEX DIFFERENCES AND IMPLICATIONS FOR PERFORMANCE

Growth. All human characteristics follow a bimodal curve; all traits except those directly related to reproduction overlap. The sexual differences increase with maturity as the result of both biological and cultural influences. Indeed, at times it is difficult to decide which has the greater effect.

The general growth curves of the two sexes more or less parallel one another until the ninth year, when the girl starts her prepubertal growth. At that time the linear growth of the girl decelerates, and with the onset of the menarche (the beginning of the menses), usually between the ages of 12 and 14 years, breadth increases. Growth in general terminates between the fifteenth and sixteenth year, when full maturity is achieved, whereas the male achieves full maturation and ultimate size at the age of 20 to 21 years. In the age range of 14 to 18 years, girls tend to show an increase in fat and boys in muscle.

Skeletal changes. Assessment of the degree of ossification is the most accurate method of determining maturity. Such assessment is usually made by means of x-ray studies of the metacarpal bones and the phalanges. Ossification is the process whereby bone salts are deposited in the organic matrix (the intercellular center) of bone, producing a hardening of the bone itself and a closure or bony union between the primary and secondary growth centers. The ossification dates provide a type of physiological clock that runs according to an exceedingly accurate schedule. However, the rate of ossification can be altered by nutrition, health, endocrine secretions, and other factors.

A growing girl at any age has reached greater maturity than a boy of the same age. X-ray assessment of the carpals and metacarpals indicates that these bones ossify sooner in the female than in the male. The pisiform bone of the female is usually completely ossified at the ages of 9 and 10 years, whereas complete ossification in the male does not occur until about the age of 13 years. The same pattern may be seen in the epiphyseal union of the metacarpals and phalanges, which is completely ossified in the female at the age of 16 years and at the age of 19 years in the male. The long bones of the body reveal a similar pattern. Generally speaking, growth in the length of the long bones will be completed some 1 to 3 years sooner in the female than in the male.[12]

A comparison of mature male and female skeletons reveals other significant differences. In general appearance the skeleton of the male is more rugged, the bones more massive and of greater density, and the long bones longer. The joints of the male are relatively larger and present a greater articular surface. However, if the knee joint is examined in terms of its width in proportion to height, the female has an advantage in that her wider knee joint probably provides more stability in relation to her size. The overall skeletal size and ruggedness give the male a decided superiority in leverage, arc of movement, and other aspects.

15

Trunk. If one were to draw two geometric figures, one to indicate the general proportions of the female trunk and the other those of the male, the former would be a truncated pyramid with the narrow portion uppermost, whereas the latter would be the reverse. The trunk of the male presents a wedge-shaped appearance because of his wider shoulders and narrower hips, whereas the female generally has a wider pelvis in relation to the width of her shoulders. Also, the female pelvis is more shallow than that of the male. The presence of fat pads over the hips serves to accentuate her pelvic width. Since there are extreme variations in the skeletal morphology of both sexes, generalizations are subject to criticism. Certainly more anthropometric studies need to be made before such generalizations can be accepted as fact.

Pelvis. The pelvis consists of two sections, each composed of three bones, the *ilium,* which is the upper portion at the side of the hip; the *ischium,* which is below and to the rear; and the *pubis,* which is below and forward. The pelvis is held together by three extremely strong ligaments. In front the two pubes are separated by a heavy cartilaginous disc but are firmly held together by other strong ligaments. During pregnancy the ligaments soften and relax as a result of the action of certain hormones, permitting some degree of movement at the symphysis pubis and therefore expansion of the pelvis. This phenomenon occurs to a lesser degree during menstruation.[11]

Chest. Chest measurements of both sexes vary at different age levels so that it is difficult to make a generalization. Up to the age of 3 years the female has the greater chest girth relative to height, but beyond this point the male has a greater girth. The chest circumference of the male is greater except possibly at the ages of 12 and 13 years, when the girl, because of the adolescent spurt, will frequently equal or surpass him. The thoracic index, found by dividing chest width by chest depth and multiplying by 100, indicates that the maximum is attained at the age of 11 years for girls and 14 years for boys. Beyond these ages a slight increase in this index is manifested by the girl, whereas the index for the boy rises quite rapidly so that at the age of 16 years he exhibits a broader chest than the female.

Shoulder width. Measurements of shoulder width indicate that in the age span from 11 to 15 years the girl has relatively wider shoulders than the boy, and that at age 13 years she exceeds him in measurements of shoulder width relative to height. From the age of 15 years on, the shoulder width of the male increases, until at age 19 years it is noticeably larger.

Abdomen. Although the male has a larger thoracic region, the female, conversely, has a larger abdominal cavity. This segment contains relatively larger visceral organs and the additional organs of reproduction.

Upper extremities. Hrdlička,[6] in measuring thousands of male and female humeri, found the upper arm of the female to be shorter and smaller than the forearm. In males and females of the same height the upper arm was found to be longer in the male.

Lower extremities. The male shows a relatively longer length in this measurement also. The leg length of men is about 52% of their height, whereas that of women is 51.2% of their height. Typically a girl's leg is longer than a boy's from age 7 years to about 12 years, whereupon the boy takes over the lead and never surrenders it. The lower leg of the girl is relatively much shorter than that of the male; the male's foot is of greater length and breadth.

Height. From birth, the male has a slight advantage in terms of height. This difference, however, is so small as to be barely discernible. At about the age of 9 or 10 years the female begins to surpass him, and, with the onset of puberty, the rapid acceleration of growth will give the girl an edge of at times as much as 2 inches over her male counterpart. However, this superiority is short-lived. At the age of 15 years the boy begins his growth spurt and maintains the height advantage from then on. In general, females stop growing in height between the ages of 18 and 20 years, whereas males continue to grow until the age of 20 to 23 years. The mean height of the female is 5 to 6 inches shorter than that of the male.

Weight. The weight pattern approximates that of height in that accelerated pubertal growth may give the girl a weight advantage of 4 to 5 pounds by the time midadolescence is attained. Once again the boy catches up and surpasses the girl at the age of 15 years and continues; when he reaches maturity, he has a weight advantage of approximately 25 pounds. One must keep in mind that we are speaking only in terms of bone structure and lean muscle mass.

Center of gravity. The center of gravity is considered to be that point within the body at which the total weight of the body is concentrated. It is a most important concept, particularly in the areas of physical education and athletics, since the center of gravity determines balance. It has been found that the mean center of gravity in man is located at a point 56.7% of his height above ground, whereas woman's mean center of gravity is at 56.1% of her height, a difference of 0.6%.[13] Man's greater height, shorter torso, wider shoulders, and narrower hips account for the difference. The shorter legs and broader pelvis of the female establish a lower center of gravity and hence endow her with better balance than the male, who would need to widen his stance somewhat in a given situation to obtain a comparable degree of balance (Fig. 2-1).

Adiposity. The tendency of the female to accumulate fat over the hips, on the thighs, in the tela adiposa (the ventral apron of fat), and the breasts explains her relatively greater weight in relation to her size. The average female possesses approximately 7 pounds more subcutaneous fat than does her male counterpart. The percent of fat to body weight is 22% to 25% for the female as compared to 14% for the male. This accumulation of fat appears as early as the age of 4 years, when the girl already has a greater proportion of fat and continues to increase this percentage until she reaches maturity.[8]

Although this tendency toward accretion of adiposity does pose some disadvantages, there are some advantages as well. The female exhibits a greater buoyancy (some 10% greater) than does the male, loses much less body heat in cold water, and can tolerate heat better than does the male.

Heart size. Various studies have shown that, with the exception of the twelfth and thirteenth year, the male heart is larger. The transverse diameter of the heart indicates this difference; mean measurements for men and women are 12.13 and 10.67 cm., respectively. The difference may well be accounted for by the male's larger physical size and greater percentage of lean muscle mass, whereas the female has a greater percentage of adipose tissue. There is also a strong difference in the ratio of heart weight to body weight. From the age of 10 years to the age of

Fig. 2-1. The woman athlete's lower center of gravity is an advantage in events requiring good balance.

60 years the average value for females is only 85% to 90% of the value for males. After the age of 60 years the values are similar.

Effectiveness of neuromuscular response. In the age group of 6 to 18 years there is little if any difference between girls and boys insofar as efficiency in the use of small muscles is concerned. De Vries[2] reports that the female generally has greater manual dexterity than the male. According to research aimed at determining the difference in reaction time between men and women, there is no significant difference between the sexes in speed of reaction to a visual stimulus. Men, however, do have a faster movement time. Athletes of both sexes respond faster than do nonathletes.[4,5,10]

Muscle mass and strength. As stated earlier, the male possesses a larger muscle mass; consequently, his strength-to-weight ratio is greater. Since his muscles are of greater bulk and strength potential is directly related to the physiological cross section of the muscle itself, he possesses greater strength in terms of muscle contraction. This advantage, coupled with the advantages he enjoys in respect to leverage and angles of pull, makes it possible for him to perform at levels of strength not possible for women. The average muscle strength of women is about two thirds that of men; with the same kind of training stimulus, strength increases more and faster in men than in women, indicating that the difference in muscle strength can increase after training.[14]

Prior to puberty the girl holds her own, often surpassing the boy in terms of strength performance. After puberty, however, because of the change in the strength-to-weight ratio, the male is stronger.

There are differences between the male body and female body not only in proportions of various tissues but also in the chemical constituents of those tissues. For example, there is approximately 23% more sulfur present in female skeletal muscle tissue and a difference in creatinine coefficients when compared to male tissues.[2] The precise significance of these values in terms of muscle metabolism and performance is presently unknown, but future research should be able to determine their implications.

Body efficiency. The human body operates at an efficiency factor of approximately 25% to 30%. Out of a possible 100% potential energy available for performing any task, some 70% to 75% is expended to overcome gravitational forces, manipulate skeletal levers, metabolize food, and overcome inertia, muscle viscosity, and unfavorable angles of pull. The center of gravity, which is relatively high in the human, affects the stability of the body. Because of the high center of gravity, stability becomes somewhat tenuous in the erect posture if the body is subjected to external forces. A person standing is easily moved off balance, particularly if the external force is projected laterally. To offset this loss in efficiency, one needs to lower the center of gravity by widening the stance, thus gaining greater stability. Given situations require the body to make compensatory adjustments, all of which contribute to some loss in efficiency.

Performance implications. A number of anatomic factors predispose the male to be superior in athletic performance. His overall greater muscularity and strength, longer limbs, and greater lean body mass contribute to an ability to develop faster acceleration of body segments, higher final velocities, and subsequently greater momentum to sports objects as well as to himself in running and jumping events. Consequently, males enjoy an advantage in almost all sports events, and particularly so in those events that largely depend on strength, speed, and power.

Greater muscularity in the shoulders of the male endow him with a greater ability potential in events requiring shoulder and arm strength, such as throwing, pole vaulting, and parallel bars.

The female's anatomic characteristics have been compared to those of the male, not to demonstrate the superiority or inferiority of one sex over the other, but merely to provide a baseline for objective assessment of these factors and to show relationships between structural characteristics and athletic performance.

Separate categories of athletes. The structural and physiological differences between the sexes emphasize the need for separate but equal competitive opportunities for the female and the male athlete. In many sports, individuals are classified according to height and weight, with athletes competing within their own category. The light-weight wrestler is no less a champion than is the heavyweight. Simon de Beauvoir, in *The Second Sex*,[1] expresses the concept well:

> And in sports, the end in view is not success independent of physical equipment; it is rather the attainment of perfection within the limitations of each physical type.

We suggest that the female athlete is indeed in a class by herself and should have every opportunity that she desires to pursue excellence within the realm of sport.

PHYSICAL CHARACTERISTICS OF FEMALE ATHLETES

A review of literature on studies pertaining to the physique of female athletes, including comparisons of female athletes with nonathletes, and of differences in body structure between athletes engaged in different sports.[7,9,14,15] Some generalizations follow.

Comparisons with nonathletes

Height-weight. Investigations indicate that sportswomen are taller and heavier than nonathletic women, but this is partially a function of the sport population studied. For example, the low height of gymnasts, swimmers, and distance runners, when combined with the tallness of other Olympic competitors, resulted in an average height not significantly different from that of the nonsportswomen. But mean weights of female athletes tend to be heavier, probably because of the greater muscularity of these active women (Fig. 2-2).

Fig. 2-2. The female athlete is typified by a smaller muscle mass and slightly greater adiposity in comparison to her male counterpart. Yet sportswomen are higher in mesomorphy than are nonathletic women.

Body composition. Although estimates of body fat in average college females have ranged from 23% to 25.6%, relatively little data is available for women athletes. There is some evidence to indicate, however, that the amount of body fat varies between athletes engaged in different sports. Wilmore[14] found that highly trained female runners had relative fat values of less than 10%. On the other hand, women track and field athletes specializing in the throwing events displayed a slightly higher percent of body fat than did the nonathletic population (Fig. 2-3).

Somatotype. Sheldon developed a system to classify body form on the basis of three primary components termed "ectomorphy," "mesomorphy," and "endomorphy." Endomorphy is characterized by a predominance of visceral tissue; mesomorphy by a predominance of muscle tissue; and ectomporphy by a predominance of skin, appendages, and the nervous system. Sportswomen have been found to be higher in mesomorphy than nonathletes, whereas nonsportswomen are more endomorphic than are sportswomen.

Comparisons between sport groups

Height-weight. The tallest, heaviest athletes are those excelling in the track and field throwing events—shot put, discus, and javelin. Shot-putters in one study averaged 5 feet, 6 inches in height and 178 pounds in weight. This is an interesting contrast to a study in which the average height of gymnasts was found to be 5 feet, 3 inches (159.34 cm) and the average weight 118 pounds (53.52 kg.).

Malina[9] investigated the participants in the National Intercollegiate Track and Field Competition for Women and found height, weight, and body type differ-

A   **B**   **C**

Fig. 2-3. Phenotypes. **A,** Endomorph. **B,** Mesomorph. **C,** Ectomorph. Success in a given activity often depends on body type. (Photo by William Stuart, Huntington Beach, Calif.)

ences between athletes in different events, as well as between athletes and the nonathletic control group. The data indicated that all athletes except distance runners were taller than the nonathletic control group. The sprinters tended to be muscular and short-legged, with muscular arms—the latter ascribed to the pumping action of the arms in a sprint. Jumpers were of the linear type, longer-legged, and muscular, whereas the throwers were physically the largest, being taller and heavier, with broader shoulders and hips. Distance runners were small but evidenced longer legs relative to their height and slight muscularity. The control group of nonathletes had more body fat and larger shoulder and hip widths. In general, the physical characteristics identified with the particular type of sport agreed very well with similar studies made of male athletes. The conclusions of the researchers was that body build and body composition determined to a large degree the limits of an individual's athletic ability in track-and-field events.

A study comparing the phenotypes of women basketball players with those of hockey players concluded that mesomorphy was more prevalent among hockey players, indicating a blockier body mass, whereas basketball players tended more toward ectomorphy.[9] In both sports, defensive players were taller and heavier than offensive players. The conclusion was that phenotype could be a useful index in selecting hockey players. The results of this study also compare favorably with the results of studies conducted with male athletes.

Body composition. Malina's investigation also revealed that the percent of body fat of track and field athletes was related to the type of event in which they specialized. Throwers had a higher percent body fat, around 26%, compared with about 20% in runners and jumpers. Swimmers, basketball players, and volleyball players in another study showed body fat percentages more similar to the college-age nonathletic population, whereas Wilmore[14] found national-class distance runners' percentage of body fat to be less than 10%.

REFERENCES

1. de Beauvoir, S.: The second sex, New York, 1953, Alfred A. Knopf, Inc.
2. de Vries, H. A.: Physiology of exercise for physical education and athletics, ed. 2, Dubuque, Iowa, 1974, William C. Brown Co., Publishers.
3. Gerber, E., et al.: The American woman in sport, Reading, Pa., 1974, Addison-Wesley Publishing Co.
4. Henry, F. M.: Influence of motor and sensory sets on reaction latency and speed of discrete movements, Res. Q. Am. Assoc. Health Phys. Educ. **31:**459, 1960.
5. Henry, F. M., and Rogers, D. E.: Increased response latency for complicated movements and a memory drum theory of neuromotor reaction, Res. Q. Am. Assoc. Health Phys. Educ. **31:**448, 1960.
6. Hrdlička, A.: Practical anthropometry, Philadelphia, 1939, Wistar Institute of Anatomy and Biology.
7. Johnston, R. E., and Watson, J. M.: A comparison of the phenotypes of women basketball and hockey players, N.Z. J. Health Phys. Educ. Rec. **3:**48, 1968.
8. Klafs, C. E., and Arnheim, D. D.: Modern principles of athletic training, ed. 4, St. Louis, 1977, The C. V. Mosby Co.
9. Malina, R. M., Harper, A. B., and Avent, H. H.: Physique of female track and field athletes, J. Am. Coll. Sports Med. **3:**32, 1971.
10. Pierson, W. R., and Lockhart, A.: Effect of menstruation on simple reaction and movement time, Br. Med. J. **1:**796, 1963.
11. Rasch, P. J., and Burke, R. K.: Kinesiology and applied anatomy, ed. 4, Philadelphia, 1971, Lea & Febiger.

12. Ulrich, C.: Women and sport. In Johnson, W. R., editor: Science and medicine of exercise and sports, New York, 1960, Harper & Row, Publishers.
13. Wells, K. F.: Kinesiology, ed. 5, Philadelphia, 1966, W. B. Saunders Co.
14. Wilmore, J. H.: Strength, endurance and body composition of the female athlete. Paper presented to the National Conference on the Medical Aspects of Sports, Anaheim, Calif., December 1, 1973.
15. Wilmore, J. H.: Athletic training and physical fitness, Boston, 1977, Allyn & Bacon, Inc.

3 □ Physiological capabilities

In a biological comparison of the sexes the physiological parameters provide much interesting information, for it is here that certain distinct differences manifest themselves and play an important role in determining the capabilities of the individual in regard to sports. Contrary to common opinion, the female is not so handicapped in these respects as most people assume. Social and subcultural mores have a great deal more to do with the relegation of the female to certain prescribed roles than any particular physiological limitations; this has been particularly true in Western society, wherein she has been forced into a secondary role from which she is finally emerging, albeit at not so rapid a rate as desirable. Such cultural patterns have erected a restrictive barrier in the past insofar as physical performance was concerned. Current recognition and acceptance of the fact that girls and women are fully capable of participation in any and all sports, regardless of the physiological demands, has resulted in a veritable rash of record-breaking performances and, in particular, by very young females. These record-breaking performances are bringing to attention the fact that women are capable of and appear to thrive on strenuous physical activity. See Fig. 3-1.

As more and more positive information about biological responses to stress comes to light, the more apparent it becomes that the female can hold her own in most activities heretofore considered the domain of the male. This is not to say that the best female performer can perform at par with the best male performer in every sport. Both structural and physiological entities favor the male in activities requiring strength and he will therefore continue to dominate in those areas. We must recognize that the female performer, within her range of capabilities, can still improve performance to the point where it will be comparable to that of the male in terms of their potentialities. However, the absolute working capacity of the female has been established to be approximately 20% less than that of the male.[11] See Fig. 3-2.

Genetic differences

Differences between the sexes commence in utero, the female embryo being created by the joining of two X chromosomes and the male embryo by the joining of an X and a Y chromosome. It appears that the formation of the female embryo through a double X chromosome linkage is a decided advantage in terms of survival in that if one chromosome with a defective gene of the recessive type is present, the other normal matching gene may block the effect of the defective gene. However, should there be a defective X chromosome in the case of the male embryo, there is no matching normal gene present to block the defective one. As a result, spontaneous abortion or some genetic imperfection may result.[22]

Fig. 3-1. Olympic gymnast Cathy Rigby shows excellent shoulder and arm strength in executing a one-handed walk-over.

PHYSIOLOGICAL SEX DIFFERENCES
Cardiovascular system

Blood constituents. Blood may be considered a typical connective tissue with numerous components and performing certain specific duties. It is composed of a fluid portion, the plasma; a fibrous portion, which appears only during the clotting phase; and a cellular portion, the red and white blood cells. Blood platelets, which are a part of the clotting mechanism, and chylomicrons, little fat droplets, are also found in the fluid portion. The duties of blood are twofold. Its first role is to transport oxygen, glucose, and nutrients to the tissues and wastes such as car-

Fig. 3-2. Ann Meyers of U.C.L.A. illustrates superb leg strength. (Photo by Tony Kawashima.)

bon dioxide and lactic acid away from the tissues for subsequent reconstitution or removal from the body. The second role is that of buffering, effected through the weakening of acid wastes produced through metabolic activity, thus preventing sharp changes in the chemical reactions of the tissues.

Exercise produces changes in blood composition, particularly in the red blood cells. Even after brief but intensive exercise, for example, running 200 meters, an increase in the number of red blood cells is noted.[22] The increase will depend on such factors as the work load and the duration of the exercise. At rest the average number of red blood cells in the male is 5 million/mm.³ of blood and that in the female 4½ million/mm.³. Postexercise values for the male range from 5,200,000 to 6,180,000, although the increase seldom reflects a rise of more than 10%, returning to preexercise levels in from ½ to 2 hours. Values for the female relate to her lower resting value. The rise is indicative of a compensatory adjustment to assure a more adequate oxygen supply. In the age group of 20 to 30 years, women have approximately 15% less hemoglobin and 6% less erythrocytes per cubic millimeter of blood.[10] This would indicate that men have a greater oxygen-carrying capacity than women. The specific gravity of the blood also reflects a difference, that of the female being lower than that of the male.

Blood pressure. Both the systolic and the diastolic blood pressure values are usually about 5 to 10 mm. Hg higher in the male. In girls the increase in systolic pressure at puberty is much less pronounced than in the male and is often followed by a decrease until the eighteenth year, at which time it assumes the pattern of the male, steadily increasing as one ages.[28] The systolic pressure of the female, after menopause tends to increase slightly over that of the male.

Heart weight. Heart weight in all mammals is directly proportional to body weight and can be found by multiplying 0.0066 times the body weight.[3] Although this ratio holds true in mammals from the smallest, such as a mouse, up to those the size of a horse, mammals that are capable of severe exercise have a heart-to-body weight ratio of greater than 0.6 (heart ratio = heart weight × 100 divided by body weight), whereas those incapable of sustained heavy work have a ratio of less than 0.6. The male possesses a larger heart than the female, probably because he has more muscular tissue and consequently a greater circulation. Inasmuch as heart rate is proportional to body size, a larger individual would have a slower heart rate. Accordingly, the female heart rate is some five to eight beats faster than that of the male.

Cardiac output and cardiac cost. Cardiac output is defined as the volume of blood ejected by the heart in a given unit of time, usually expressed liters per minute (L./min.). Åstrand and Rodahl[3] have found that the cardiac output required to transport 1 liter of oxygen during a submaximal work load was 9 liters of blood for women and 8 liters for men. The measured oxygen content in the blood was 16.7 ml. of oxygen/100 ml. of blood for women and 19.2 ml. oxygen/100 ml. of blood for men. It seems that the more efficient cardiac output of the male, along with his greater circulatory effectiveness, may be explained by the greater hemoglobin content of his blood as well as his greater heart size.

Oxygen pulse. This measure is used to ascertain how effectively the heart functions as a respiratory organ. It is a relative measure, taking into consideration blood volume, hemoglobin content, and body weight, and calculates the oxygen consumption in milliliters per heartbeat. During exercise the oxygen pulse increases rapidly at a rate comparable to that of the heartbeat increase. It reaches a maximal value ranging from 11 to 17 ml. when the heart rate is 130 to 140 beats per minute. It has been shown that there is a close relationship between the oxygen pulse rate of young women and young men who have similar heart rates while engaged in exercise of approximately 3,600 foot-pounds of work per minute. From 12 to 15 years of age, oxygen pulse rates are the same for both sexes. However, from the age of 15 years up to the age of 31 to 35 years, the male demonstrates a rapid increase in values (up to three times that of the female's rate, which remains unchanged).[10]

Respiratory system

Vital capacity. Vital capacity is the volume of air moved through the lungs from a maximal inspiration to a maximal expiration. This volume bears a direct relationship to body size, surface area, and height, the female thus having a smaller breathing capacity (about 10% less than that of a comparable male). This fact may be partially accounted for by her lower metabolic rate, which demands less oxygen. However, since she registers a higher per minute respiratory rate than the male, it may well be that her lower metabolic rate does not completely balance her smaller lung capacity.[3]

A large vital capacity is not in itself an indication of superior ability, nor may it be used as a prognosticator of physical capability. Rather, it is the effectiveness and the efficiency with which the vital capacity is used that determines these qualities. To a limited degree, vital capacity can be increased through training, but the principal benefit derived from training is more efficient utilization of one's inherent capacity. Karpovich and Sinning[22] have shown that the ratio of skin surface to vital capacity is greatest in male athletes and least in sedentary women. Their studies have also indicated that the average vital capacity of women college students is 3.4 liters. Åstrand and Rodahl,[3] in a study conducted on well-trained women physical education students, whose average age was 25 years, found that the women had an average vital capacity of 4.25 liters as compared to 5.70 liters for a comparable group of men. Men tend to breathe more abdominally or diaphragmatically, whereas women breathe higher in the chest, or costally. A good training regimen tends to produce diaphragmatic breathing in the female.

Maximum aerobic power. Maximum aerobic power (V_{O_2} max.) is defined as the greatest oxygen uptake attained by an individual while breathing air at sea level during the performance of physical work. Researchers have found maximum aerobic power to be the best way of determining endurance capability. Prior to the ages of 11 and 12 years, there appears to be no significant difference between boys and girls in respect to maximum aerobic power, but after this period

Fig. 3-3. Joan Lind, Olympic silver medalist, Single Sculls, registers an extremely high oxygen-uptake capacity.

the female drops to some 70% to 75% the power of the male. Both sexes peak at 18 to 20 years, followed by a gradual decrease as the years advance. It appears that within the competitive age range (12 to 21 years) the effect of training on the maximum aerobic power is independent of age, that is, age per se does not appear to influence the magnitude in gain of increased aerobic power.[12] See Fig. 3-3.

If the lean muscle mass of the female is compared with that of the male, it is evident that they have approximately the same oxygen uptake values per kilogram of body weight. Since women have a smaller body size, it would seem that the values should be higher. It has been postulated that again the difference may be attributable to the smaller hemoglobin concentration in the woman, which might restrict the complete utilization of the cardiac output for oxygen transport. Young girl swimmers show a much higher maximal oxygen uptake than do more sedentary girls.[2]

Erholungsquotient. De Vries,[10] reporting on a study done by Nocker and Bohlau in Germany, states that the *Erholungsquotient* ("recovery quotient," EQ), a measure of increased oxygen utilization during work to increased oxygen utilization during the recovery period, indicates the degree of physical work capacity possessed by individuals. EQ values for females are lower than those of males at all ages, indicating less intrusion upon anaerobic reserve by the male for a given amount of exercise.

Metabolism

The term "metabolism" designates the various chemical reactions that occur in the conversion of food to energy and subsequent use of such energy by the body. The *basal metabolic rate* (BMR) is the rate of conversion measured under so-called *basal conditions* — after 8 hours of restful sleep, 12 to 18 hours after the last meal, and without any physical activity or emotional excitement before the test, which is conducted at a comfortable temperature. The caloric expenditure of the body in relation to body surface area is the usual mode of expression; this measure gives a good indication of how effectively the body functions in converting food into energy. A synonym for the term "metabolic rate" could be "rate of heat production." The BMR represents the minimum amount of heat the body must produce in a given time to keep itself alive, the heat being supplied by the conversion of either stored food (in the body itself) or ingested food. Since the BMR is not identical for all individuals because of varying factors such as size, it must be computed on the basis of body surface area (BSA), sex, and age.

The metabolic rate of the female is lower than that of the male at all ages. It is probable that the greater proportion of adipose tissue to lean body mass is responsible to a considerable extent. The somewhat smaller size of the female is another factor. However, when the BMR is compared to lean muscle mass rather than to body surface area, the sex difference disappears. The metabolic rate, as such, has no bearing on the effectiveness and efficiency of muscular activity. It is significant, however, when considered in its relation to heat dissipation.

Women in the age range of 18 to 19 years usually average around 37 kcal.*/ m.² of body surface area per hour in caloric expenditure, and over a 24-hour

---

*Kilocalorie (kcal.) is also referred to as kilogram calorie and Calorie.

period will reflect basal rates ranging from 1,200 to 1,400 kcal., whereas young men of the same age and comparable body structure show values close to 40 kcal./m.^{2} of body surface area and basal rates in the neighborhood of 1,668 kcal. for a 24-hour period. Men oxidize their food approximately 5% to 7% faster than women; therefore their basal metabolic rate will be approximately 5% higher. At puberty the differential begins to increase slightly, until at around 20 years of age a gradual decrease sets in. The moderately active young woman needs about 2,400 kcal. per day, whereas her male counterpart requires 3,000 to 3,200 kcal. Younger persons tend to have higher values. Variations in metabolic rate are apparent during the menstrual cycle. The rate of metabolism also appears to have some effect upon red blood cells, hemoglobin content, and the specific gravity of blood as well as upon the rate of respiration.

The calcium metabolic rate of the female is apparently higher than that of the male since ossification of the bones occurs earlier in females. The bones of the male are denser and more rugged than those of the female, probably because of the slower rate of ossification and the greater calcium retention subsequently.

Heat adaptation

As stated previously, the female possesses about 10% more adipose tissue than does the male. This serves as insulation to prevent excessive heat loss from the internal organs. The skin temperature of the female is higher in warm weather and lower in cold weather than that of the male. Additionally, she possesses a slightly higher sweating threshold (2° to 3° F.) than the male; hence she does not begin sweating until the environmental temperature is 2° F. above the male's sweating threshold, and her amount of sweating is less. The temperature gradient from the body core temperature to the shell temperature is smaller, so that a physiological cost of maintaining heat balance in a hot environment is greater and appears to be more limiting in terms of physical performance.

Muscular strength

It is a truism that persons with a larger muscle mass have greater muscular strength than those possessing a smaller muscle mass. The strength of muscle is also related to the strength of the bones, joints, tendons, and connective tissue, which provide safe and reasonably efficient movement. By virtue of his larger, more rugged anatomy, the male usually has greater muscular strength, an advantage he enjoys from childhood on. The girl's closest approximation of the boy's strength occurs at 10 to 11 years of age. The greatest increment occurs between the ages of 12 and 13 years, and her muscular strength continues to increase until maturity.[8] After reaching maturity there is some diminution. The same kind of training stimulus produces a faster and greater increase in male strength, hence the increase in strength differences.[19] There is considerable difference between the sexes in respect to the trainability of muscle. Young adult males are able to improve their strength to a greater degree. Edington and Edgerton attribute this difference to the greater sex difference in maximum oxygen uptake rates found in trained subjects (see *maximum aerobic power,* p. 28). They further postulate that there appears to be a relationship, although perhaps not as a causative factor, to the higher anabolic hormone levels found in males.[11] A boy shows his greatest increase at 15 to 16 years of age and reflects a continuous, strong rise that peaks around the age of 20 years.

The strength-to-weight ratio after puberty favors the male, not so much because of any significant histological difference inherent in the muscle tissue itself but rather because of the female's greater adiposity in relation to lean muscle mass, as previously indicated. The muscle mass in the male may exceed that of the female by as much as 50%. The adult woman has about 65% of the strength of the adult man.[19] Some of this difference may be explained by differences in height. However, when this factor is eliminated, she still has but 80% of the strength of her male counterpart.[3,15] Body composition and proportions vary in a woman and man of a given height, thus accounting for the difference in overall strength; however, if age and the degree of training are the same, her strength per square centimeter is the same, and the proportion of fast- and slow-twitch muscle fibers appears to be about the same in most muscles as that of the male. Strength values, which vary from muscle to muscle, range from 3.6 to 10 kg./cm.^{2}. Strength usually decreases quite suddenly a few days preceding menstruation and remains at a lower level throughout the menstrual period. Strength can be greatly increased when women are put on a program of progressive resistance exercises (PRE) (see Chapter 6). Wilmore and others in recent studies, have shown strength increases ranging from 15% to 44% with little muscle hypertrophy resulting.[5,6,35] Muscle hypertrophy (that is, an increase in muscle size or bulk) is probably related to the plasma production of testosterone; hence males, having higher levels, would indicate greater hypertrophy as strength increases. Females who possess high natural levels of testosterone would tend to bulk up similar to males.[35]

In the performance of such activities as sprints and jumps, girls below the age

Fig. 3-4. A fast reaction time is an asset to the skillful fencer.

of 12 years perform as well or just slightly below boys of similar age, but from the ages of 12 to 18 years, boys show considerably more ability than girls. Such improvement can be accounted for by the increase in body size, which is probably hormonal in origin.

Neuromuscular coordination, reaction time, and movement time

The speed with which one recognizes, interprets, and physically responds to a stimulus is known as *reaction time*. Strength as such is not necessarily a factor, but one's ability to identify a stimulus and elicit the proper response in a minimal amount of time is an important factor in athletic success. It has been shown that athletes manifest a faster reaction time than do nonathletes.[22,37]

Reaction time varies between individuals as well as the same individual (Fig. 3-4). Extrinsic as well as intrinsic factors—the nature of the stimulus, age, internal and external body temperatures, degree of fatigue, ambient temperature and humidity, time of day (diurnal variation), and limb dominance—will affect the response time. A complex stimulus requires a longer reaction time than does a simple stimulus. Reaction time gradually improves with age, peaking between the ages of 18 to 21 years, then, from the mid-20s it shows a gradual decline.[21,33]

Movement time is defined as that period of time between the start of recordable movement and the completion of that movement. Men register a faster movement time than women, although the response to a visual stimulus appears to be the same in both sexes (Fig. 3-5).[24]

Fig. 3-5. Barbara Brushert serving volleyball.

In comparing the sexes from the ages of 6 to 20 years, there does not appear to be any noticeable difference in movement time.[21,33] In motor learning no significant differences appear unless strength is a factor and then the male registers superiority. Women, on the other hand, exhibit greater dexterity and manual skill, factors that were put to use in the assembly of aircraft and radio components during World War II.[24]

Trainability

Girls and women are less responsive than men in their ability to improve a given performance involving strength through a training program. Although strength training values are relatively similar prior to the age of 20 years, after this age the female values drop some 10% to 15% below that of the male, and in the age span from 20 to 30 years she has a strength training response of only 50% that of the opposite sex.[19] She starts at a lower level and attains a lower maximum. When the results of comparable training programs for high school and college boys and girls are computed and then compared on a percentage basis, girls and boys show the same amount of improvement.[15]

Endurance

It is interesting to note that girls and women have always been believed incapable of turning in creditable performances in events requiring great endurance; until recently, women performing in any sort of distance run or endurance event was taboo. The psychophysiological responses to such activity are no different for the female than for the male. The 800-meter run was believed to be the upper limit in terms of endurance for the "weaker" sex, but currently the event is being run in less than 2 minutes and it has been predicted that there will be an 8-second decrease.[20]

Women champion distance runners who run from 50 to 100 miles weekly in training have been carefully studied. They are shown to have a greater ventilatory capacity than average, with a maximum oxygen consumption approaching that found in male championship long-distance runners. Wilmore and Brown recently studied 11 women long-distance runners of national and international prominence in respect to their $\dot{V}_{O_2}$ max. values and found that the average values of these athletes were quite a bit higher than those of the average male or female and only slightly lower than the values achieved by male athletes of similar age. When these values were expressed in relation to the lean body weight (that is, the weight exclusive of body fat, which in the female is greater in amount) the values were quite close.[36]   Ikai,[21] who has made comparison studies of females and males in the age range of 12 to 17 years, found that the maximum endurance after training increased considerably for the boys, whereas the girls showed no improvement. However, participation of prepubescent girls in endurance type of athletic competition, wherein a group of girls aged 8 through 13 years ran cross-country from 3 to 7 miles daily, 4 or 5 days weekly, and engaged weekly in competitive races of 3/4 to 1 1/2 miles, indicated an increased maximum oxygen uptake with no untoward effects whatsoever, in a carefully controlled study by Brown et al.[4] If one carefully considers the various physiological and anatomic parameters discussed in this and the preceding chapter, one may conclude that the girl reaches her peak at ages 12 to 14 years, whereas the boy has not as yet achieved his, hence the differential indicated by Ikai. Now that psychosocial barriers are being broken down and more and more girls and women enter endurance events, evidence supports the contention that the female is capable of severe endurance competition. A number of women have recently competed with men in marathon races (a distance slightly over 26 miles) with considerable success and, although greatly outnumbered, have finished well up in the pack (Fig. 3-6).

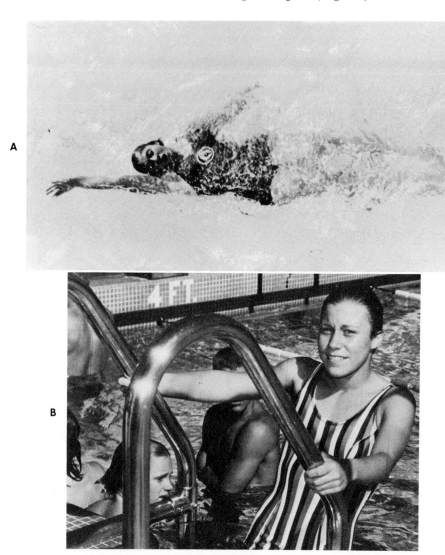

Fig. 3-6. A, Cathy Ferguson Cullum followed a strenuous training regimen in preparation for the 1964 Olympics in Tokyo. She won the gold medal in the 100-meter backstroke at the age of 16 years. **B,** Patty Caretto, holder of the United States and world records in the 1,500-meter freestyle in 1964, 1965, and 1966, was 13 years of age when she first broke the existing world record.

Swimming seems to offer an area for favorable comparison. It is only in those events requiring great strength or "explosive" power that the sex differences in performance appear more distinct (Table 3-1). Limitations in respect to female performance appear only when the athlete seeks to compete with the male on a common ground. Here the male's greater size, strength, and speed give him an undeniable advantage. In addition, the influence of psychosocial factors and the degree of training may function as inhibiting or limiting factors in the athletic performance of women.

Work capacity

Work capacity can be thought of as energy expenditure as quantified in terms of calories (or kilocalories*). As previously stated, the absolute work capacity of males exceeds that of females by 20% or more, but should the workload be iden-

*One kilocalorie represents a large calorie and indicates the amount of heat needed to elevate the temperature of one kilogram of water (2.2 lb.) one degree Celsius.

Table 3-1 □ Comparison of women's and men's records at Montreal (1976)

Event	Women	Men	Approximate percent
Track (meters)			
100	11.0	9.9	90
200	22.4	19.8	88
400	51.08	43.8	86
800	1:58.6	1:44.3	87
1,500	4:01.4	3:34.9	89
400 relay	42.8	38.19	89
1,600 relay	3:23.0	2:56.1	86
Field (feet)			
High jump	6' 3⅝"	7' 4¼"	86
Long jump	22' 4½"	29' 2½"	77
Swimming (meters)			
Freestyle			
100	58.59	51.22	87
200	2:03.56	1:52.78	91
400	4:19.4	4:00.27	93
Backstroke			
100	1:05.78	56.58	86
200	2:19.19	2:02.82	88
Breaststroke			
100	1:13.58	1:04.94	88
200	2:41.71	2:21.55	88
Butterfly			
100	1:03.34	54.27	87
200	2:15.57	2:00.70	89
Individual medley			
400	5:02.97	4:31.98	90
400 medley relay	4:20.75	3:48.16	88

tified in reference to per kilogram of body weight, the difference drops approximately 5%. In certain types of work performance some females can equal and, in some instances, outperform males.

Response to stress

Sport is a combination of physical, social, and psychic stresses forming an integrated pattern to which the person responds in toto, invoking both a physiological and a psychological pattern of response. Over the years certain standards of behavior categorized as "sportsmanship" have evolved; sports participants are expected to measure up to these standards. Deviations from expected behavior are characterized as "poor" sportsmanship and are not tolerated by the mores of our society. It has long been accepted, whether justly or unjustly, that women are emotionally unstable in stressful situations; therefore it was believed that the intensities of severe competition could result in unpleasant or harmful aftereffects to the female psyche. This *idée fixe* simply does not hold true. Emotional control in stressful situations is usually stabilized through experience and is more of a psychological than a physiological manifestation. An intensive study of young girl competitive swimmers from the ages of 12 to 16 years revealed no particular nervous symptoms or emotional instability as the result of either an intensive training program or competition.[2] This age group is somewhat notorious for emotional instability. Constant exposure to or experience under stress can result in the development of the ability to function adequately in stressful situations.

There is no scientific evidence that indicates that females are more psychologically or emotionally unstable than males. Stress reactions are similar in both sexes. Sports participation and competition exert a healthy influence upon one's sociopsychological qualities, and participation can only result in the acquisition of beneficial traits.

Age

In today's world of competitive sports, literally millions of girls and women are participants at all levels of competition. Currently, the competitive age span is increasing. At the championship level of competition, girls 13 and 14 years of age are not unusual, nor are married women, mothers, and grandmothers. More than half of the female finalists in the 1952 Olympics were married and many had children; many were over the age of 35 years and at least two were grandmothers.

Vastly improved standards of living, nutrition, and general health have produced a generation of girls and women who are physically more mature and stronger than those of the past. This has resulted in an earlier entrance into the competitive picture as well as a longer stint as a competitor. In the past, most women retired from sports after marriage and subsequent motherhood. Today they do not feel that marriage or parenthood sets any particular limitations; many women continue in competition. The constant improvement of health care appears to have slowed the aging process; women 30 years of age and over are no longer content to remain sedentary and "grow old gracefully," but would rather look, act, and perform like their younger counterparts. De Vries[10] has found that physical activity has a delaying effect on the aging process. The beneficial effects of active sports participation at any age level upon the body processes far outweigh the rather dubious results attained through overuse of cosmetics and application of various artificial aids often used to disguise that wherein nature has failed.

The constant setting of new records and top-level performances by very young girls indicate what exercise physiologists, supported by many reputable studies, have long maintained—that girls 12 to 15 years old are at their physiological peak and are both sociologically and psychologically more trainable than at any other time. Certainly the current record-breaking spree helps bear out this contention.

Altitude

Women seem to adapt to altitude more readily than men despite a lowered hemopoietic (formation of red blood cells) response, which is believed to be attributable to iron deficiency.[18] Although this deficiency may be chronic in nature and present prior to high-altitude exposure, high altitudes appear to be associated with such deficiencies since it has been shown that increased iron turnover and intestinal absorption of iron and an elevated iron requirement accompany such exposure.[18,31]

Menstrual function seems to undergo some changes at medium to high altitudes that are a disruptive influence on the cycle, resulting in either a cessation of flow or a greatly increased flow. During the International Sports Week, held prior to the Olympic Games at Mexico City, seven female athletes were carefully studied during competition. It was found that the women tolerated the altitude of 2,300 meters better than did the men, despite the fact that three out of the seven women were menstruating at some time during their competition.[17]

At high altitudes, women experience some weight loss, but it is considerably less than that experienced by men. A slightly higher tachycardia (abnormal rapidity of the heart action) and some loss of blood volume occur. However, changes in pulmonary function are similar to those in the male.[18]

Morbidity and mortality

In the majority of diseases, morbidity and mortality are less for women than they are for men. Cancer, coronary heart disease, diabetes, ulcers, and respiratory diseases occur more often in men. Because of the lower incidence of such diseases and disabilities in women, the aptitude for endurance could be developed considerably further in girls and women than is now the case.

GYNECOLOGICAL FACTORS
Periodicity

Until recently, both public and medical opinions have been that participation during menstruation was not only unwise but could be physiologically harmful. A considerable amount of research has established that this view is not justified (particularly when the participant is healthy). Training and competition do not materially affect either the menarche (the onset of menstruation) or the menstrual function proper.[14] Environmental influences, and socioeconomic influences in particular, seem to be among several of the key factors influencing the menarche, but the specific effect that vigorous physical activity has upon the hormonal influences that bring about menarche remains to be discovered. There seems to be some disagreement as to what age the menses normally begin. Tanner[34] has indicated that there has been a steady decrease from about 17 years of age in 1840 to 13½ years of age in 1962. Others state that the decline is not so sharp. Menarche, like menstruation, is regular in its irregularity and may commence between the ages of 13 and 15 years.

In a study involving 111 women track-and-field athletes, 55% showed no performance decrement during the menses, whereas the remainder showed some decrease in performance.[22] Some of the athletes performed better during menstruation. The best performances were given in the immediate premenstrual period. Studies indicate that circulatory responses during the first 2 or 3 days of the menstrual period are somewhat unfavorable insofar as performance involving physical loads of considerable intensity is concerned.[13,14,16] During this same time, minimum arterial blood pressure values increase considerably and pulse rate responses to exercise and pulse recovery rates are some 20 to 60 seconds longer. Physical efficiency is highest during the intermenstrual period, although no periodicity with respect to speed, skill, or accuracy of motion has been identified. Erdelyi,[14] in a study of 729 Hungarian female athletes, found that there were no untoward problems encountered either with the onset of menarche or during the menstrual period proper. Other research seems to bear out these findings.[2,38] Apparently the hormonal cycle that causes menstruation may affect performance either positively or negatively, and the time in the menstrual period when such effect is greatest is as variable as menstruation itself. This observation is borne out by the study carried out by Zaharieva[38] of the menstrual cycle, pregnancy, and childbirth in the Olympic athletes at Tokyo.

The general consensus of doctors is that women should avoid extremely strenuous activity and, in particular, activity that produces excessive jarring, torque, or strain, especially to the pelvic floor, during the first 2 days of the menstrual period. At this time the womb is engorged with blood and heavier. Such symptoms as depression, fatigue, irritability, nervousness, and water retention, which sometimes accompany menstruation, are induced by psychological and hormonal factors that normally attend this phenomenon. A decrease in strength occurs a few days prior to the onset of menstruation; this lowered level persists throughout the period.

Dysmenorrhea (painful or difficult menstruation) occurs when ischemia (a lack of normal blood flow to the sexual organs) or a possible hormonal imbalance is present. There is no simple explanation of this syndrome, which is identified by cramps, low abdominal pain, aching in the thighs, nausea, headache, and occasionally emotional lability. Muscular exercise is beneficial in relieving pain and also in ameliorating and preventing dysmenorrhea.[13,27,30] Mild to vigorous exercises are regularly prescribed for those suffering from this syndrome. The incidence of dysmenorrhea is materially lower among athletes than among more sedentary women.

As a rule, physicians recommend regular participation in sports activities during the menstrual period if the level of performance does not drop below that which is customary. A higher percentage of menstrual and inflammatory diseases are found among gymnasts, divers, swimmers, skiers, and tennis players than among the rest of the athletic population. There also appears to be a less effective level of performance among these athletes during menstruation.[23] Erdelyi has found that athletes in those sports that require great physical effort over a long period of time (for example, rowing, skiing, tennis) have menstrual disorders more often than that of other athletes.[13]

Olympic and world records have been set by women in all phases of the menstrual cycle; it is difficult to say precisely which phase is more positive or negative with respect to performance. Of all the factors that influence physical performance, none appears more variable in its effect than menstruation. Generally it can be said that performance during the menses is well tolerated and appears to have a beneficial effect.

Effect of physical activity on pregnancy, childbirth, and the postpartum period

Over the years one of the major arguments against female participation in strenuous sports activities has been that the stresses and strains of such competition should be avoided because they could permanently damage the reproductive organs. Research indicates that this point of view simply is invalid. Another widely held view asserts that women athletes tend to have narrower pelves than normal; hence they are subject to more complications during pregnancy and childbirth. Again, scientific evidence reveals that this is not true.

The reproductive organs are remarkably well protected. The body provides natural safeguards to the uterus by absorbing external shocks to the body; any force that reaches the uterus is greatly diminished. Paramore's experiment points out that the uterus is surrounded with structures of approximately the same specific gravity as itself, normally with no air space around it. Hence it floats freely in the pelvic viscera, like a raw egg floating freely in a jar filled to the rim with water and tightly capped so as to exclude air. Any forces transmitted to the external housing, short of smashing the jar itself, will be dissipated by the external surface and the transmitting medium to such an extent that the egg will remain uninjured. Try this graphic experiment, for it indicates most vividly that the pelvic organs are indeed adequately protected against external forces.

Fertility and gestation among women athletes are within normal ranges. Outstanding women athletes, including Olympic performers, have no particular problems in respect to childbearing and childbirth. In fact, Erdelyi[13] found that the duration of labor was considerably shortened and that complications per se were not at all excessive. At the time of this writing, research dealing with the effects of physical activity upon pregnancy, childbirth, and the postpartum period is somewhat limited. To date, shorter periods of labor and convalescence and fewer childbirth complications have been noted in athletes.[13,14,30]

In 1950 Pfeiffer[25] studied twenty-four women athletes, all Olympic competitors and holders of world records. The majority gave birth relatively quickly with little pain and had both shorter delivery and convalescent periods. Upon resumption of athletic competition after childbirth, many of the women showed a pronounced improvement in their physical performances. He postulated that hormones that were activated by pregnancy might account for the relative ease of parturition and the improvement in performance. Klaus and Noack[24] studied fifteen women athletes. Six of the fifteen established record performances after pregnancy, five dropped out of sports activities, two maintained their status quo as regards performance, whereas the others established better performances than previously. All the women stated that they had more strength, endurance, and tenaciousness after pregnancy. These investigators see pregnancy as a training period for the maternal organism, since the increases in blood volume and metabolism make intensive demands upon the physiological systems. Therefore pregnancy should be viewed as a time of intensive conditioning or training so that the body is able to meet these demands adequately. Myotonometric measurements indicate a high level of muscle tonicity in pregnant women.[24] From the evidence at hand it would seem that no undue concern should be felt regarding the effects of strenuous exercise before or after childbirth. Generally speaking, competition continued well into the third month of pregnancy appears permissible, unless bleeding or cramping, or both, are present. Most athletes usually stop strenuous activity during the fourth month, not because of discomfort, but rather because the performance level drops. Some athletes have continued well beyond this point and with success. During the first three months, however, the dangers of disturbing the pregnancy are the greatest, since the pregnancy usually stabilizes itself by the end of that period. Each situation must be considered on an individual basis. Such activity should be viewed from a positive aspect as a means of providing a protective and preventive function in making pregnancy, childbirth, and the postpartal period less stressful.

Femininity

Participation in sports does not masculinize women. Hormonal secretions of androgen, estrogen, progesterone, and testosterone vary greatly, resulting in considerable variations insofar as muscular strength and general morphology are concerned.[23] Carpenter[7] developed a table for assessing the degree of femininity or masculinity in women. Girls whose physiques are more masculine are stronger per unit of weight and enjoy certain mechanical advantages over girls who rate low in masculinity and boys who rate high in femininity.[9] *It is inherent endocrinological and morphological factors that are responsible for femininity and masculinity and not vigorous physical activity, which too often is held to blame.* Such activity makes a woman more graceful and feminine. Femininity is the rule rather than the exception among today's women athletes.

Today's athlete is extremely different from the mannish, muscular type that has often been associated in the past with the term "female athlete." Young girls in particular often fear that hard, vigorous exercise will result in unsightly bulging muscles and the masculinizing of the body. Careful study of available evidence negates this fear. For example, a study of young American black women who had performed hard physical labor during youth revealed no significant degree of masculinity in body build.[1] Girls and women should have no fear that strenuous exercise or intense competition will affect their appearance in any other than a beneficial way, inducing better muscle tonus, replacing fatty tissue with firm musculature, and improving fitness, to mention a few.

Sex determination

As the result of some rather bizarre and unscrupulous practices in international and Olympic competition wherein males disguised as women competitors (how many will probably never be known) took part in world championships, the various international governing bodies were compelled to establish compulsory medical examinations to determine the true sex of women athletes. The International Olympic Committee established such standards at the Tokyo Olympiad and ruled that such physical and laboratory examinations would be mandatory at all future games. Examinations to establish sexual validity include both visual inspection and laboratory tests conducted by gynecologists in such a manner as to preserve secrecy and protect the athlete from embarrassment.

Many instances of men posing as women in international competition have been well documented.[29,32] In 1938 a world high-jump record was set by "Dora," who turned out to be a man who for the "honor and glory of the Third Reich" had been forced to pose as a woman. At Oslo in 1946 the bronze medal in the 100-meter sprint was won by "Claire," now known as Pierre, the father of a child and residing on a farm near Metz, France.

More unfortunate "females" who have received a great deal of unpleasant publicity have been intersexed individuals. Truly bisexual individuals are extremely rare. More common is abnormal gonadal development, called *dysgenetic male pseudohermaphroditism,* in which the sex glands (gonads) and the chromosomes are male but the external virilization is incomplete, often with a resultant female appearance. A male infant born with certain noticeable defects in the anatomy of the penis and scrotum may resemble a female externally but still lack her reproductive ability. Conversely, a female infant possessing an overgrown clitoris that resembles a penis is still a female with a female's reproductive capabilities.

Often at birth a misdiagnosis of sex is made because of abnormal genitalia; as a result, such individuals are raised as members of the opposite sex, usually until puberty, when the predominant sex hormones manifest themselves. Under such circumstances, a supposed "female" would have greater strength and athletic ability. "Lea," one of "Claire's" teammates, won the bronze medal in the 200-meter sprint and then teamed up with "Claire" and two other women to take the silver medal in the 400-meter relay at Oslo. A subsequent operation converted "Lea" to "Leon," who then entered the French Air Force.

One of the more recent intersexed individuals to undergo surgical change was Erika Schinnegger, the Austrian skier, winner of the women's downhill skiing championship in 1966, who withdrew from the last Winter Olympic Games because of difficulty in proving total femininity at the age of 19 years. After four difficult operations and almost 7 months of hospitalization, Erika was successfully and officially transformed into Eric and is now pursuing not only his skiing career but is engaged in bicycle racing as well. A number of Middle European representatives withdrew from the Olympic Games at Mexico City rather than undergo the mandatory examinations.

In the normal female and male there are twenty-three pairs of chromosomes that includes one pair of sex chromosomes, XX for the female and XY for the male. Sex determination is effected at fertilization. If the ovum is fertilized by a sperm carrying a Y chromosome, the paired chromosomes (XY) will produce a male offspring, whereas if the sex chromosomes are constituted so as to effect an XX combination, the offspring will be female. The intersexed individual carries an abnormal combination of sex chromosomes such as XYY or just X.

Sex determination is obtained by securing a buccal smear (that is, from inside the mouth, usually the cheek) and studying the sex chromatin granules. The presence of a significant number of Barr bodies (a clump of chromatin at the nuclear rim) verifies that the individual is genetically female. The presence of Y chromosomes is identified through fluorescence. If the result is not satisfactory, a complete karyotyping (a systematized arranging of the chromosomes of a single cell, typical of an individual) is carried out, complemented by blood tests and a gynecological examination. A procedure introduced at the Olympics in Munich in 1972 involves testing cells from a hair root. This test is much simpler and more accurate.[29] Such tests preclude the appearance of genetically unqualified individuals from competition and ensure that women compete only against other women.

SUMMARY

A review of the information presented in this chapter reveals the following significant facts:
1. Woman is competent to participate in strenuous activity under all conditions in which the man can participate.
2. She has not in any way reached her potential in terms of performance and is thoroughly capable of attaining much greater heights.
3. Physiologically, she compares favorably to the male in most parameters. However, in the area of power or strength she will always function at a 20% to 30% handicap because of her size and structure.
4. Obstetrical and gynecological data obtained to date refute the idea that severe exercise is damaging and the cause of undesirable effects.
5. Endurance performance is no more damaging or overtaxing to the female than to her male counterpart. She is capable of great endurance.
6. The female's emotional reactions under stress are no different from those of the male; so-called "emotional" reactions are more likely to be the result of social and cultural mores than psychophysiological factors.
7. Such differences as do exist between the sexes must be kept in mind when selecting physical activities and sports for the female. Activities should be designed or modified when necessary to take advantage of both her body structure and functions.
8. Age is not, nor should it be permitted to be, a barrier to sports activity and competition. The values of such participation are pointed up not only by the beneficial aspects that can accrue but by the fact that participating mothers are most insistent that their daughters should be activity conscious.

REFERENCES

1. Adams, E. H.: A comparative anthropometric study of hard labor during youth as a stimulation of physical growth of young colored women, Res. Q. Am. Assoc. Health Phys. Educ. **9:**102, 1961.
2. Åstrand, P. O., Engström, L., Erikson, B., et al.: Girl swimmers with special reference to respiratory and circulatory adaptation and gynaecological and psychiatric aspects, Acta Paediatr. Scand., suppl. 147, 1963a.
3. Åstrand, P. O., and Rodahl, K.:. Textbook of work physiology, New York, 1970, McGraw-Hill Book Co., Inc.
4. Brown, C. H., Harrower, J. R., and Deeter, M.: The effects of cross-country running on preadolescent girls, Med. Sci. Sports **4:**1, 1972.

5. Brown, C. H., and Wilmore, J. H.: The effect of maximum resistance training on the strength and body composition of women athletes, Med. Sci. Sports **6:**174, 1974.
6. Capen, E. K., Bright, J. A., and Line, P. A.: The effects of weight training on strength, power, muscular endurance, and anthropometric measurements on a selected group of college women, J. Assoc. Phys. Mental Rehab. **15:**169, 1972.
7. Carpenter, A.: Strength, power, and femininity as factors influencing the athletic performance of college women, Res. Q. Am. Assoc. Health Phys. Educ. **9:**120, 1938.
8. Chikin, V. T.: Age changes in muscular strength in girls of school age, Yessis Translation Rev. **2:**36, 1967.
9. Cress, C. L., and Thorsen, M. A.: Morphological bisexuality as a factor in the motor performance of college women, Res. Q. Am. Assoc. Health Phys. Educ. **35:**408, 1964.
10. de Vries, H. A.: Physiology of exercise for physical education and athletics, ed. 2, Dubuque, Iowa, 1974, William C. Browne Co., Publishers.
11. Edington, D. W., and Edgerton, V. R.: The biology of physical activity, Boston, 1976, Houghton Mifflin Company.
12. Eisenman, P. A., and Golding, L. A.: Comparison of effects of training on $\dot{V}O_2$ max. in girls and young women, Med. Sci. Sports **7:**136, 1975.
13. Erdelyi, G. J.: Effects of exercise on the menstrual cycle, Physician Sportsmed. **4:**79, Mar. 1976.
14. Erdelyi, G. J.: Gynecological survey of female athletes, J. Sports Med. Phys. Fitness **2:**174, 1962.
15. Falls, H. B.: Exercise physiology, New York, 1968, Academic Press, Inc.
16. Garlick, M. A., and Bernauer, E. M.: Exercise during the menstrual cycle: variations in physiological baselines, Res. Q. Am. Assoc. Health Phys. Educ. **39:**533, 1968.
17. Goddard, R. F.: United States Olympic Committee swimming team performance in international sports week, Mexico City, October 1965. In International symposium on the effects of altitude on physical performance, Chicago, 1967, The Athletic Institute.
18. Hannon, J. P., Shields, J. L., and Harris, C. W.: High altitude acclimatization in women. In International symposium on the effects of altitude on physical performance, Chicago, 1967, The Athletic Institute.
19. Hettinger, T.: Physiology of strength, Springfield, Ill., 1961, Charles C Thomas, Publisher.
20. Hodgkins, J., and Skubic, V.: Women's track and field records (analysis and predictions), J. Sports Med. Phys. Fitness **8:**36, 1968.
21. Ikai, M.: Work capacity of Japanese related to age and sex, J. Sports Med. Phys. Fitness **6:**100, 1966.
22. Karpovich, P. V., and Sinning, W. E.: Physiology of muscular activity, Philadelphia, 1971, W. B. Saunders Co.
23. Klafs, C. E., and Arnheim, D. D.: Modern principles of athletic training, ed. 4, St. Louis, 1977, The C. V. Mosby Co.
24. Klaus, E. J., and Noack, H.: Woman and sport, Stuttgart, 1961, Georg Thieme Verlag.
25. Pfeiffer, W. A.: Top performance of women and their influence on constitution, fertility, and proceedings of birth, Rev. Anal. Educ. Phys. Sport **8:**2, 1966.
26. Pierson, R., and Lockhart, A.: Effect of menstruation on simple reaction and movement time, Br. Med. J. **1:**796, 1963.
27. Pros, J. R.: Physical movement and sports as prevention and therapy of dysmenorrhea, J. Sports Med. Phys. Fitness **2:**125, 1962.
28. Ruch, T. C., and Fulton, J. F.: Medical physiology and biophysics, Philadelphia, 1965, W. B. Saunders Co.
29. Ryan, A. J.: Sex and the singles player, Physician Sportsmed. **4:**39, Oct. 1976.
30. Ryan, A. J.: Sports during pregnancy, other questions explored; discussion, Physician Sportsmed. **4:**82, March 1976.
31. Ryan, A. J.: The Olympic Games at altitude. In American Academy of Orthopaedic Surgeons Symposium on sports medicine, St. Louis, 1969, The C. V. Mosby Co.
32. Stiles, M. H.: Olympic doctors face controversial problems: sex testing and drug use by athletes, Mod. Med., pp. 60-64, Sept. 9, 1968.
33. Takano, K., and Fujiyoshi, H.: A study on timing in sensory motor performance viewed from the developmental stages, J. Sports Med. Phys. Fitness **5:**50, 1965.
34. Tanner, J. M.: Growth at adolescence, Oxford, England, 1962, Blackwell Scientific Publications.

35. Wilmore, J. H.: Alterations in strength, body composition, and anthropometric measurements consequent to a 10-week weight training program, Med. Sci. Sports **6:**133, 1974.
36. Wilmore, J. H., and Brown, C. H.: Physiological profiles of women distance runners, Med. Sci. Sports **6:**178, 1974.
37. Younger, L. A.: A comparison of reaction and movement times of athletes and non-athletes, Res. Q. Am. Assoc. Health Phys. Educ. **30:**349, 1959.
38. Zaharieva, E.: Survey of sportswomen at the Tokyo Olympics, J. Sports Med. Phys. Fitness **5:**215, 1965.

SUGGESTED READING

Wilmore, J. H.: Athletic training and physical fitness, Boston, 1977, Allyn & Bacon, Inc.

PART THREE

Physical conditioning

4 □ Evaluation of the athlete

Every girl participating in an organized athletic program is entitled to expert medical care and sound health supervision. In the assessment of the fitness of the athlete to participate in the sports program, two comprehensive types of examination should be given, the preseason medical examination and the physical fitness examination given respectively by the medical doctor (either team physician or family doctor) and the trainer or coach, or both. Such examinations ensure the welfare of those desiring to participate in the organized sports program.

MEDICAL ASSESSMENT

Before any girl is permitted to participate in either training or competitive programs, she must undergo a thorough, comprehensive medical examination by a qualified medical doctor. There are three reasons for such a requirement. First, it is a matter of protection for the athlete. The examination serves to identify any incipient physical condition that, through strenuous activity, could develop into a serious or dangerous complication. The physician can exercise his judgment as to whether the prospective athlete should be excluded from, restricted, or permitted to participate in the sports program. Frequently such conditions are relatively minor and steps can be taken that may completely ameliorate the condition and permit uninhibited physical participation. Second, a medical examination should prevent unwarranted medical disqualification of any athlete who desires to participate in the program. Third, such an examination protects the trainer, coach, and the school district legally, should the performer suffer injury as the result of sports participation. The legal liability for such injury could well be attributed to negligence on the part of the trainer, coach, or school district, should the athlete not have undergone a medical assessment. In all respects, there must be a close liaison between the physician, the coach, and the trainer. They must work cooperatively, with the physician's word prevailing in all instances pertaining to the medical well-being of the athlete.

MEDICAL EXAMINATION

The medical examination is a screening device wherein all facets of the athlete's anatomy, physiology, and sociopsychological aspects come under the scrutiny of the physician. If at all possible, the athlete should undergo examination at least yearly. The examination should be scheduled far enough in advance of the start of training or conditioning that, if necessary, appropriate diagnosis, consultation, and treatment can be instituted. Unless the individual has experienced a significant injury, illness, or surgery since the last evaluation, an annual medical examination should suffice.

The examining physician has two significant responsibilities: (1) to withhold the sportswoman from participation if medical reasons warrant such action and (2) to prevent unwarranted medical disqualification of a sportswoman with the

47

desire to participate. In the first instance, the physician is concerned with a disease or process that would prevent the athlete from either participation or competition with "normal" individuals or where a disease or process that is present could be significantly or even permanently aggravated by sports participation. In the second instance, there are incidents wherein a girl with, for example, an erratic blood pressure reading or a nonpathological heart murmur, neither of which pose a threat to her well-being but because of which it has been concluded, perhaps by her parents, that she should be restricted in respect to any type of physical activity. A careful medical examination might indicate that she was capable of participating in any or all activities or perhaps restricted from some specific types only.

The following areas should be covered in the preparticipation examination.

Medical history. Complete knowledge of past illnesses, injuries, operations, and immunizations should be made part of the record. Such information as allergic responses, medications, etc., should be recorded.

Respiratory area. Efficient respiratory function is crucial and synonomous with good sports performance; hence any potentially disqualifying respiratory abnormalities should be identified. There is a number of respiratory anomalies that may prove limiting, and the physician will need to consider whether the condition justifies disqualification from certain types of activities. The respiratory movements are observed and the rate and character of respiration noted.

A chest x-ray examination, for the purpose of identifying lung and heart anomalies is often desirable, although the expense and time involved, especially on a mass basis as in athletics, frequently precludes its use.

Cardiovascular area. This is a critical area and extremely important because of the number of conditions frequently present attributable to the psychological response to the examination. For example, blood pressure elevations, nonpathological heart murmurs, or pulse irregularities that are transient and not indicative of a pathological condition. None of these should limit performance.

Disqualifying conditions might include valvular or cyanotic heart disease, significant pulse irregularities, hypertension, or an active carditis. These would disqualify the sportswoman from either endurance of contact type of sports.

The trunk. The general shape and size of the chest, any deformities, any tumors or growths, the distribution of hair, and the condition of the glands are noted. The breasts are examined for growths or lumps within the tissue.

Kidneys, hernias, and genitalia. Acute and chronic kidney diseases (which are renal insufficiency, glomerulonephritis [Bright's disease], and nephritis) are not compatible with any form of significant exertion and would disqualify an individual from sports.

Femoral hernia occurs at the femoral ring, an opening in the groin, located just below the inguinal ligaments, and, though not a particularly common hernia, is more prevalent among females than among males.

The inguinal hernia occurs at the inguinal canal, located at the extreme lower border of the abdomen, and is a relatively weak place in the abdominal wall. Weak abdominal muscles, injury, or excessive intra-abdominal pressures (such as those resulting from lifting a heavy object) will predispose a person to inguinal hernia.

With the permission of the athlete and the parents, a vaginal examination should be made. Vaginal abnormalities can thus be identified, and ameliorative or corrective measures can be instituted. A Pap smear is suggested as a part of the medical examination.

A history of the menstrual patterns as to flow, duration, cramps, and irregularities should be recorded. Menstrual patterns may affect physical performance.

Musculoskeletal area. Body structure plays a vital role in sports performance and can influence the degree of efficiency or the success attained. It has been well established that certain types of body build have definite advantages in certain sports. Generally speaking, structural abnormalities that exist must be carefully considered by the physician as to whether they are compatible with the sport or the skills involved. Such spinal conditions as spondylolisthesis (slippage between vertebrae), "ruptured" (herniated) nucleus pulposus (particularly in the cervical area), previous surgery, fracture, or dislocation should disqualify an athlete from all sports involving contact.

Postural conditions such as lordosis (swayback) or scoliosis (lateral spinal curvature) are frequently limiting factors in physical performance and may predispose the performer to injury. The physician will need to evaluate such conditions individually and may refer the athlete for corrective work.

Head and neck. Abnormal skin and scalp conditions are identified and noted. The mouth and throat examination is confined principally to observation for the presence of oral and sinus infections and any abnormal skin conditions. The dental examination can be carried out by a school dentist, if available. Cases of mouth abnormalities such as broken teeth, dental caries, or mouth and gum infections should be screened out and remedial measures instituted.

Although dental sports injuries appear, at present, nowhere as prevalent among females as among males, it would, nonetheless, be wise to provide individually fitted mouthpieces in some contact sports. It has been conclusively established that dental mouthpieces significantly reduce dental injuries and injuries to the soft tissues of the face and mouth and have been effective in reducing cerebral concussions. To be most effective, mouthpieces should be custom-made and fitted by a dentist. Stick injuries to the face are not uncommon, and as females move into the more rigorous contact sports, mouthpieces will become a necessity.

Since the advent of soft-plastic contact lenses, the awkwardness, discomfort, and dangers associated with wearing eyeglasses in sports have been largely eliminated. Most women find the use of contact lenses less handicapping and worrisome during physical performance.

The eye examination is usually comprised of a visual examination to determine the presence of an eye infection or aberration. In some instances a vision test may be given. The ears are checked for hearing problems and possible infection. If practicable, a hearing test (audiometer) can be given.

Body weight and growth pattern. The body weight should be taken and recorded. Using this value as a base, a regular program of recording the weight should be instituted by the coach or trainer. Weight loss in excess of 5% calls for an investigation as to cause (unless the athlete is considerably over what is considered normal weight). In the case of young athletes, careful growth and maturation records should be kept and referral to a physician made if strong deviation from normal patterns is observed.

HEALTH HISTORY

Date _____

(This part is to be filled out and signed by the athlete.)

Name _____ Phone _____

Address _____

School _____ Sport(s) _____

Name of person to be notified in case of emergency

_____ Phone _____

Address _____

Date of last: Medical examination _____

　　　　　　　Dental examination _____

Name and address of family physician _____

_____

Family history (State present health; if deceased, cause of death.)

Father　_____　Mother　_____

Sisters　_____　Brothers　_____

　　　　_____　　　　　　_____

　　　　_____　　　　　　_____

Have you ever had any of the following? (Answer "yes" or "no." Give dates and explanation.)

Allergies _____ Whooping cough _____

Frequent colds _____ Rheumatic fever _____

Bronchitis _____ Scarlet fever _____

Influenza _____ Chorea _____

Diphtheria _____ Epilepsy _____

Pleurisy _____ Convulsions _____

Pneumonia _____ Kidney disease _____

Tuberculosis _____ Poliomyelitis _____

Asthma _____ Appendicitis _____

Chickenpox _____ Mumps _____

Measles _____ Skin disease _____

Other _____

Do any of the following occur? (Answer "yes" or "no.")

Impaired hearing _____ Vomiting _____

Impaired vision _____ Abdominal pains _____

Eye infections _____ Indigestion _____

Frequent headaches _____ Constipation _____

Blackouts _____ Diarrhea _____

Fainting spells _____ Frequent urination _____

Sleeplessness _____ Painful menstruation _____

Loss of weight _____ Painful joints _____

Severe accident (nature of injuries) _____

Surgical operation (nature) _____

_____

Signature _____

Fig. 4-1. Health history.

Special considerations

Laboratory examinations. If at all possible, a urinalysis, a hemoglobin test, a tuberculin test, and a chest x-ray examination are recommended. The urinalysis provides a means of detecting unsuspected renal disease, diabetes, and, in those geographic areas where heat exhaustion is a possibility, electrolyte imbalance.

Immunizations. Athletes should be immunized against tetanus and poliomyelitis.

Allergies. A history of any allergy and the medication used should be noted. Some allergic young people develop asthma when they are involved in strenuous

---

PHYSICIAN'S REPORT

General appearance _____ Body type _____

Weight _____ Height _____ Posture _____

Deformities _____

Nose and sinuses _____ Speech defects _____

Vision without glasses   R _____ L _____

Vision with glasses   R _____ L _____

Ears _____ Hearing (audiometer 4A) R _____ L _____

Throat _____ Tonsils _____

Breath _____ Teeth _____

Thyroid _____ Lymph glands _____

Chest _____ Lungs _____

Heart _____

Blood pressure   S _____ D _____ Pulse rate _____

Abdomen _____ Hernia _____

Genitourinary _____

Menstruation _____

Nutrition _____

Nervous system _____

Reflexes _____

Mental or emotional stability _____

_____

Special laboratory tests, when necessary for diagnostic purposes:

Urine (albuminuria) _____ Glycosuria _____

Blood: Red _____ White _____ Hemoglobin _____

Name of athlete _____ School _____

Physical findings:

I hereby certify that the foregoing is a full, true, and correct record of an examination of the person named herein, conducted by me on _____ . Based upon such examination and upon the accompanying medical history declared by the student, it is my opinion that she be permitted to participate in sports competition with the following restrictions: (If none, so indicate.)

_____

_____

Date _____ Signature of physician _____

Fig. 4-2. Medical examination.

ACCIDENT REPORT FORM

School _____ Date _____ Time _____
Name _____ Address _____
Place of accident _____

Type of accident

Abrasion _____	Incised _____
Bleeding _____	Laceration _____
Bruise _____	Puncture _____
Burn _____	Scratch _____
Concussion _____	Shock _____
Dislocation _____	Sprain _____
Eye injury _____	Strain _____
Fracture _____	Other _____

Briefly, how did the accident happen? What was the athlete doing?

Were there any unsafe conditions existing? Was the act that precipitated the injury an unsafe act or was it one customarily performed without undue risk?

Was first-aid treatment administered? Type and by whom?

Fig. 4-3. Sample medical record for athletes.

exercise. In such cases a stress test is used to establish if they begin wheezing.

All athletes should have and are entitled to a most careful and comprehensive health evaluation. The American Medical Association has proclaimed that the aims of such an examination are as follows:

1. Determine the health status of candidates prior to exposure to participation and competition.
2. Provide appropriate medical advice to promote optimum health and fitness.
3. Arrange for further evaluation and prompt treatment of remediable conditions.
4. Counsel the atypical candidate as to the sports or modification of sports that for her would provide suitable activity.
5. Restrict from participation those whose physical limitations present undue risk.*

*This statement is based on *A Guide for the Medical Evaluation of Candidates for School Sports,* prepared by the American Medical Association on the Medical Aspects of Sports, Chicago, 1966, The American Medical Association.

ACCIDENT REPORT FORM—cont'd

Disposal

Sent to: School nurse _____ Home _____ Doctor _____

Hospital _____ How was transport carried out? _____
(Car, ambulance, other)

Location of accident	**Type of activity**
Apparatus	_____
Athletic field	_____
Dressing room	_____
Gymnasium	_____
Locker room	_____
Pool	_____
Shower	_____
Toilet	_____
Training room	_____
Washroom	_____
Other	_____

Remarks _____

_____

Recommendations for preventing other accidents of this type _____

_____

Signed: Person in charge _____

Administrative officer _____

This report is to be filled out in triplicate and signed the day the accident occurred.

Fig. 4-3. cont'd. Sample medical record for athletes.

Sample health history and medical report forms and accident report forms are presented in Figs. 4-1 to 4-3.

FITNESS APPRAISAL

It is sound practice to conduct a preseason fitness assessment of athletes in addition to the health examination. Such assessment makes known to the coach, the trainer, and the athlete where training emphasis should be placed in the coming weeks, and should some organic defect, not readily apparent in static health examinations, exist, its presence can usually be brought to light when the athlete is placed under physical stress. The athlete can then be remanded for more extensive medical examination. It is well worth the time and effort on the part of the coach and the trainer to institute fitness appraisal to get an overview of the state of fitness her athletes are in at the start of a season.

Basically, fitness testing involves three areas, cardiorespiratory, strength, and flexibility. A battery of three tests, one in each category, is usually sufficient although the battery can be expanded to include several tests in each area.

Cardiorespiratory fitness

The heart rate during or after exercise can be used as a measurement of cardiovascular (CV) fitness and can also be used to evaluate respiratory fitness in terms of a general estimate of the ability of the body to use the oxygen being transported by the blood ($\dot{V}_{O_2}$ max.).

Several approaches can be used in testing this area. A stress test designed to raise both circulatory and respiratory responses to levels approximating 60% to 70% of the athlete's maximum and to have the athlete sustain this level of work for at least 6 minutes, with heart rate or blood pressure being monitored, will give the examiner a good indication of her subject's cardiorespiratory (CR) fitness. A good rule is to subtract the subject's age from 220 to establish a maximum heart rate from which the working rate (60% to 70%) can be established. The use of the nomogram to find the $\dot{V}_{O_2}$ max. is a simple matter (Fig. 4-4). The athlete can perform on a treadmill, if one is available, or can use the 12-minute running test. Probably the simplest and quickest way to assess CR fitness is through the use of bench stepping. The test consists of having the athlete step up and down, alternating the feet, on a 16-inch bench at the rate of 30 steps per minute for a period of 5 minutes. Postexercise heart rates are taken at 1 to $1^{1}/_{2}$, 2 to $2^{1}/_{2}$, and 3 to $3^{1}/_{2}$ minutes for 30 seconds' duration, and the sum of the three pulse rates are then put into the following formula:

$$\text{Fitness index} = \frac{\text{Duration of exercise in seconds}}{2\,(\text{Sum of pulse rates in recovery})} \times 100$$

The derived index is then applied to Table 4-1 to ascertain the athlete's fitness.

The Kasch pulse recovery step test, a variation of the original step test, is another easily administered test that can be used to assess exercise tolerance or exercise classification (Table 4-2).

Fig. 4-4. Aerobic work capacity in men and women. The nomogram is used to predict $\dot{V}_{O_2}$ from heart rate in cycling, running, or the step test. One can estimate $\dot{V}_{O_2}$ by reading horizontally from the body-weight scale (step), or work load (cycle) to the oxygen-uptake scale. The point on the oxygen-uptake scale ($\dot{V}_{O_2}$, 1) should be connected with the corresponding point on the pulse rate scale and the predicted $\dot{V}_{O_2}$ value read on the middle scale. Examples: Note the dotted lines for a female, 61 kg. at 156 heart rate and 2.4 L./min. (step test). Also, a male on the bicycle ergometer at 1,200 kilogram meters per minute and 166 heart rate has a value of 3.6 L./min. Step rate = 22.5/min. and duration = 5-6 min. for both tests. (From Åstrand, I.: Aerobic work capacity in men and women, Acta Physiol. Scand. **49,** Suppl. 169, 1960.)

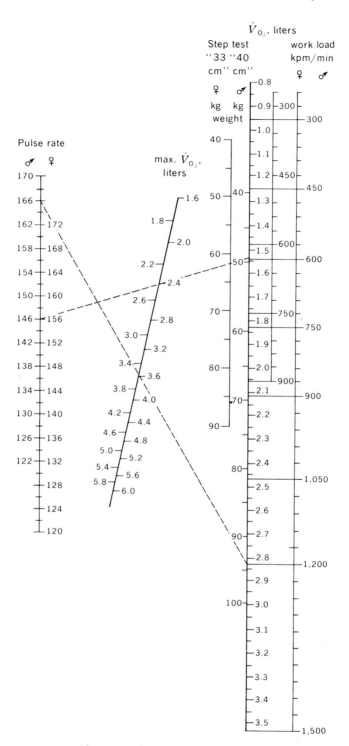

Fig. 4-4. For legend see opposite page.

Table 4-1 □ Harvard step test scoring table (3-pulse count method)

Recovery pulse rate	Rating	Brouha score	Recovery pulse rate	Rating	Brouha score	Recovery pulse rate	Rating	Brouha score
100	Excellent	150	168	Average	89	234		64
102		147	170		88	236		64
104		145	172		87	238		63
105		144	174		86	240		62
106		142	176		85	242		62
108		139	178		84	244	Good	61
110		136	180	Good	83	246		61
112		134	182		82	248		60
114		132	184		81	250	Low average	60
116		129	186	Below average	81	252		59
118		127	188		80	254		59
120		125	190		79	256		58
122		123	192		78	258		58
124		121	194		78	260		58
126		119	196		77	262		57
128	Very good	117	198		76	264		57
130		115	200	Mean	75	266		56
132		114	202		74	268	Very poor	56
134		112	204		73	270		56
136		110	206	Poor	73	272		55
138		109	208		72	274		55
140		107	210		71	276		55
142		106	212	Average	71	278	55 and below is poor physical condition	54
144		104	214		70	280		54
146		103	216		69	282		53
148	Above average	101	218		69	284		53
150		100	220		68	286		52
152		99	222		68	288		52
154		97	224	Very poor	67	290		52
156		96	226		66	292		51
158		95	228		66	294		51
160		94	230		65	296		51
162	Average	93	232		65	298		50
164		91				300		50
166		90						

(Brouha score column note: 90 or above is excellent)

HOW TO USE TABLE: Add sum of three pulse counts, 1-1½, 2-2½, 3-3½, i.e., 80 + 65 +55 = 200. Find 200 under recovery pulse rate and note score of 75 under Brouha score.

Devised by F. W. Kasch, from Cureton, T. K.: Physical fitness workbook, St. Louis, 1947, The C. V. Mosby Co., and Brouha, L.: The step test; a simple method of measuring physical fitness for muscular work in young men, *Research Quarterly*, vol. 14, no. 1, March 1943.

The Kasch pulse recovery step test (Fred W. Kasch,* 1976). The 3-minute pulse recovery step test consists of a 12-inch bench, 24 per minute stepping rate for exactly 3 minutes' duration. Its purpose is to broadly determine the exercise tolerance or exercise classification of human subjects. It is not intended to be a diagnostic test, but for (1) screening and classification of fitness as a means of prescribing an exercise program, (2) evaluating the subject's fitness in comparison to normals, and (3) following the progress of a person undergoing training or recuperating from a low fitness level or illness.

The test is administered as follows:

1. The subject steps up onto bench with left (L) foot, then right (R), then down with L, and next with R in a four-count sequence. This is done 24 times per minute, or two complete steps each 5 seconds.
2. Start stepping at 11 on the clock sweep second hand (see p. 58), counting up two, three, one; up two, three, two; up two, three, three; etc. for 24 steps, ending at 11 on the sweep second hand. Repeat this procedure thrice or for a duration of 3 minutes.
3. After 3 minutes and at 11 on the clock sweep second hand, step over bench, and sit down. Find pulse, wait until sweep reaches 12 and count the heart rate (HR) for 1 minute either total count or in 10-second intervals. Record.

*Kasch, F. W.: A comparison of the exercise tolerance of postrheumatic and normal boys, J. Assoc. Phys. Mental Rehab. **15**:35-40, 1961.

Kasch, F.: Heart rate response of children to standard exercise. Proc. Fourth Int. Symposium, Pediatric Work Physiology, Wingate Institute, Israel, April 1972.

Kasch, F. W., and Boyer, J. L.: Adult fitness, Palo Alto, Calif. 1968, National Press Books.

Table 4-2 □ Table for use with Kasch pulse recovery test (1976); suggested standards: recovery heart rate, 0-1 minute after exercise in sitting position

Classification	6-12 years		18-26 years		27-60 years	
	Boys	**Girls**	**Men**	**Women***	**Men**	**Women***
Superior	74	82	68	73	69	74
Excellent	74-83	83-93	69-75	74-82	70-78	75-83
Good	84-92	94-103	76-83	83-90	79-87	84-92
Average	93-103	104-115	84-92	91-100	88-99	93-103
Fair	104-112	116-125	93-99	101-107	100-107	104-112
Poor	113-121	126-136	100-106	108-114	108-115	113-121
Very poor	122	137	107	115	116	122
Mean	98	111	88	95	93	98
Range	74-126	83-142	72-104	—	60-115	—
SD	9.9	11.2	9.8	—	9.5	—

*Arbitrary data.

4. Compare 0-1 minute recovery HR to table of standards (Table 4-2). Classify subject and then review results with him or her. Advise.

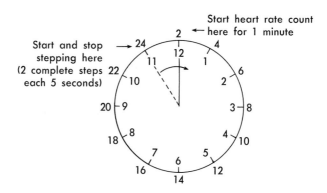

Another excellent method of assessing cardiovascular fitness is through the Cooper 12-minute fitness test.* This test measures oxygen uptake without the use of laboratory equipment, since the tables developed by Cooper after extensive testing reflect a high correlation with the true values of oxygen uptake measured in relation to the total distance in miles traveled by the individual in 12 minutes, either walking or running. In testing athletes it is suggested that they pace themselves to run the entire 12 minutes. Table 4-3 projects the values for the age groups. The test is easily administered by having the athletes run a measured mile distance, preferably on a quarter-mile running track, so that segments of the distance can be easily calculated and the 12-minute total applied to the chart to ascertain the degree of fitness. Retesting at intervals gives a good indication as to how the athlete is progressing in her training program.

*Cooper, K. H.: The new aerobics, New York, 1970, M. Evans & Co.

Table 4-3 □ 12-minute cardiovascular fitness test

Fitness category	Distance covered in miles	
	Under 30 years	30 to 39 years
Very poor	<0.95	<0.85
Poor	0.95-1.14	0.85-1.04
Fair	1.15-1.34	1.05-1.24
Good	1.35-1.64	1.25-1.54
Excellent	1.65+	1.55+

"<" means "less than."
From Cooper, K. H.: The new aerobics, New York, 1970, M. Evans & Co.

Strength testing

Strength may be measured in a number of ways, either through instrumentation (Fig. 4-5) or through physical performance without the use of instruments. One must bear in mind that the strength of one particular muscle group cannot serve as a general indicator of other muscle groups, since strength per se depends on the challenge to and amount of use the group gets during daily activities. Hence, in strength testing one would be wise in getting assessments of several muscle groups; for example, the arm-shoulder complex, the abdominal group, and the leg-hip complex would give a good picture of the all-around general strength of the individual. A simple test battery can easily be set up using, for example, parallel bar dips or push-ups (modified, if desired), abdominal curls, and the vertical jump. Such pattern would give a good indication of the state of tonus and strength. The use of a hand dynamometer to measure grip strength is very specific but such measurement should be used only in addition to other measurements, especially if grip strength is a factor in the sport. It is indeed fallacious to use grip strength as an index of arm strength.

Flexibility testing

Flexibility refers to the range of motion of the joints. Insufficient flexibility is a distinct handicap in physical performance; excessive flexibility is also handicapping in most sports. The coach or trainer should assess the tightness-looseness factor of each athlete under her. Girls or women showing limited flexibility should be put onto a stretching program that will develop desirable ranges of motion in the affected joints. Those athletes who exhibit excessive flexibility should be placed on a strength-building program that will increase the density of the muscles and the collagenous tissues until they have achieved more acceptable levels.

Flexibility, like strength, is highly specific not only to each joint, but also a distinct pattern of flexibility is identifiable with each sport since the activity performed makes distinctive demands upon the performer. For example, a gymnast

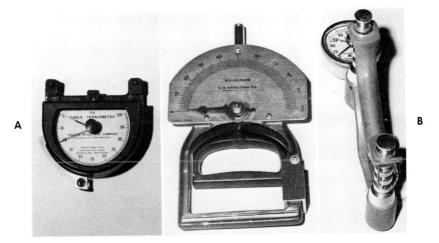

Fig. 4-5. A, Cable tensiometer used in strength testing. **B,** Two types of hand dynamometers for measuring grip strength.

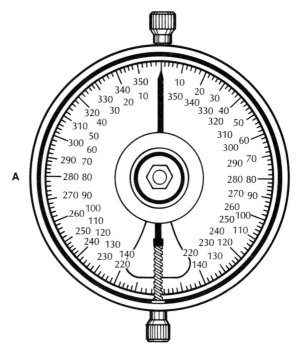

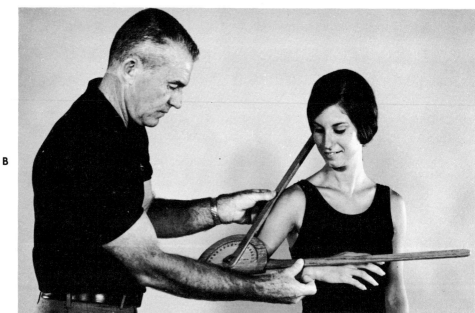

Fig. 4-6. A, Leighton flexometer. **B,** Homemade goniometer in use. (**A** from Morehouse, L. E.: Laboratory manual for physiology of exercise, St. Louis, 1972, The C. V. Mosby Co.; **B** from Arnheim, D. D., Auxter, D., and Crowe, W. C.: Principles and methods of adapted physical education, ed. 3, St. Louis, 1977, The C. V. Mosby Co.)

requires different ranges of flexibility as opposed to a softball player, and a dancer will have different ranges developing as opposed to a swimmer.

After injury, a degree of flexibility in the injured joint is lost, usually as the result of immobilization. That which is lost must be reestablished during the rehabilitative period before the athlete is permitted to reenter her sport. It is helpful to make a record of each athlete's ranges of motion to assist the trainer, should injury occur.

In assessing flexibility a number of different methods may be utilized. Instruments such as a Leighton flexometer or a goniometer (Fig. 4-6) are most often used for reasonably accurate measurement. However, there are a number of movement tests that can also be used that will give the assessor a fairly good indication of the tightness-looseness factor.

Hip joint. The sit-and-reach test is easily administered, and the device utilized is easily constructed. The test may be performed either sitting or standing (see Fig. 4-7). After three preliminary trunk bobs, with the knees extended and locked, the subject reaches as far forward or downward as she can. The distance reached is recorded as the measure of flexibility in positive or negative values (inches or centimeters) with point zero coinciding with the position of the soles of the feet.

Spine. A lower back condition, not uncommon among females, is lordosis (swayback). This is an exaggerated anterior lumbar curve in the spine and is caused by an imbalance between the abdominal and hip flexor muscles. Although

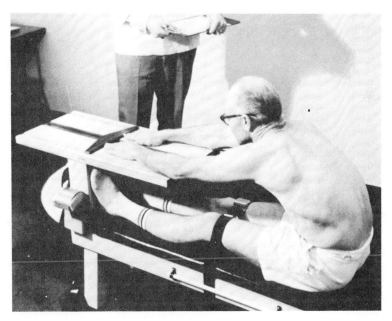

Fig. 4-7. Sit-and-reach test. (From Morehouse, L. E.: Laboratory manual for physiology of exercise, St. Louis, 1972, The C. V. Mosby Co.; courtesy County of Los Angeles, Department of Personnel, Occupational Health Service.)

lordosis is considered normal for a preschool child, usually one grows out of the condition as sufficient abdominal strength is gained to offset the downward pull of the hip flexors on the anterior pelvis. A number of factors can cause lordosis. Weak abdominals, weak gluteal muscles or hamstrings, overly tight lumbar extensors, and strong hip flexors are all causative factors, since they cause a downward tilting of the anterior pelvis, resulting in an exaggerated posterior concave curve in the lumbar spine. Lordosis is frequently the predisposing cause of lumbosacral or sacroiliac strain, coccygalgia (pain in the coccygeal area) or hamstring pull, the bane of runners and sprinters. Excessive lordosis can lead to trauma during active exercise.

Hip flexors may be tested as follows: Have the athlete lie supine on the training table, one leg extended and hanging completely over the end of the table, the other leg flexed at the knee, which is brought to the chest and clasped by the arms. Normal flexibility is present if the athlete can keep the knee flexed tight to the chest while simultaneously lowering her other leg to 180 degrees in line with her trunk.

Another test for flexibility of the hip flexors involves having the athlete assume a straight seat on the floor, legs together, knees extended, back erect, and at 90 degrees to the thighs. She now attempts to flatten the backs of the knees firmly against the floor while maintaining the back-thigh relationship. Inability to press the knees firmly to the floor or to completely extend the knee joints indicates tight hip flexors, and hamstring- and quadriceps-strengthening exercises such as quad setting should be assigned.

The *spinal extensors* may quickly be tested as follows: the athlete lies supine upon a table or the floor and attempts to rotate the anterior pelvis upward thus flattening the lumbar spine bringing it into full contact with the floor or table. She can also perform the same maneuver while standing with the heels and the back against the wall surface. Inability to accomplish lumbar flattening indicates tight hip extensors and a program of exercises such as abdominal curls or the knee-chest curl should be assigned.

Ankle, knee, wrist, elbow, and shoulder joints. These joints are more effectively tested through instrumentation. Undoubtedly, the single best instrument currently in use for such testing is the Leighton flexometer (Fig. 4-6, *A*), which is a device consisting of a weighted 360-degree dial and a weighted pointer enclosed within a case. Any limb-joint position 20 degrees or more removed from horizontal can be measured objectively. Complete instructions and testing procedures for the flexometer can be found in Mathews, D. K.: *Measurement in Physical Education*, ed. 2, Philadelphia, 1963, W. B. Saunders Company.

Should a flexometer be unobtainable, a goniometer may be used. This instrument consists of two shafts fastened together at one end to either a 180- or a 360-degree protractor (Fig. 4-7, *B*). The axis is centered over the joint; one shaft is held in place on the rotating limb and the other held against the opposite segment. The degree of flexibility is recorded as indicated in the degrees of movement on the protractor. The goniometer is vulnerable to operator error when in use and the results depend to a great degree on the skill and experience of the operator. However, it can be used successfully with care and particularly where gross measurements are desired.

SUGGESTED READINGS

American Heart Association: Exercise testing and training of apparently healthy individuals: a handbook for physicians, New York, 1972, American Heart Association.

Åstrand, P. O., and Rodahl, K.: Textbook of work physiology, New York, 1970, McGraw-Hill Book Co.

Boyer, J. L.: Round table; what to cover in office evaluation for exercise, Physician Sportsmed. **4:**82, 1976.

Committee on Medical Aspects of Sports, A. M. A.: A guide for medical evaluation of candidates for school sports, ed. 2, Chicago, 1966, The American Medical Association.

Cooper, K. H.: The new aerobics, New York, 1970, M. Evans & Co.

de Vries, H. A.: Physiology of exercise for physical education and athletics, ed. 2, Dubuque, Iowa, 1974, William C. Brown Co., Publishers.

Houston, G.: Pediatrician's role in sports medicine mainly preventive, Med. Sports, vol. 9, no. 1, Jan. 1969, Rystan Co., Mt. Vernon, N.Y.

Karvonen, M. J.: Effects of vigorous exercise on the heart. In Rosenbaum, F. F., and Belknap, E. L., editors: Work and the heart, New York, 1959, Paul B. Hoeber, Inc.

Kasch, F. W.: Exercise physiology laboratory manual, San Diego, 1970, F. W. Kasch, publisher (San Diego State University).

Klafs, C. E., and Arnheim, D. D.: Modern principles of athletic training, ed. 4, St. Louis, 1977, The C. V. Mosby Co.

Lane, R. M.: Medical qualifications for participants in interscholastic athletics in Maine: J. Natl. Athletic Training Assoc. **5:**1, 1970.

Mathews, D. K.: Measurement in physical education, ed. 2, Philadelphia, 1963, W. B. Saunders Co.

New York State Sports Medicine Symposium: High school sports medicine, Med. Sports, vol. 10, no. 5, Sept. 1970, Rystan Co., Mt. Vernon, N.Y.

Reiheld, R. E.: The high school team physician, Proc. 7th National Conference of the Medical Aspects of Sports, Chicago, 1965, The American Medical Association.

Tips on athletic training VIII: The health examination for athletic participation, pp. 1-3, Chicago, 1966, The American Medical Association.

5 □ Principles of conditioning

DEFINITION AND PURPOSE

Conditioning is the methodical application of an exercise program carefully formulated to bring the athlete's physiological capacities to their peak in preparation for competition.

New performance records continue to be set each year by men and women athletes alike. In some instances these improvements can be attributed to better designed equipment (for example, the fiber-glass pole for the pole vault) and to better analysis and application of mechanical principles affecting sports performance. But by far the most important factor underlying the success of the modern athlete has been the application of new techniques and procedures in the conditioning program. The willingness of today's high-level competitor to dedicate herself to long hours of strenuous daily training should also be recognized (Fig. 5-1).

BASIC PHYSIOLOGICAL CAPACITIES

The three basic capacities that the athlete attempts to improve through conditioning are strength, endurance, and flexibility.

Strength. Strength refers to the capacity of muscles to exert force or to their ability to do work against a resistance. Adequate muscular strength is probably the single most important capacity contributing to successful athletic performance, particularly those in which short, explosive bursts of power and speed are necessary. Strength is developed by requiring the various muscle groups to perform work against a resistance, as in lifting a weight, or the weight of a body part against the force of gravity, as in sit-ups. Such exercises cause the muscles to work isotonically in shortening and lengthening contractions, thus resulting in motion of the limb or body part involved. Or the muscles can be made to work isometrically, in which case the muscles are tensed or contracted maximally for a period of 6 to 10 seconds. But no body motion occurs in isometric exercise, for there is no lengthening or shortening of the muscles as in isotonic work.

Endurance. Cardiorespiratory endurance is the ability to sustain intense, vigorous activity for a prolonged period of time before the onset of fatigue and the ability to recover quickly. Good endurance is dependent on efficient respiratory, cardiac, and circulatory function. This capacity is extremely important in events of longer duration such as track, swimming, field hockey, and lacrosse (Fig. 5-2).

Endurance is developed by performing an activity vigorously enough to cause a noticeable increase in heart rate (approximately double the resting pulse rate or more) and in the rate and depth of breathing. The exercise should be performed for a minimum of 10 to 15 minutes or longer, with short rest pauses as necessary, until endurance improves. If the individual perspires, this is a good indication that the exercise is sufficiently strenuous to produce beneficial effects.

Flexibility. Flexibility refers to the range of motion of the joints. The flexible

Fig. 5-1. The modern woman athlete has shown her willingness to dedicate long hours to strenuous training.

Fig. 5-2. Good cardiorespiratory endurance is particularly important in sports, such as in lacrosse.

individual can move her trunk and limbs with ease. This capability is influenced by the stretching capacity of the muscles and fascia (connective tissue surrounding muscle), the shape of the bones at the joints, and the relative looseness of the ligaments and joint capsule. Flexibility is absolutely essential in many sport specializations, including the hurdles, gymnastics, swimming, and modern dance. It is also an asset in those sports in which it might provide a reach advantage over a less flexible opponent (Fig. 5-3).

Fig. 5-3. The excellent flexibility demonstrated by Olympic gymnast Cathy Rigby is one of many attributes contributing to her success.

Flexibility is improved by assuming a body position that stretches the desired muscle group. Stretching exercises, unlike strength and endurance activities, are best done very slowly, avoiding rapid, bouncing motions. Slow, gradual stretching has been found more beneficial in improving flexibility and in reducing muscle soreness; rapid, ballistic stretching may induce tissue damage and residual soreness.

PHYSIOLOGICAL IMPROVEMENTS ATTRIBUTABLE TO TRAINING

A variety of physiological responses can be altered by conditioning that will contribute to improving the athlete's competitive performance. On the average the function of each body system can be improved approximately 25%. But the sum of these systemic responses may result in a 100% improvement in total performance capacity in terms of both magnitude and duration of work that the athlete can accomplish. Brouha[5] identifies some of these functional improvements as follows:

1. Increased muscular strength
2. Greater maximum oxygen consumption
3. Higher maximum cardiac output (greater volume of blood pumped by the heart) and less of an increase in pulse rate and blood pressure during submaximal exercise
4. More economical lung ventilation during exercise and a greater maximum lung ventilation
5. Increased capacity to perform more work aerobically, thereby decreasing the tendency to incur an oxygen debt and lactic acid buildup, which causes fatigue
6. Quicker recovery in pulse rate and blood pressure after exercise
7. Better heat dissipation during exercise

PRINCIPLES OF CONDITIONING

Certain basic principles of conditioning must be followed in order to improve the athlete's strength, endurance, flexibility, and concomitant systemic functions. These principles apply equally to the development of all three parameters.

SAID principle. The SAID principle refers to the fact that the human body is extremely adaptable in its ability to accommodate itself to the various kinds of stresses imposed upon it. Physical exercise, that is, muscular work, is one such type of stressor. The progressive adaptation to the stress of muscular work results in an increased ability to perform subsequent muscular activity.[26] However, the adaptation is very specific to the type of demand (stressor) imposed. SAID, a coined word that explains this concept, means "specific adaptation to imposed demands."

Therefore, if a strength demand (strengthening exercise) is imposed upon the body, the body specifically adapts by improving in strength. Endurance is improved only by placing endurance demands upon the body's circulatory and respiratory systems; flexibility can be improved only by performing stretching exercises. Because of the body's tendency to adapt in such a specific manner to the type of demand (stress) imposed, the conditioning program must be comprehensive in content and include activities that place strength, endurance, and flexibility stressors on the athlete if she wishes to improve in these capacities.

Overload. The overload principle must be applied when performing exercises if improvement is made. The particular activity being performed, whether designed to improve strength, endurance, or flexibility, must be such that it exceeds in either intensity or duration the demands regularly made on the individual.[25] It makes sense that one is not going to improve in strength, for example, unless she taxes her present strength capacity. One must make sure, however, not to apply too much overload at once, for this can result in painful residual muscle soreness and discouragement.

Progression. This principle complements and works hand in hand with overload. If the individual applies overload, she will improve in that particular capacity. As improvement is achieved, slightly greater demands must be made if improvement is to continue. In strengthening exercises, progression can be achieved by increasing the number of repetitions, the resistance, or both, as is the case in progressive resistance exercise programs. Progression in endurance is provided by increasing either the speed of the exercise (running, swimming, cycling, etc.), the distance, or a combination of the two. In the case of flexibility, progression is accomplished by increasing the range of motion, that is, that extent to which the muscle group is stretched by stretching further.

Regularity. To improve basic physiological capacities, the individual must work out regularly and frequently. High competitive levels demand daily workouts, even if a satisfactory fitness level has been achieved.

Maintenance. The maintenance principle refers to the fact that once a desired fitness or performance level has been achieved, it is easier to maintain that level than it was to attain it. Maintaining is easier than attaining. This principle also is a reminder that the beneficial effects of conditioning—that is, improved physiological function—are not permanent and will be lost if the athlete fails to continue her maintenance conditioning program. This explains why the athlete quickly gets "out of shape" at the end of the season and must again work extra hard to get back into shape prior to the next competitive schedule. Consequently, it would be to the athlete's advantage if she pursued a maintenance conditioning program between seasons.

WEIGHT TRAINING (PROGRESSIVE RESISTANCE EXERCISES)

In line with the growing acceptance of the premise that woman can, without physiological trauma, do that which man can do, the use of weight training as a corollary of the conditioning program has come into being (Fig. 5-4). Many individuals tend to confuse weight lifting with weight training. Weight lifting is a competitive event wherein one employs certain prescribed lifting techniques in an endeavor to lift a greater maximal amount in each technique than one's competitors. It is a sport calling for sheer power and endurance. Weight training, on the other hand, utilizes a series of resistive exercises performed with progressively increased resistance (most often, but not necessarily, with weights) to develop strength and endurance of the muscle groups so exercised. Weight training is usually designated as progressive resistance exercises (PRE) and is based on the De Lorme system, which utilizes the *overload* principle, the physiological

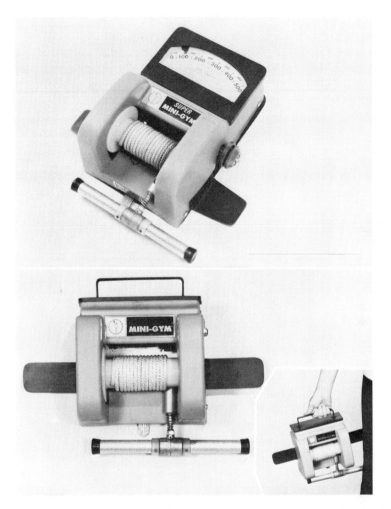

Fig. 5-4. Modern equipment such as the Mini-Gym allows strength to be developed in specific sport-skill movement patterns.

principle upon which the development of strength is dependent.[10,14] Any gains in the strength of the muscle can only be achieved when that muscle or muscle group is worked against a resistance greater than that to which the muscle is accustomed. Conversely, if the muscle falls into a state of relative disuse, atrophy or wasting away of the muscle takes place.

To enable the reader to gain better understanding of strength development, the following terms used in progressive resistance exercises are defined:

power Composed of strength and speed. Defined as the amount of energy per unit of time. It is the ability to exert a muscular force rapidly, such as by a single dynamic movement.
tension Internal force contained within a muscle when the muscle contracts.
overload Use of a resistance greater than that to which the muscle is accustomed.

hypertrophy Increase in the size of skeletal or cardiac muscle, resulting from the increased use of that muscle against heavy resistance.

repetitions Number of consecutive times a particular exercise is performed.

set Number of groups of repetitions of a particular exercise done without rest, usually three.

repetitions maximum (RM) The greatest weight that can be lifted ten times.

isotonic contraction The contraction usually employed in progressive resistance exercises. It is a contraction wherein the muscle visibly shortens.

isometric contraction A contraction wherein there is no visible shortening of the muscle. Most often performed either with no equipment or immovable equipment. Exercise involving this type of contraction are detailed later in this chapter.

Increases in muscular strength as a direct outcome of progressive resistance exercises are a well-established fact; strength gains of as much as 25% are not uncommon.[4,6,12,20] Currently there are numerous variations of the De Lorme system being used. However, the basic principles are the same, and if desirable, the trainer-coach can develop her particular pattern based upon these principles. De Lorme's pattern utilizes the following:

> 1 set of 10 repetitions of $1/2$ RM
> 1 set of 10 repetitions of $3/4$ RM
> 1 set of repetitions of RM

The performer is first pretested to ascertain her maximum effort in a particular exercise. Her training program, utilizing the pattern just given, is then performed from three to five times weekly, depending on the amount of other activity in which she is engaged. When she is able to perform the complete pattern for two successive work sessions, the RM is increased in an increment of either 3 or 5 pounds, such increase being progressively made as the athlete achieves the ability to complete the series successfully in two or more consecutive work bouts.

There seems to be some support for using fewer repetitions than ten, perhaps between four and eight.[4] The instructor should experiment and determine the number of repetitions that give her students the best results. It is useful to keep progress records, either in the form of record cards or a graph; the latter is an excellent motivational device since it utilizes a competitive factor. Strength testing prior to starting the weight-training program, from time to time throughout the program, and at regular intervals after the intensive program enables both athlete and coach to ascertain progress as well as the maintenance of desirable strength levels. The use of a cable tensiometer (Fig. 4-5, *A*) for such strength assessment is recommended.*

Strength retention. Once the desired level of strength has been attained, it will persist in proportion to the length of time spent in developing it. The frequency of workouts may now be reduced and progressive resistance exercises performed to the degree necessary to maintain the status quo. A slight decrease in strength may be noted a few days preceding menstruation.

Muscular endurance. Strength and endurance increase proportionally with

---

*Instructions for the use of the tensiometer are found in Clarke, H. H., and Clarke, D. H.: Developmental and adapted physical education, Englewood Cliffs, N.J., 1963, Prentice-Hall, Inc.; and Clarke, H. H.: Muscular endurance, Englewood Cliffs, N.J., 1966, Prentice-Hall, Inc.

physiological hypertrophy.[14] However, these qualities are undoubtedly dependent on changes brought about in the central nervous system as concomitants of the increases in muscular endurance, which occur only when repetitive exercise is performed against a heavy resistance (Fig. 5-5).

Flexibility. The development of strength without the accompanying maintenance of good flexibility can be exceedingly disadvantageous to the

Fig. 5-5. Strength is developed through the use of modern weight-training equipment.

athlete. As muscles grow in power and in size, the connective tissues—tendons, ligaments, fascial structures, and investments—also increase in size and density, and unless full range of motion of the joints is maintained, the gains in muscle strength in terms of performance may well be negated by movement restriction. Exercises to maintain and increase desirable flexibility should be used. Excessive flexibility should be avoided since it, too, can work to the performer's disadvantage. (See Fig. 5-6.)

Points to stress

1. Be certain that all weight collars are securely fastened and that all equipment is in good working order. It is advisable to use spotters in certain exercises when the equipment is difficult to manage or the terminal position of the lift is somewhat precarious.
2. Precede all progressive resistance exercises with a general warm-up of proper duration.
3. Perform all exercises slowly and deliberately. Speed is not of the essence.
4. Inhale on the lifting maneuver; exhale on the return maneuver. NOTE: There is usually a tendency to hold the breath, particularly when a maximum or near-maximum effort is being made, thus involving the *Val-*

Fig. 5-6. This athlete has developed excellent abdominal, shoulder, and arm strength to perform on the uneven parallel bars.

salva phenomenon. By closing the glottis, intrathoracic and intra-abdominal pressures are built up, thus inhibiting venous blood return to the heart, which results in a decline of arterial blood pressure. Arterial pressure decline reflexly increases heart rate. After the resistance has been overcome, the sudden surge of venous blood greatly increases pulmonary arterial pressures. Systolic pressures higher than 200 millimeters of mercury (mm. Hg) may result.[10] The danger here is not to the healthy individual who possesses a good circulatory system but rather to the individual who may harbor some undetected organic or circulatory deficiency.

5. When lifting with the trunk inclined to approximately 90 degrees, *do not lock the knees*. To prevent possible low-back injury, bend the knees to approximately 15 degrees of flexion or rest the forehead on a padded table to stabilize the lower back and reduce the stress. Either of these techniques will eliminate undue pressure on the spinal discs.
6. On all lifts, keep the back as nearly vertical as possible. Initiate low lifts by flexing the knees; then begin the lift through extension of the knee joints.
7. Perform a complete set before proceeding to the next exercise.
8. Take each exercise through the full range of joint movement.
9. Plan your program so that each set develops a different body part. The entire body must be exercised.
10. Warm-down. Utilize warm-up procedures in inverse order so as to permit a gradual circulatory readjustment.

ISOMETRIC EXERCISES

Recently the development of strength through the use of isometric exercises has become extremely popular. News media have exploited isometrics as the "easy way" to health and fitness through exercise. They have stressed the idea that one can gain considerable strength merely by sitting at one's desk and devoting a few minutes daily to isometrics, all this without perspiring or suffering discomfort. Some of the more enthusiastic adherents have further claimed that isometric exercises can develop the body so completely that virtually no other types of activities are needed. Statements of this kind are utterly false. A program of isometric exercises can indeed result in strength gains, but there are some definite limitations that must be recognized. First, the principle of specificity applies in that such strength gains will reflect increases in isometric not isotonic strength. Second, isometric exercises do not sufficiently challenge nor do they improve cardiovascular strength or endurance. The use of isometric exercises as part of a well-rounded physical conditioning program will contribute much to the individual, and such exercises have particular value in physical restoration after injury when the individual is unable to exercise isotonically.

The use of isometric or "dynamic" tension exercise was first popularized in the 1920s by Charles Atlas, a well-known "physical culturist" who advertised that he could take a 90-pound weakling and, through the use of "dynamic tension," make him into a superb physical specimen. His claims received some scientific support years later. In 1953 Hettinger and Müller of the Max Planck Institute at Dortmund, Germany, reported the results of their studies, which validated muscular strength gains achieved through isometric exercises. Since that time isometric training has undergone a great deal of investigation, from which conflicting results have emerged, particularly in respect to the duration of held contractions and strength gain.[3,22-23] It has been shown that isometric strength gains are specific to the joint angle at which the exercise is performed. To use isometrics effectively, one should execute exercises throughout the full range of joint motion during each workout.

In isometric exercises the muscles are forcefully contracted, but no change in the length of the muscle occurs, although the production of metabolic heat by the muscle indicates that work is being accomplished. One may attain a contraction of this type by contracting opposing groups of muscles equally and maximally, or muscular force may be expended against a completely immovable object (for example, standing within a doorway and pushing maximally against the jamb on either side.) Although in the foregoing examples maximal force is being applied, there is no visible change in the length of the muscle. Hettinger and Müller used such static contractions at about two thirds maximal effort, holding the contraction for 6 seconds. Although weekly strength gains of approximately 5% were reported, subsequent investigators showed somewhat lower increases. On the basis of the most recent investigations, it appears that employing one maximal contraction for a sustained 10-second period is the most effective. A program of isometric exercises is presented in *Modern Principles of Athletic Training*.[17] Other programs may be found in any of the current texts dealing with exercise programs. Isometric exercise training must be viewed as only one form of training in the overall program and must not be considered as either a panacea or a method calculated to preclude hard physical work. When isometric exercise training is properly carried out, positive results can be obtained. Bear in mind that isometrics do not appear to contribute significantly to isotonic strength, skill, or endurance, nor do they increase cardiopulmonary endurance. Their contribution lies solely in the improvement of the strength components of physical fitness.[11,13]

Points to stress

1. Little difference appears to exist between the end results of isometric and isotonic exercises; so one may use them interchangeably, bearing in mind that each is specific to itself in terms of strength.
2. Either because of a time factor or because of a pathological condition, isometrics can lend themselves particularly well to physical restoration.
3. Performance of a series of isometric exercises should be done at least five times a week.
4. A near-maximum or maximum contraction sustained for 10 seconds should be followed by a few seconds of rest and should then be repeated once or twice, constituting a series.
5. A series should be performed involving the muscle groups of each of the following: the neck, shoulders and arms, legs, and trunk.
6. Isometric exercises should be used as complementary exercises to the program as a whole rather than as an end in themselves.

CIRCUIT TRAINING

Circuit training is one of the most versatile training systems of physical conditioning. It was developed at the University of Leeds in the post–World War II era by Morgan and Adamson[19] to train and condition athletes more expeditiously through the use of a systematized and orderly program. Circuit training gained almost instant popularity and is widely used from the secondary school level on up. There are several favorable aspects that enable this system to be used not only in the sports program but in the general physical education program as well. It is self-motivating and may be easily tailored to individual needs. It can be set up to utilize various pieces of equipment and apparatus or it can be designed so that no such aids are necessary. It can be devised to develop strength, speed, skill, endurance, and cardiopulmonary efficiency. It makes use of the principles of overload, repetition, and specificity and in addition can employ time as a factor as well. It permits careful gauging of the strenuousness of the activity in terms of the performer's level of condition and allows constant adjustments to be made throughout the training period. See Fig. 5-7.

The following terms are used in circuit training:

circuit Performing all the required exercises at each station in their proper sequence in the allotted time, that is, performing one complete tour of the entire course.
lap Synonymous with circuit.

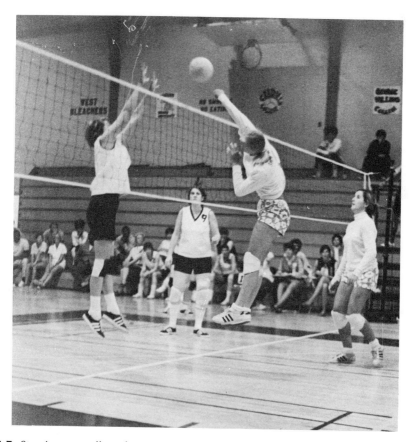

Fig. 5-7. Stamina as well as the arm and leg strength needed in spiking and blocking can be developed by means of circuit training.

stations Designated places on the circuit, at each of which a prescribed activity is performed. There are usually from six to nine stations on a circuit.

target time Specific time limits set up for completing one or more circuits. As training progresses, the target time is lowered accordingly, hence speeding up the rate of performance at each station.

maximum repetitions Number of exercise repetitions of which the performer is capable. These may be performed either within a specified time interval (usually 1 minute) or without regard to time.

The circuit-training program usually consists of three laps of the entire circuit, with the last lap requiring maximal effort at each station. The preceding laps are usually scaled below maximum (about 60% to 70% maximum) both in time and effort. In establishing a circuit-training program one must bear in mind the following considerations:

1. Select exercises with regard to specificity so that one lap of the circuit will involve all desired muscle groups and the cardiopulmonary system.
2. The intensity and duration of each exercise must be established to provide enough of a challenge to be meaningful and still permit sufficient reserves for an all-out effort on the final lap.
3. Regardless of whether time or repetitions are used, the performer must adhere to the established program. She is permitted no shortcuts.
4. In determination of the training dosage a procedure similar to that used in progressive resistance exercises is employed. The performer executes each exercise maximally in sequence and within a specified time period (30 or 60 seconds), depending on the type of exercise. Careful count of the number of repetitions achieved at each station is kept and a 1-minute rest interval is permitted before proceeding to the next station. The dosage for each of the three circuits is then established as follows:

   Circuit 1 Performed at one half of maximum
   Circuit 2 Performed at three fourths of maximum
   Circuit 3 Performed at maximum

5. After the dosage has been determined, the performer then completes all three circuits, resting between exercises, and establishes a target time. The target time is computed on a subsequent day after adequate rest. A timed rest interval, arbitrarily determined, is permitted after each circuit. The total elapsed time for the completion of the three laps, exclusive of the rest periods, represents the target time.
6. The athlete is now ready to perform each of the exercises in the circuit in the required dosage (time or repetitions) and completes three full circuits against the clock. When she has reached the point of equaling or bettering the target time, she is again evaluated and new dosages and target time established.

As may be seen, circuit training is a variation of the progressive resistance exercise program. Fig. 5-6 illustrates sample circuits. The flexibility of this program is one of its desirable features. Activities are easily changed, the number of stations increased or decreased, the intensity of the activities varied, and the time factor varied or adjusted as the situation warrants. The preliminary time and

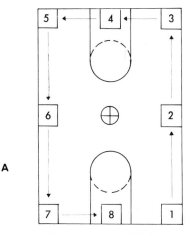

1. Half squats, barbell behind neck
2. Abdominal curls
3. Bench stepping (16 inches)
4. Push-ups
5. Rope skipping
6. Flexion exercises
7. Squat thrust (four-count burpee)
8. Hamstring stretch

1. Forearm curls
2. Knee extensions—quadriceps
3. Abdominal curls—weight behind head
4. Knee flexions—prone—hamstrings

Fig. 5-8. A, Weight-training circuit (general conditioning). **B,** Weight-training circuit (strength). Note that all exercises are done against a weight resistance.

planning in establishing this program are well worth the effort since the program, once established, virtually runs itself; the athlete is her own competition (Fig. 5-8).

INTERVAL TRAINING PROGRAM

Today, probably the most universally used training procedure in track and field and in swimming (particularly to improve endurance) is the interval training program (ITP). Basically this is a time-oriented program or system in which a measured distance is covered using five factors:

1. A flat measured track or swimming pool
2. A prescribed distance to be covered
3. A prescribed number of repetitive performances over the distance
4. A prescribed recovery interval between each performance
5. A set or fixed pace for the performances

This type of program is extremely permissive in that it permits the program to be developed in terms of specificity for both athlete and event. As with some of the previous programs presented, the principle of *overload* is the basic premise of interval training. However, the subsequent improvement in endurance is gained through a decrease in the length of rest intervals rather than through an increase in the work load, as is the case in both progressive resistance exercises and circuit training.

The concept of the interval training program was developed in Germany some years ago by Reindell and Harbig, along with a track coach named Gershler. Almost immediately the system found universal acceptance, and today it is undoubtedly the most widely used program in conditioning for track and field and for swimming in particular. The program uses a number of well-established physiological principles:

1. Greater work loads can be tolerated if they are broken down into smaller increments or bouts, interspersed with rest periods.[1,7]
2. Work is assessed on the basis of overload.
3. An increase in aerobic capacity is incurred, which is reflected in greater cardiorespiratory endurance.
4. Because of its inherent specificity, it utilizes learning through the use of those neuromuscular components peculiar to the sport itself.
5. It assists the athlete in her mastery of pace.
6. It delays the onset of fatigue by not reaching so deeply into the lactic acid system.[18]*
7. As the intensity of the work increases, the lactic acid system improves; thus the athlete is allowed to develop a greater tolerance toward the lactic acid accumulations in the tissues.
8. Work intervals sufficiently stressful to maintain heart rates above 150 beats per minute must be established so that desired cardiopulmonary improvements will occur.

The program may be developed for slow-interval or fast-interval training, depending on whether the sport is one primarily involving distance or speed.[27] Slow-interval training stresses aerobic endurance, whereas fast-interval training is geared toward anaerobic endurance. The following terms are used in interval training:

sprinting Running or swimming at maximum speed.
striding Running speed anywhere between jogging and sprinting.
work interval Portion of the program in which work of high intensity is performed.
relief interval Recovery period that follows the work interval, usually consisting of walking or jogging, or in swimming, sustaining a leisurely pace. The term "rest interval" is often used.
set A series of alternating work and relief intervals.
repetitions Number of work intervals performed in one set. For example, six work intervals of 110-yard runs interspersed with a like number of rest intervals would constitute one set of six repetitions.
training time Prescribed speed at which the prescribed work interval is performed.

Procedure. Prior to embarking upon an interval training program, a reasonably well-conditioned sportswoman should spend a week or 10 days in a general conditioning program involving jogging, running, or swimming. The emphasis should be on duration of activity rather than intensity or speed, or both. The sportswoman who is at a lower level of fitness needs approximately 3 to 5 weeks of a jogging and general exercise program preparatory to entering a concentrated interval program. No individual should be permitted to push herself to a stressful

---

*Lactic acid is formed in muscle tissue by the breakdown of glycogen (glycolysis) during exercise, and since it is incompatible with muscular economy, it is the most common limiting factor of muscular activity. The body has a tolerance level that limits one's ability to continue physical work.[8,16]

point. Work is best done at about 75% to 80% of maximum and should be accomplished so as to avoid muscle soreness and undue fatigue. Such preliminaries ready the individual for the more taxing interval program.

Slow-interval training. Slow-interval training is usually restricted to distances of up to and including 1/2 mile. It stresses the athlete through an alternation of fast and slow intervals and should be sufficiently strenuous to elicit heart rates of 180 beats per minute and above during the work intervals. It employs a given number of repetitions at a prescribed distance performed at a set pace and is used to develop the athlete's aerobic endurance. Usually the target or pace times for the work intervals are empirically determined upon the basis of the athlete's best performance or she may be pretested and her speed determined over the workout distances. *A running start should be used.* The performance speed during the work interval must be faster than that attained by the athlete during a continuous performance.

For example, a half-miler has a best effort of 2:10; therefore her average for each 110 yards is 16.25 seconds. In determining her target time for a 110-yard work interval, we must keep in mind that *her work speed must be faster than the speed of her continuous performance.* Therefore, by arbitrarily adding 5 seconds to the average of 16 seconds (the fraction is dropped for the sake of convenience), we arrive at a target time of 21 seconds for each of her 110-yard work intervals. Depending on her state of training, we could add 4 or even 6 seconds to her continuous performance time.

As the training program advances, both target times and work loads must be intensified. Careful planning should result in the final one fourth to one third of the schedule being infinitely more difficult than the initial phases. Inasmuch as this program is tailor-made to the performer, there will be differences in loads and time adjustments for the various performers. The number of repetitions to be done in each set are determined empirically, common practice usually establishing the number as between four and ten when training for distances up to and including 800 meters. The number of repetitions must be governed by the work load and the race for which the athlete is training. Distances over 1/2 mile will require more repetitions per set and a somewhat higher target time. Experience in coaching is of considerable assistance in making the necessary adjustments logically. A suggested initial slow-interval training program for a hypothetical miler is as follows:

1. Two or three sets of ten each—110-yard runs in 21 seconds, each followed by a 60-second jog and a 2- to 3-minute walk set interval
2. Three or four sets of ten each—220-yard runs in 42 to 45 seconds, each followed by a 220-yard jog and a 3- to 5-minute walk set interval
3. Three or four sets of ten each—440-yard runs at 84 to 90 seconds, each followed by a 440-yard jog and a 5-minute set interval.

As one can see, there is a great deal of leeway in establishing a program. With some experience, one can do a good job in setting up a program that brings gratifying results to both coach and participant.

Fast-interval training. Fast-interval training is usually instituted after the slow-interval program and is used to develop one's anaerobic endurance. Here again, the work interval must be sufficiently stressful to evoke heart rates of 180 beats per minute and above. The program is developed in a manner intended to develop the ability of the athlete to withstand the pain and discomforts of fatigue when the oxygen supply to the working muscles is inadequate. Fast-interval training appears to result in a greater tolerance of lactic acid and other by-products of muscle metabolism. The program is more stressful than slow-interval training and is used by those who must run longer distances since it seems to develop an ability to sustain a faster pace for a longer period of time. The procedure described in slow-interval training is used to determine the target times. However, for the 110- and 220-yard distances it is suggested that the athlete be pretested over each distance *with a running start* and then 3 to 5 seconds *added* to her time to constitute the work load. For the 440-yard phase, if the athlete is competing in the half-mile or in the mile run, it is suggested that her best 440-yard average be taken and then from 1 to 4 seconds *subtracted* from that average. Let us assume that in pretesting our hypothetical runner came up with times of 17 and 30 seconds for the 110- and the 220-yard runs, respectively. Her best time for the half-mile was 2:10, which would give her an average of 1:05 for each 440 yards. In the first two instances we add 3 seconds so that her target times would be 20 and 33 seconds, respectively, for the 110 and 220. In the latter instance we subtract 3 seconds for her 440 time, thus establishing a target time of 1:02. A suggested fast-interval initial program might be as follows:

1. Two or three sets of ten each—110-yard runs in 20 seconds, each followed by a 100-yard jog and a 3- to 5-minute walk set interval
2. Three sets of five to ten each—220-yard runs in 33 seconds, each followed by a 220-yard jog and a 5-minute walk set interval
3. Three to five sets of ten each—440-yard runs in 1:02, each followed by a 440-yard jog and a 5-minute walk interval

If the athlete keeps within 3 seconds of her target time, she is doing well. Here again, a knowledge of pace is essential and is developed while performing at set speeds.

Recovery period. After strenuous exertion a period of light activity must be pursued. During exertion, as the exercising muscles require more and more oxygen, the heart rate and blood volume must increase to meet these demands. Upon cessation of the activity, as the heart rate decreases, the excess blood volume must be returned to the viscera from where most of it comes. A period of light activity such as walking prevents blood pooling and maintains venous return, which in turn expedites reducing the blood volume toward preexercise levels. Usually walking for 3 to 4 minutes is adequate. The term "cooling out" is often applied to the postexercise recovery period. Jogging may be substituted for walking. However, jogging or slow running requires half again as much energy as walking; recovery may take somewhat longer. Most athletes favor walking during recovery.

The athlete should learn to take her own pulse during training, either by palpating the carotid artery in the neck or the radial artery on the thumb side of the wrist, using the first two fingers, never the thumb. A 10-second count, taken with a stopwatch, multiplied by six to get the minute rate, will assist her, particularly during interval training where it is necessary to be cognizant of the heart rates during both the work and recovery intervals. The heart rate should return to two thirds of the *immediate postexercise rate* before the next set of work intervals is attempted. For example, a heart rate of 180 beats per minute should return to 120 beats per minute about 1 minute after exercise. Recovery is then sufficient to begin the next work interval.[1,8,24]

Karvonen[16] has indicated that pulse rates of 150 beats per minute are necessary if improvement in cardiac performance is to be realized. It is therefore necessary that work loads elicit heart rates above that figure if improvement in performance is to occur. Decreases in target times or increases in the number of repetitions are in order if the stress is insufficient to reach a rate of 180 beats per minute. Keep in mind that the normal heart is invulnerable to exercise inasmuch as neuromuscular fatigue will occur well before physiological limits are attained.[26]

Frequency. Interval training workouts should be confined to four or five weekly during the training or precompetitive season and from three to four during the competitive season. This dosage may vary with the individual, depending on her state of training, but it does provide a guide for the trainer-coach.

REFERENCES

1. Åstrand, I., Åstrand, P. O., Christensen, E. H., and Hedman, R.: Intermittent muscular work, Acta Physiol. Scand. **48:**448, 1960.
2. Åstrand, P. O., Cuddy, T. E., Saltin, B., and Stenberg, J.: Cardiac output during submaximal and maximal work, J. Appl. Physiol. **19:**268, 1964.
3. Berger, R. A.: Comparison between static training and various dynamic training programs, Res. Q. Am. Assoc. Health Phys. Educ. **34:**131, 1963.
4. Berger, R. A.: Comparison of the effects of various weight training loads on strength, Res. Q. Am. Assoc. Health Phys. Educ. **36:**141, 1965.
5. Brouha, L.: Training. In Johnson, W. R., editor: Science and medicine of exercise and sports, New York, 1960, Harper & Brothers.
6. Chui, E.: The effect of systematic weight training on athletic power, Res. Q. Am. Assoc. Health Phys. Educ. **21:**188, 1950.
7. Christensen, E. H., Hedman, R., and Saltin, B.: Intermittent and continuous running, Acta Physiol. Scand. **50:**269, 1960.
8. Cooper, K. H.: Aerobics, New York, 1968, M. Evans & Co.
9. Corbin, C. B., Dowell, L. J., Lindsey, R., and Tolson, H.: Concepts in physical education, ed. 2, Dubuque, Iowa, 1974, William C. Brown Co., Publishers.
10. De Lorme, T. L., and Watkins, A. L.: Progressive resistance exercise, New York, 1951, Appleton-Century-Crofts.
11. Falls, H. B., Wallis, E. L., and Logan, G. A.: Foundations of conditioning, New York, 1970, Academic Press, Inc.
12. Golding, L. A., and Bos, R. R.: Scientific foundations of physical fitness programs, Minneapolis, 1970, Burgess Publishing Co.
13. Hansen, J. W.: The training effect of repeated isometric contractions, Int. Z. Angew. Physiol. **18:**474, 1961.
14. Hellebrandt, F. A., and Houtz, S. J.: Mechanisms of muscle training in man, experimental demonstration of the overload principle, Phys. Ther. Rev. **36:**371, 1956.
15. Hettinger, T.: Physiology of strength, Springfield, Ill., 1961, Charles C Thomas, Publisher.
16. Karvonen, M. J.: Effects of vigorous exercise on the heart. In Rosenbaum, F. F., and Belknap, E. L., editors: Work and the heart, New York, 1959, Paul B. Hoeber, Inc.
17. Klafs, C. E., and Arnheim, D. D.: Modern principles of athletic training, ed. 4, St. Louis, 1977, The C. V. Mosby Co.
18. Mathews, D. K., and Fox, E. L.: The physiological basis of physical education and athletics, ed. 2, Philadelphia, 1976, W. B. Saunders Co.
19. Morgan, R. E., and Adamson, G. T.: Circuit training, New Rochelle, N. Y., 1961, Soccer Associates.
20. O'Shea, P.: Effects of selected weight training programs on the development of strength and muscle hypertrophy, Res. Q. Am. Assoc. Health Phys. Educ. **37:**95, 1966.

21. Rarick, G. L., and Larson, G. L.: Observations on frequency and intensity of isometric muscular effort in developing static muscular strength in post-pubescent males, Res. Q. Am. Assoc. Health Phys. Educ. **29:**333, 1958.
22. Rich, G. Q., Ball, J. R., and Wallis, E. L.: Effects of isometric training on strength and transfer of effect to untrained antagonists, J. Sports Med. Phys. Fitness **4:**217, 1964.
23. Royce, J.: Re-evaluation of isometric training methods and results, a must, Res. Q. Am. Assoc. Health Phys. Educ. **35:**215, 1964.
24. Rushmer, R. F.: Cardiovascular dynamics, ed. 2, Philadelphia, 1961, W. B. Saunders Co.
25. Steinhaus, A. H.: Toward an understanding of health and physical education, Dubuque, Iowa, 1963, William C. Brown Co., Publishers.
26. Wallis, E. L., and Logan, G. A.: Figure improvement and body conditioning through exercise, Englewood Cliffs, N. J., 1964, Prentice-Hall, Inc.
27. Wilt, F.: Training for competitive running. In Falls, H. B., editor: Exercise physiology, New York, 1968, Academic Press, Inc.

6 □ Designing the conditioning program

ROLE OF CONDITIONING IN SPORTS PERFORMANCE

A well-designed conditioning program is an absolute essential in contemporary athletics. In the highly competitive environment that characterizes the sports world of today, as performance levels continue to improve, the physical fitness base of the athlete must be more than adequate if only to achieve moderate success. For the national and world-class athlete, victory is achieved not only through faultless technique but through a willingness to devote countless hours in a conditioning regimen designed to bring and maintain the body to an ultimate peak of conditioning and physical capability. But optimal fitness does even more than enhance athletic performance; it is probably the single most important factor that keeps the athlete "healthy" by reducing (but not entirely eliminating) the risk of incurring an injury. Indeed, experts in the field of sports medicine refer to good conditioning as the best preventative medicine available in avoiding injury.

Physical fitness factors

The four parameters of physical fitness that will enhance the athlete's performance potential and reduce the risk of injury are (1) muscular strength, (2) muscular endurance, (3) flexibility or range of motion, involving mainly connective tissue (fascia, which surrounds muscles; ligaments; tendons and joint capsules), and (4) aerobic and anaerobic capacity.

Improving performance potential

Strength. Strength is one of the single most important factors contributing to successful sports performance. The athlete's only source of force essential to putting herself into the fast, vigorous motions involved in sports—running, jumping, throwing, striking, kicking, etc.—comes from the actual force of her muscles pulling on the bony segments of the body. And the stronger the muscles, the greater the force that can be developed. See Fig. 6-1.

This force, in turn, is used to accelerate arms and legs quickly, thereby achieving high final velocities of these body parts. High final velocity, coupled with the athlete's mass, allow her to impart great momentum to sport objects (such as ball, javelin, shuttlecock, and her own body) that she is throwing, kicking, or striking. This causes the object to travel faster, farther, or higher, as the case may be. What this really amounts to is *power*, or rate of work. Power is essential in jumping, sprinting, and swimming (projecting one's own body) and in kicking, striking, and throwing activities. The stronger the athlete, the greater power she can develop whenever the situation demands. In volleyball, good leg strength enables the athlete to jump higher while spiking and blocking; good back and arm strength allows her to hit the ball harder while spiking and serving.

Strength further aids performance by improving the athlete's ability to make sudden starts, stops, and changes in direction, essential to many sports, especially

Fig. 6-1. Arm and leg strength is important in all sports. **A,** Badminton. **B,** Jumping. **C,** Base running. (**A,** Photo by William Foy, Manhattan Beach, Calif. **B,** Photo by William Stuart, Huntington Beach, Calif. **C,** Photo by Phyllis Stevens, Anaheim, Calif.)

field games (soccer, field hockey) and court games (basketball, volleyball, tennis, and badminton). The ability to execute sudden changes in velocity and direction is often termed *agility*. As strength (power) is necessary to overcome momentum and then regain the momentum in a new direction, a high level of agility is impossible without adequate strength.[1]

Muscular endurance. Being strong also helps the athlete to resist fatigue. She can perform the same activity for a longer period of time before experiencing a drop in performance level, compared with a weaker player. Strength, then, is a major factor contributing to muscular endurance, or the ability to use muscles repetitively over an extended period of time. With good muscular endurance, the volleyball player's jumping height and hitting power can remain near their maximum levels through an extended match.

Flexibility. Good flexibility, or the ability to move one's body segments freely, easily, and throughout a wide range of motion, is of utmost importance in improving sports performance. One obvious reason is that many sport skills require the athlete to assume certain positions that demand flexibility. Examples would be the back of the hurdler's lead leg as she clears the hurdle, or the gymnast's low back, as she executes a back bend on the beam. Yet another way in which flexibility contributes to good performance is by enabling the athlete to get into the proper preparatory position or wind-up during the execution of a skill.

In throwing and spiking activities, a big backswing (requiring free range of motion at hips, trunk, and shoulder) provides the athlete more distance and time in which to apply force to the object being thrown or hit. This is well demonstrated by the javelin thrower, whose hips, trunk, and arm on the throwing side are rotated far backward just preceding the actual forward "power" phase of the throw, during which time the hip, trunk, and arm are rotated forcefully forward. In addition to providing more time in which to apply force, the full-range preparatory motion has the added effect of putting the athlete's "power" muscles on *stretch,* thereby, enabling them to contract even more forcefully.

Good flexibility also allows the so-called power muscles to pull their bony segments (arms, legs, etc.) through their complete range without being hampered by tightness of opposing muscle groups. Tight antagonistic muscles can restrict this essential motion, thereby decreasing the athlete's efficiency, resulting in greater fatigue.

Aerobic and anaerobic capacities. Athletic events lasting approximately 3 minutes or longer place large demands on the body's oxygen-transport system. This is especially true for the field sports (soccer, lacrosse, field hockey), which require a great deal of continuous running, but it is also an important factor in court sports as well. It is probably of least importance in the throwing events in track and field. Even in sports that might be classified as mainly anaerobic (softball, volleyball, tennis) a good aerobic base should be established prior to the introduction of the high-intensity, short-duration, repeat work associated with developing anaerobic capacity. See Figs. 6-2 and 6-3.

If these capacities are not well developed during the preseason conditioning period, the athlete's performance, even when fresh, will not be at her best; in addition, fatigue will occur much earlier in the game, causing a further decrement in power, speed, agility, reaction time, and coordination.

Fig. 6-2. Distance events make severe aerobic demands on the body. (Photo by William Stuart, Huntington Beach, Calif.)

Reducing the risk of injury

As stated earlier, bringing players to an optimal level of conditioning constitutes the best form of preventive medicine in minimizing the chances of sports injury. It is a truism that the poorly conditioned athlete is an injury-prone athlete. A higher percentage of injuries occur during the early part of the competition season, usually because the athlete is not yet in good physical condition and may often be overweight as well.[2]

Strong muscles help provide stability at weight-bearing joints. Strength training also increases the toughness of tendons and ligaments, providing additional stability. Developing balanced strength between antagonistic muscle groups (for example, knee extensors and knee flexors) minimizes the chance of pulled muscles. Strong muscles are more resistant to fatigue, thereby minimizing injury resulting from slowed reaction time and loss of coordination.

Good flexibility can reduce the chance of overstretch injuries, such as muscle strains and shin splints. A high level of endurance delays the onset of fatigue and its concomitant problems.

Adminstrators of statewide athletic federations and local leagues should formulate policies and establish competitive schedules that provide sufficient time

Fig. 6-3. Olympian Kathy Schmidt demonstrates excellent form in an anaerobic event. (Photo by William Stuart, Huntington Beach, Calif.)

for adequate conditioning programs to be conducted. Responsibility for designing and implementing conditioning programs should be mutually shared by the team physician, athletic trainer (if one is available), and the coach. Responsibility for fully participating in the program, in order to bring herself to an optimum level of conditioning and reduce the propensity for injury, rests ultimately on the athlete herself, with good parental encouragement and support. An athlete who for any reason is not in adequate condition when the competitive season begins should be prohibited from competing until she is well-conditioned and therefore less prone to injury.

DESIGNING THE CONDITIONING PROGRAM

Planning a conditioning program that will bring the athlete to an optimum level of fitness requires knowledge of the sport itself, the ability to analyze specific sport skills in terms of joint and muscle actions and some understanding of the physiological principles of conditioning.

Some general guidelines to consider when designing a program for a specific competitive sport are offered, as follows.

Adequate time

Provide adequate time to achieve a training effect. Improvement in strength flexibility, aerobic and anaerobic capacities will require approximately 6 to 8 weeks, depending on the fitness level of the athlete as she begins the program. Individuals will vary in response to training, with some improving faster than others. Some athletes will also need to lose weight (fat); as weight loss should not exceed about 2 pounds per week, this will require time.

Principles of conditioning

Principles of conditioning must be considered in planning and implementing the program, if desired improvements are to occur. Included are the principles of overload, progression, and specificity of training response. Gains in strength occur only if muscles are made to work slightly beyond their present capability. Flexibility is improved only when a certain body segment or muscle group is put on stretch slightly more than that to which it has been accustomed. Improvement in aerobic capacity occurs only if the aerobic system is slightly overtaxed beyond its present level. As improvements occur, the demands made upon these systems must be *progressively increased* if improvement is to continue.

Because the body adapts (responds) to the demands placed upon it in a *highly specific* manner, all the components that are required in a given sport must be carefully identified. Then, conditioning activities, appropriate for improving each of these specific factors must be included in the conditioning program. For example, volleyball involves repetitive spiking and blocking. Both of these skills require good leg strength. Consequently, exercises designed to improve leg strength should be included in the preseason program.

Analyze and identify requirements

As explained above, *every facet and skill* of the game or event must be analyzed in terms of the following (Tables 6-1 to 6-7):
  1. Muscle groups that require *strength*
  2. Muscle groups, body positions, and motions that require *flexibility*
  3. Extent to which *aerobic* and *anaerobic capacities* are required
  4. Potential for injury

Design the program

After the sport has been thoroughly analyzed in terms of its specific requirements, the content of the program can then be planned. Activities and exercises appropriate to improving the athlete's specific needs in strength, flexibility, aerobic and anaerobic capacities are included. Each exercise performed by the athlete contributes toward a specific purpose of the overall conditioning program, with the ultimate goal being an improved fitness level designed to help the athlete achieve her highest performance potential with a minimal risk of injury.

Modify as appropriate

The guidelines outlined above refer mainly to the preseason conditioning program in which the main emphasis is on improving the athlete's fitness level in preparation for competition. In-season and off-season programs will vary in purpose and consequently in intensity and content.

Text continued on p. 97.

Table 6-1 □ Conditioning requirements for volleyball

Skill/movement	Strength	Flexibility	Endurance	Injury susceptibility
Spike	*Lower body* Ankle, knee, and hip extensors *Trunk* Stabilizers—abdominals and sacrospinalis *Upper body* Scapular abductors, adductors, upward and downward rotators Shoulder—horizontal adductors and inward rotators Elbow extensors Forearm pronators Wrist flexors and adductors	*Lower body* Ankle, thigh, and hip—flexors and extensors *Trunk* rotators; low back *Upper body* Shoulder—outward rotation movement should be extensive; stretch anterior joint capsule, ligaments, and tendons	Muscular (strength) Mainly anaerobic, some aerobic Interval training techniques recommended	Ankle and knee sprains Shoulder joint and tendon inflammation Low backache—overuse
Serve	Same as spike	Same as spike	Same as spike	Shoulder joint inflammation Low back pain—overuse
Set	Same as spike plus finger flexors	Same as spike	Same as spike	Finger and thumb hyper-extension sprains
Block	Same as spike for ankle and trunk plus: Scapular downward rotators Shoulder flexors Elbow extensors Wrist and finger flexors	*Trunk*—low back and lateral trunk *Upper body* Shoulder—obtain free range of motion in extension	Same as spike	Finger and thumb sprains Acute sprains of ankle and knee

Continued.

Table 6-1 □ Conditioning requirements for volleyball—cont'd

Skill/movement	Strength	Flexibility	Endurance	Injury susceptibility
Roll	*Lower body* Ankle, knee, and hip flexors and extensors Foot inverters *Trunk*—flexors (abdominals) *Upper body* Shoulder, wrist, and neck flexors	*Lower body* Hip extensors *Upper body* *Trunk* Low back muscles *Upper body* Neck extensors	Muscular—for aiding momentum when regaining upright stance	Vertebral contusions Gluteus maximus contusion
Pass	Same as set	Same as set	Same as set	Same as set

Table 6-2 □ Conditioning requirements for gymnastics (uneven parallels)

Skill/movement	Strength	Flexibility	Endurance	Injury susceptibility
Uneven parallel bars	*Lower body* Hip flexors and extensors Knee flexors and extensors Ankle extensors *Trunk*—abdominals and sacrospinalis *Upper body* Scapular downward rotators Shoulder flexors and extensors Elbow flexors and extensors Forearm pronators Wrist and finger flexors	*Lower body* Hip flexors Thigh—hamstrings Ankle—anterior tibialis for full range of motion in extension *Upper body and trunk* Shoulder—full range of motion Back—upper and lower	Largely muscular (strength) Mainly anaerobic, some aerobic Interval training technique recommended	*Overuse* Callouses Blisters Shoulder joint inflammation Low back sprains *Trauma* Ankle and knee sprains on dismount Hip contusions

Table 6-3 □ Conditioning requirements for track and field (sprints)

Skill/movement	Strength	Flexibility	Endurance	Injury susceptibility
Start	*For power* Ankle, knee, and hip extensors Shoulder flexors and extensors *For stabilization* Trunk flexors and extensors	Ankle flexors and extensors Knee flexors Hip flexors and extensors Low back	Muscular (strength) Almost entirely anaerobic Recommend interval training techniques	Muscle spasms Muscle strains
Sprinting	*For power* Ankle, knee, and hip flexors and extensors Hip abductors and adductors Scapular abductors and adductors Shoulder flexors and extensors *For stabilization* Trunk flexors and extensors	Same as above, plus: Quadriceps Hip adductors Shoulder joint—complete mobility Lateral trunk	Muscular Cardiorespiratory: mainly anaerobic	Gastrocnemius, hamstring, quadriceps spasms (cramp) Plantar fasciitis Shin splints Patella inflammation or chondromalacia, or both Knee inflammation of capsule, ligaments, tendons Blisters

Table 6-4 □ Conditioning requirements for track and field (field events—throwing)

Skill/movement	Strength	Flexibility	Endurance	Injury susceptibility
Shot, discus, javelin	*Lower body* All muscle groups in all joint actions *Trunk* Flexors, rotators, lateral flexors, back extensors *Upper body* All muscle groups but especially Scapula: abductors and upward rotators Shoulder—horizontal adductors and inward rotators, flexors Elbow extensors Forearm pronators and supinators Wrist flexors, extensors, abductors, adductors	Muscle groups of entire body but especially: Hamstrings Hip flexors Trunk rotators Shoulder—anterior joint capsule, ligaments, and muscles Low back	Mainly anaerobic Recommend interval training techniques	Sprains from overuse—ankle, knee, hip, low back Hamstrings—tears or spasm Shoulder, elbow, wrist—tenosynovitis, from overuse, strain, and improper technique

SPECIAL NOTES: 1. Balance important throughout full body glide for building momentum and explosive force.
2. Diaphram—proper breathing.

Table 6-5 □ Conditioning requirements for soccer

Skill/movement	Strength	Flexibility	Endurance	Injury susceptibility
Running (speed; stop and start; change of direction)	*For power* Ankle, knee, and hip muscles in *all* joint actions Shoulder flexion and extension Scapular adductors *For stabilization* Trunk flexors and extensors	Leg—anterior and posterior Thigh quadriceps and hamstrings Hip flexors, abductors, adductors Trunk—low back, lateral trunk	Muscular (strength) Cardiorespiratory: anaerobic and aerobic Include interval training methods	Plantar fasciitis Ankle and knee sprains Shin splints Contusions of thigh: quadriceps, hamstrings, adductors Strains of quadriceps, hamstrings, adductors Stress fractures of tibia
Kicking	Same as above	Same as above	Anaerobic	
Heading	Neck flexors, extensors, rotators Scapula—all upper back muscles Shoulder—all shoulder joint muscles	Neck flexors, extensors, lateral flexors, and rotators		

Table 6-6 □ Conditioning requirements for swimming backstroke and breaststroke

Skill/movement	Strength	Flexibility	Endurance	Injury susceptibility
Backstroke	*Power in kick* Ankle and knee flexors and extensors Hip flexors, extensors abductors, adductors, inward and outward rotators *Power in arm pull* Scapular downward rotators and depressors Shoulder adductors and inward rotators Elbow extensors Forearm pronators Wrist flexors and adductors *Stabilize trunk* Trunk flexors and extensors	Leg—anterior and posterior Thigh hamstrings Trunk—low back Shoulder—complete mobility in full circle Hip flexors	Muscular (strength) Anaerobic and aerobic depending on length of event Recommend interval training techniques	Shoulder joint inflammation
Breaststroke	Same	Same	Same	Same plus knee extension overuse

SPECIAL NOTES: Weight train on pulleys and Mini-Gym, along with regular weight training to gain strength in the identical arm and leg motions used while swimming.

Table 6-7 □ Conditioning requirements for swimming freestyle

Skill/movement	Strength	Flexibility	Endurance	Injury susceptibility
Freestyle	*Power in kick* Ankle, knee and hip extensors Ankle, knee and hip flexors *Power in pull* Scapular downward rotators and depressors Shoulder extensors *Stabilize body* Trunk flexors and extensors Hip adductors and abductors	Same as backstroke	Same as backstroke	Same as backstroke

SPECIAL NOTES: See backstroke (Table 6-6).

Off-season conditioning. The main purpose of off-season conditioning is to maintain the athlete's fitness level, or at least to minimize the loss of fitness that would occur without any maintenance program. Activities designed to maintain adequate levels of strength, flexibility, and aerobic and anaerobic capacities should be included, perhaps twice weekly. When possible, it would be helpful for the athlete to engage in an active sport of her choice, which would provide some variety while maintaining a desirable fitness base.

If a young girl or woman aspires to become an athlete of national or world-class caliber, then there really is no such thing as an "off season." These highly dedicated people maintain an extremely high level of fitness throughout the year, literally spending hours each and every day in intensive conditioning activities and technique workouts.

In-season conditioning. During the competitive season, the daily conditioning program is usually modified to perhaps twice weekly. Relatively more time is spent on improving performance skills and strategy. However, the daily practice or workout is designed to incorporate a variety of drills that combine both technique and conditioning development.

On the preceding pages are a few samples of typical worksheets that one might use when analyzing the conditioning needs for a particular sport (Tables 6-1 to 6-7). After analyzing the sport in detail and identifying the various fitness requirements, one can use them as the basis for determining specific goals of the conditioning program and for selecting the exercises that will bring about the particular training responses (improvements in fitness) desired.

SOME GENERALIZATIONS IN SPORT CONDITIONING

Although each sport has its own specific skills that the athlete must master, certain generalizations can be made about the more basic motor skill patterns that may be involved in several different sports. For example, the volleyball spike, tennis serve, and softball throw require an overhand throwing and hitting arm motion. We can therefore generalize regarding this movement in terms of strength and flexibility requirements. Some sports are court games, limiting players to relatively smaller areas of play and involving many short bursts of running speed, followed by brief rest periods. These kinds of activities demand a different kind of endurance base compared with field sports, such as soccer, played over a much larger area and with few, if any, rest "pauses."

Generalizations follow, pertaining to strength, flexibility, and endurance requirements of selected sport skill movement patterns and games.

Overhand throwing and hitting

Examples. Overhand throw, volleyball spike and serve, tennis smash and serve, badminton smash and clear, javelin and discus throws, football pass.

Strength. Throwing and hitting power can be improved by resistive exercises in which the player performs the motion against resistance such as with a pulley or Mini-Gym, as well as with regular weight training for the upper extremity.

Strong abdominal muscles help stabilize the trunk and add power through forceful trunk rotation. Trunk extensors also assist in stabilization.

Hips should be strong in rotation and extension. Knee and ankle extensors also contribute.

Flexibility. Good flexibility is required in the anterior shoulder and in trunk and hip rotators.

Jumping

Examples. Basketball lay-ups and rebounding, volleyball spike and block, high jump, broad jump.

Strength. Jumping requires good strength in all of the extensor muscles of the hip, knee, and ankle joints. Through weight training, jumping height can be improved by as much as 6 inches. Repetitive jumping drills build muscular endurance.

Kicking

Examples. Soccer, football.

Strength. Powerful kicking involves strong hip flexors and knee and ankle extensors. Kicking across the body necessitates strength in the hip adductors as well.

Flexibility. Hip flexors and hamstrings and adductors should be well stretched with a good range of motion.

Starting and stopping

Examples. Most sports, including field sports, but particularly the court games of basketball, tennis, and badminton.

Strength. Strength should be developed in both the flexor and extensor muscles of the hip, knee, and ankle. Quick starts demand power.

Table 6-8 □ Energy processes and duration of event

Area	Performance time	Major energy system(s) involved	Examples of type of activity
1	Less than 30 seconds	Anaerobic	Shot-put, 100-yard sprint, base stealing, golf and tennis swings
2	30 seconds to 1½ minutes	Anaerobic	220- to 440-yard sprints, halfbacks, fullbacks, speed skating, 100-yard swim
3	1½ to 3 minutes	Combined	880-yard dash, gymnastics events, boxing (3-minute rounds), wrestling (2-minute periods)
4	Greater than 3 minutes	Aerobic	Soccer and lacrosse (except goalies), cross-country skiing, marathon run, jogging

Modified from Fox, E. L. and Mathews, D. K.: Interval training, Philadelphia, 1974, W. B. Saunders Co.

Table 6-9 □ Anaerobic and aerobic components in sports

Sports or sport activity	Emphasis (percent) according to energy systems		
	Anaerobic	Combined	Aerobic
1. Baseball	80	20	—
2. Basketball	85	15	—
3. Fencing	90	10	—
4. Field hockey	60	20	20
5. Football	90	10	—
6. Golf	95	5	—
7. Gymnastics	90	10	—
8. Ice hockey			
a. Forwards, defense	80	20	—
b. Goalie	95	5	—
9. Lacrosse			
a. Goalie, defense, attack men	80	20	—
b. Midfielders, man-down	60	20	20
10. Rowing	20	30	50
11. Skiing			
a. Slalom, jumping, downhill	80	20	—
b. Cross-country	—	5	95
c. Pleasure skiing	34	33	33
12. Soccer			
a. Goalie, wings, strikers	80	20	—
b. Halfbacks, or link men	60	20	20
13. Swimming and diving			
a. 50 yards, diving	98	2	—
b. 100 yards	80	15	5
c. 200 yards	30	65	5
d. 400, 500 yards	20	40	40
e. 1500, 1650 yards	10	20	70
14. Tennis	70	20	10
15. Track and field			
a. 100, 220 yards	98	2	—
b. Field events	90	10	—
c. 440 yards	80	15	5
d. 880 yards	30	65	5
e. 1 mile	20	55	25
f. 2 miles	20	40	40
g. 3 miles	10	20	70
h. 6 miles (cross-country)	5	15	80
i. Marathon	—	5	95
16. Volleyball	90	10	—
17. Wrestling	90	10	—

Modified from Fox, E. L., and Mathews, D. K.: Interval training, Philadelphia, 1974, W. B. Saunders Co.

Flexibility. Court games often require the athlete to assume positions that place muscle groups on extreme stretch. If these muscles lack adequate flexibility, the individual is unable to get into the desirable positions and, in attempting to do so, will often suffer from overstretch injuries.

Endurance

Endurance may be classified as anaerobic or aerobic, depending on the duration of running or other skills involved. Anaerobic movements typically last from less than 30 seconds up to 90 seconds. Aerobic events last 3 minutes or longer. Short activities with a duration of 90 to 180 seconds depend on a combination of anaerobic and aerobic energy pathways. See Tables 6-8 and 6-9.

Anaerobic. Some sports are characterized by many repetitive starts and stops, with brief momentary pauses in between. Examples are volleyball, softball, basketball, fencing, gymnastics, downhill skiing, and sprint events in swimming and running.

Anaerobic capacity is best developed by interval training techniques that require relatively short, strenuous work intervals, followed by brief rest intervals. Drills that incorporate technique practice with strenuous demands on the individual can be developed. An example in volleyball would be a drill that requires a number of digs to be performed in rapid succession, followed by brief rest and then repeated.

However, anaerobic capacity is best developed only after an initial aerobic base has been established. So even the so-called anaerobic sports require athletes to develop cardiorespiratory (aerobic) endurance.

Aerobic. In some sports, continuous movement predominates. This is exemplified by sports such as field hockey, soccer, lacrosse, cross-country skiing, distance swimming and running, and rowing. Aerobic endurance is best developed by working out for relatively long periods of time and distance. Although interval training methods can be used, the work periods are longer, the pace is slower, and the rest periods are also longer than for "speed work."

But even these sports call for sudden bursts of extrastrenuous work at certain times. Consequently, while training for aerobic capacity dominates, one should spend a certain amount of time in "speed work," involving higher intensity, short interval repeats. This provides the athlete the ability to move continuously over a longer period, in addition to the stamina required to initiate sudden burts of speed when necessary.

REFERENCES

1. Jensen, C. R., and Schultz, G. W.: Applied kinesiology. New York, 1977, McGraw-Hill Book Co., Inc.
2. Klafs, C. E., and Arnheim, D. D.: Modern principles of athletic training, ed. 4, St. Louis, 1977, The C. V. Mosby Co.

7 □ The conditioning program in action

This chapter serves as a resource for ideas and activities to incorporate into a conditioning program and consists of three main sections.

The first section includes a series of strengthening and stretching exercises that can be used in improving the athlete's fitness level. Each of the 65 exercises is described and number-keyed to charts and illustrations that show the location of the involved muscle group (Figs. 7-1 and 7-2) and give examples of sport skills in which that muscle group is important (Figs. 7-3 and 7-4).

In the second section, national and world-class women athletes and successful coaches provide a personal glimpse into the highlights of their individual training programs, which have helped them become champions. One cannot help but be impressed with the tremendous dedication that these people display, as well as with the high fitness levels they have attained through regular, yearlong participation in highly stressful workouts.

This section also stands as a testimony and tribute to the outstanding achievements of these women in the world of sports. These women and their accomplishments serve as much-needed role models for younger girls who will become the women champions of the future.

Because running is not only a sport in and of itself but is also basic to most athletic events and used as a method for improving endurance, this activity is discussed in detail in the third section. Emphasis is placed upon sprints and distance running, the development of anaerobic and aerobic capacities, suggestions for avoiding foot and leg problems, and considerations when selecting a good running shoe.

DEVELOPING THE ATHLETE'S FITNESS BASE

Because of the very specific manner in which the body responds to the stresses imposed upon it (specific adaptation to imposed demands), each exercise in a conditioning program is designed to accomplish a particular goal. Generally, an exercise is performed to accomplish *one* of the following: (1) an increase in muscle strength, (2) an increase in flexibility or range of motion, (3) improvement in aerobic capacity, or (4) improvement in anaerobic capacity. An exercise designed to increase strength will not contribute to improved flexibility or endurance. Furthermore, a strengthening exercise will only increase the strength of the specific muscle group for which it was intended.

The significance of this basic physiological principle is that if a conditioning program is to bring about improvement in the athlete's strength, flexibility, and endurance levels, it must involve a comprehensive array of appropriate strengthening, stretching, and endurance exercises.

GENERAL CHARACTERISTICS OF EXERCISES

For strength. Exercises designed to increase muscular strength are characterized by requiring muscles to perform work against a resistance of some kind.

101

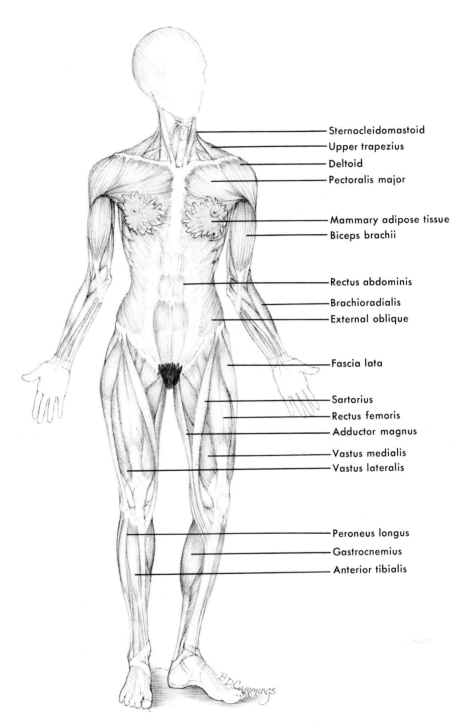

Sternocleidomastoid

Upper trapezius

Deltoid

Pectoralis major

Mammary adipose tissue

Biceps brachii

Rectus abdominis

Brachioradialis

External oblique

Fascia lata

Sartorius

Rectus femoris

Adductor magnus

Vastus medialis

Vastus lateralis

Peroneus longus

Gastrocnemius

Anterior tibialis

Fig. 7-1. Female muscle system. Anterior view.

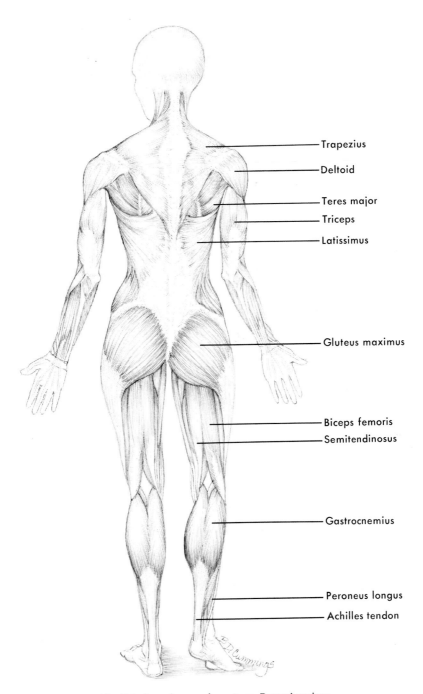

Trapezius

Deltoid

Teres major

Triceps

Latissimus

Gluteus maximus

Biceps femoris

Semitendinosus

Gastrocnemius

Peroneus longus

Achilles tendon

Fig. 7-2. Female muscle system. Posterior view.

USES IN SPORT—SUGGESTED EXERCISES

No.	Name	Uses in sport	Exercises S = Strength F = Flexibility
1	Neck flexors and rotators (sternocleidomastoid)	Stabilize head on spine Turn head	S — F—1
2	Shoulder abductors (deltoid)	Overhand throwing and hitting Volleyball block Handstand	S—1, 30, 32 F —
3	Shoulder adductors and inward rotators (pectorals, latissimus)	Overhand throwing and hitting Tennis forehand drive Breast stroke—arm pull	S—2, 3, 31, 33 F —
4	Trunk flexors and rotators (abdominals)	Stabilize trunk in all running, striking, throwing, and kicking skills Overhand, throwing and hitting skills (rotation)	S—21, 22 F —
5	Wrist adductors	Tennis—backhand topspin Allows a "cocked wrist" position preceding throwing and badminton drive	S—16 F —
6	Wrist adductors	Overhand throwing and hitting skills Batting Tennis—backspin or chop	S—16 F —
7	Hip abductors	Vaulting—spread legs to clear horse Whip kick—recovery phase	S—30 F —
8	Hip adductors	Whip kick—power phase Soccer—kick across body	S—31 F—13
9	Ankle everters	Stabilize ankle laterally	S—25 F —
10	Ankle inverters	Stabilize ankle laterally	S—25 F —

For a description of the exercises in the column to the right, refer to the same number exercise in the text.

Fig. 7-3. A, Major muscle groups. Chart for front view.

In calisthenics, such as push-ups or sit-ups, the resistance is provided by part of the athlete's own body weight. In weight training, external weights, such as steel plates, barbells, or dumbbells are used.

For flexibility. Flexibility exercises require the person to assume a body position that places a particular muscle group on stretch.

For aerobic capacity. Aerobic activities typically require that a continuous submaximal demand be placed upon the cardiac, circulatory, and respiratory systems for periods of approximately 5 minutes or longer. The exercise must be vigorous enough to approximately double the resting heart rate.

For anaerobic capacity. Exercises to increase anaerobic capacity also require the heart rate to be elevated, preferably to about 80% of maximum. This vigorous work is performed in short spurts lasting from less than 30 seconds, up to sev-

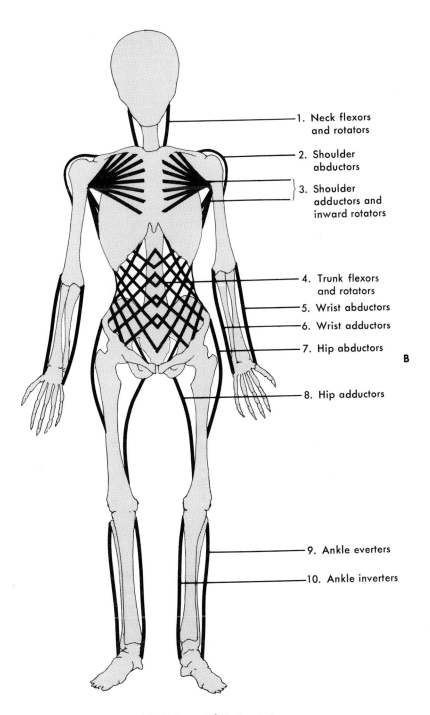

1. Neck flexors and rotators
2. Shoulder abductors
3. Shoulder adductors and inward rotators
4. Trunk flexors and rotators
5. Wrist abductors
6. Wrist adductors
7. Hip abductors
8. Hip adductors
9. Ankle everters
10. Ankle inverters

B

Fig. 7-3, cont'd. B, Front view.

USES IN SPORT—SUGGESTED EXERCISES

No.	Name	Uses in sport	Exercises S = Strength F = Flexibility
1	Neck extensors	Look upward; stabilize head on spine; backward somersault	S—24 F—1
2	Shoulder flexors (deltoid)	Chest pass; handstand; volleyball block	S—1, 2, 9, 17, 18, 23, 28 F—2, 3, 4
3	Shoulder extensors (latissimus)	Swimming—arm pull in freestyle, butter-fly breast stroke and backstroke Uneven parallels—pull-up	S—3, 18, 19, 29 F—4
4	Elbow flexors (biceps)	Tennis forehand Uneven parallel pull-up Swimming—arm pull in freestyle, butter-fly breast stroke, and backstroke	S—3, 8, 10, 19, 26 F
5	Elbow extensors (triceps)	Overhand throwing and hitting skills Basketball shooting Batting	S—1, 2, 9, 17, 18, 23, 27 F
6	Wrist flexors	Uneven parallels—grasp bar Batting—hold bat Volleyball—spiking	S—13, 15, 16 F
7	Wrist extensors	Stabilize wrist when weight-bearing	S—13, 14, 16 F
8	Low back extensors	Diving and gymnastics—arch back Stabilize trunk in all running, spiking, throwing, and kicking skills	S—24 F—8
9	Trunk flexors and rotators (abdominals)	Stabilize trunk in all running, spiking, throwing, and kicking skills Overhand throwing and hitting skills (rotation)	S—21, 22 F
10	Hip extensors	Running, jumping, landing, swimming Turn with push-off starting and stopping	S—4, 6, 11, 25, 36 F—6
11	Hip flexors	Kicking Running—bring thigh forward and up Gymnastics and diving—pike position	S—20, 23 F—9
12	Knee flexors (hamstrings)	Running—bend knee on backswing Flutter kick	S—5, 39 F—10, 11
13	Knee extensors (quadriceps)	Running, jumping, landing, starting and stopping, kicking	S—4, 6, 7, 11, 25, 40 F—12
14	Ankle extensors (gastroc-nemius, Achilles tendon)	Running, jumping, landing, starting and stopping, kicking	S—4, 6, 12, 25 F—14
15	Ankle flexors	Running—heel strike	S F—15

For a description of the exercises in the column to the right, refer to the same number exercise in the text.

A

Fig. 7-4. A, Major muscle groups. Chart for side view.

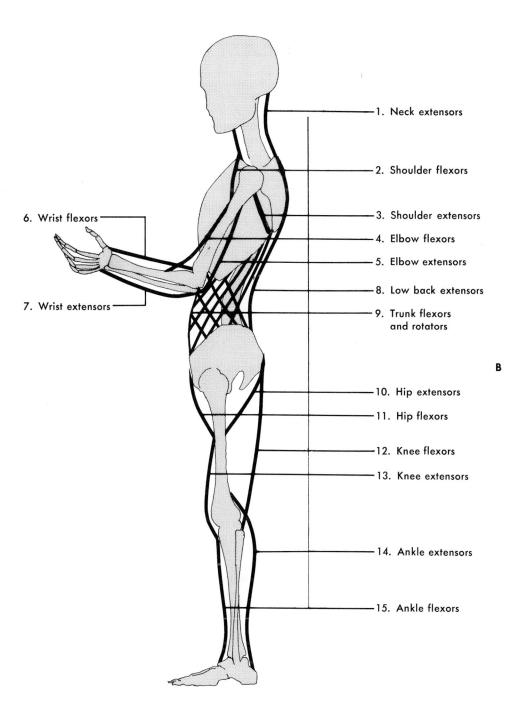

Fig. 7-4, cont'd. B, Side view.

eral minutes in duration. The short, strenuous work period or interval is followed by a brief rest interval. Alternating work and rest periods are continued, thus the name "interval training."

Guidelines

The following guidelines are suggested in conducting the conditioning program:

1. Athletes understand the purpose of each exercise. (strength, flexibility, endurance, muscle groups involved)
2. Each exercise is executed properly; the correct body position is assumed to achieve the desired results with good balance and avoidance of strain or other injury.
3. Each workout is preceded by an adequate warm-up period, which might include some easy stretching, running in place, jumping jacks, and arm circling.

Strengthening exercises

I. *Weight training*
  A. *Universal gym*
    1. Military press
    2. Bench press
    3. Lateral bar pull-down
    4. Leg press
    5. Hamstring curls
    6. Running machine
    7. Knee extension

  B. *Barbells*
    8. Rowing
    9. Bench press
    10. Curls
    11. Half squat
    12. Toe raises

  C. *Dumbbells*
    13. Wrist roll
    14. Wrist extensors
    15. Wrist flexors
    16. Figure eight

II. *Calisthenics*
    17. Bar dips
    18. Arm sprints
    19. Chin-up
    20. Pike
    21. Hanging curl-up
    22. Sit-up
    23. Push-up
    24. Back lift
    25. Bench blasts

III. *Partner resistive*
    26. Elbow flexors
    27. Elbow extensors
    28. Shoulder flexors
    29. Shoulder extensors
    30. Shoulder abductors
    31. Shoulder adductors
    32. Scapular upward rotators
    33. Scapular downward rotators
    34. Scapular abductors
    35. Scapular adductors
    36. Hip extensors
    37. Hip abductors
    38. Hip adductors
    39. Knee flexors
    40. Knee extensors

Description of strengthening exercises

Weight training
Universal gym
  1. Military press (Fig. 7-5)
     PURPOSE: Strengthen shoulder flexors; scapular upward rotators (for push-
        ing arms upward); elbow extensors (triceps).
     EXECUTION: Seated, elbows close to sides, push bar directly overhead.
     NOTE: If performed with hands farther apart, elbows away from body, the
        shoulder abductors (deltoids) will be more involved than will the
        shoulder flexors.

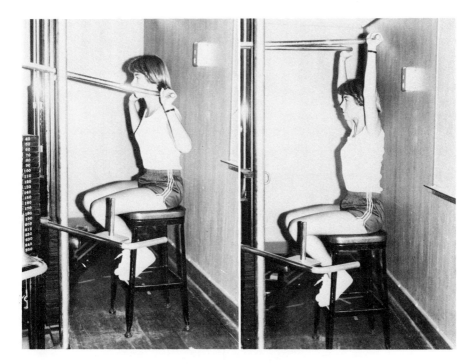

Fig. 7-5. Military press.

2. Bench press (Fig. 7-6)

PURPOSE: Strengthen shoulder flexors; scapular abductors (for pushing arms forward); elbow extensors (triceps).

EXECUTION: Lying on bench, knees bent, low back flat, elbows close to sides; push bar directly away from chest.

NOTE: Bent-knee position prevents undesirable arching of low back. If performed with hands farther apart, elbows away from body, the pectorals (shoulder adductors and inward rotators) will be more involved.

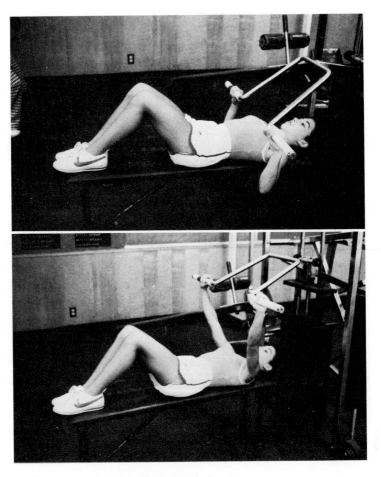

Fig. 7-6. Bench press.

3. Latissimus bar pull-down (Fig. 7-7)
   PURPOSE: Strengthen shoulder extensors and elbow flexors and extensors.
   EXECUTION: Standing, from overhead, pull bar down to shoulder height and push bar downward to full arm extension.

Fig. 7-7. Latissimus bar pull-down.

4. Leg press (Fig. 7-8)

PURPOSE: Strengthen hip, knee, and ankle extensors.

EXECUTION: Seated, knees bent; push away on pedals, pushing with toes as legs straighten.

Fig. 7-8. Leg press.

5. Hamstring curls (Fig. 7-9)

  PURPOSE: Strengthen knee flexors (hamstrings)

  EXECUTION: Prone (face toward floor), grasping bench sides, heels hooked under roller; bend knees.

  NOTE: Avoid lifting head and trunk from bench, since this results in arching the back with subsequent stress on lumbar spine.

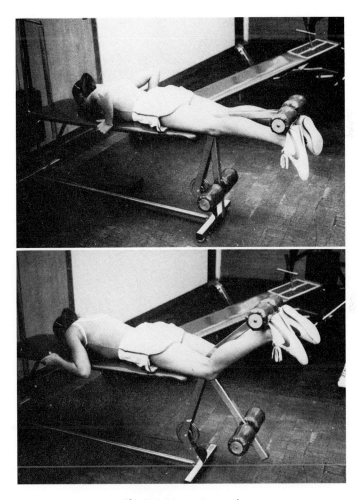

Fig. 7-9. Hamstring curls.

6. Running machine (Fig. 7-10)
   PURPOSE: Strengthen hip, knee, and ankle extensors.
   EXECUTION: Perform running motion against resistance.

Fig. 7-10. Running machine.

7. Knee extension (Fig. 7-11)

PURPOSE: Strengthen knee extensors (quadriceps).

EXECUTION: Seated, grasp sides of bench for stability, top of ankle under rollers, knees bent; straighten knees.

Fig. 7-11. Knee extension.

Barbells
8. Rowing (Fig. 7-12)

PURPOSE: Strengthen scapular adductors, shoulder horizontal abductors, elbow flexors.

EXECUTION: Standing, feet comfortably apart, knees "easy," forehead on padded table, raise barbell to chest, palms toward body.

Fig. 7-12. Rowing.

9. Bench press (see exercise 2) (Fig. 7-13)

Fig. 7-13. Bench press.

10. Curls (Fig. 7-14)

PURPOSE: Strengthen elbow flexors.

EXECUTION: Standing, feet comfortably apart, knees "easy," palms away from body; raise barbell to chest.

NOTE: Maintain a well-aligned body throughout; avoid leaning back from waist, or hyperextending knees. Performing this with back up against a wall is also recommended to promote good body alignment.

Fig. 7-14. Curls.

11. Half squat (Fig. 7-15)

  PURPOSE: Strengthen hip and knee extensors.

  EXECUTION: Standing, barbell resting across shoulders, behind head, heels on slight elevation; bend knees and hips to approximately 45 degrees.

Fig. 7-15. Half squat.

12. Toe raises (Fig. 7-16)

PURPOSE: Strengthen ankle extensors (gastrocnemius and Achilles tendon).

EXECUTION: Standing, barbell resting across shoulders, behind head, toes on slight elevation; rise up on toes; maintain good body alignment throughout.

Fig. 7-16. Toe raises.

Dumbbells

13. Wrist roll (Fig. 7-17)

PURPOSE: Strengthen wrist flexors and wrist extensors.

EXECUTION: Standing, feet comfortably apart; roll doweling, causing it to wind up a weighted sash cord; then unroll downward.

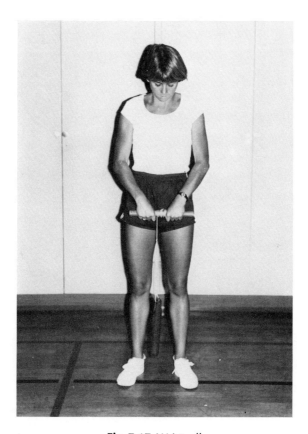

Fig. 7-17. Wrist roll.

14. Wrist extensors (Fig. 7-18)

PURPOSE: Strengthen wrist extensors.

EXECUTION: Seated, forearm supported, wrist and dumbbell extended over edge of support, palm down; lift upward.

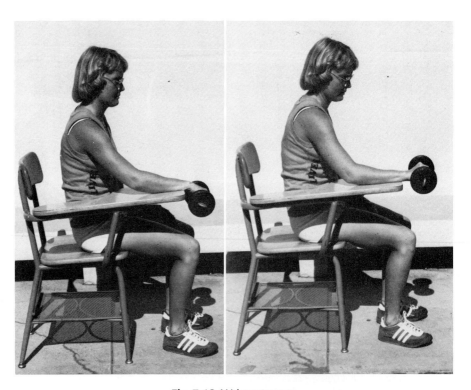

Fig. 7-18. Wrist extensors.

15. Wrist flexors (Fig. 7-19)

    PURPOSE: Strengthen wrist flexors.

    EXECUTION: Seated, forearm supported, wrist and dumbbell extended over edge of support, palm up; lift upward.

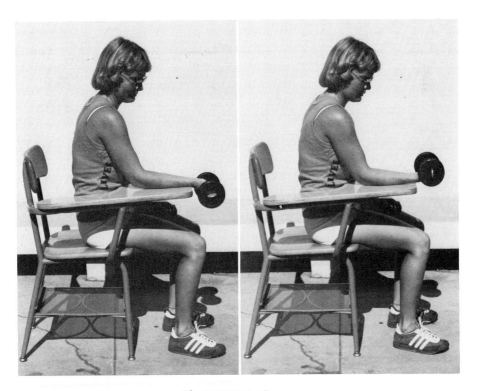

Fig. 7-19. Wrist flexors.

16. Figure eight (Fig. 7-20)
    PURPOSE: Strengthen forearm pronators and supinators.
    EXECUTION: Seated, elbow bent, on padded support; perform a figure-eight
    motion with forearm.

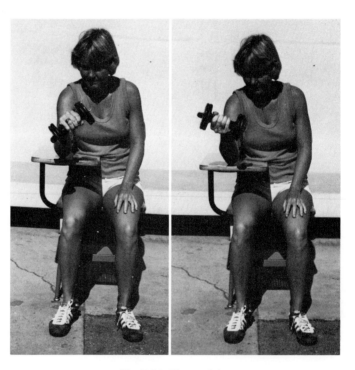

Fig. 7-20. Figure eight.

Calisthenics

17. Bar dips (Fig. 7-21)

  PURPOSE: Strengthen scapular depressors and shoulder.

  EXECUTION: Support self between parallel bars, arms extended; lower self until elbows are bent approximately 90 degrees.

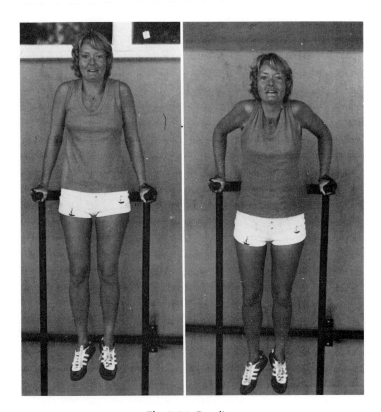

Fig. 7-21. Bar dips.

18. Arm sprints (Fig. 7-22)

    PURPOSE: Strengthen and increase muscular endurance and power of shoulder flexors and extensors and of elbow extensors.

    EXECUTION: Front-leaning rest position, arms straight on bench, trunk and legs straight. Place right arm on ground, left arm on ground, right arm on bench, left arm on bench. Repeat rapidly, using short but strenuous repeat intervals

Fig. 7-22. Arm sprints.

19. Chin-up (Fig. 7-23)

PURPOSE: Strengthen scapular downward rotators, shoulder extensors, and elbow flexors.

EXECUTION: Assume full hanging position, palms away from body; lift self, bringing chin above bar; keep body straight.

NOTE: If too weak to perform from a full hanging position, the following progression might be used, from easy to difficult.

   a. *Let-down.* Begin to chin-up position and gradually lower self to a full hanging position in 10 counts.

   b. *Half chin-up.* Execute chin-up, but beginning with elbows bent at 90 degrees.

   c. *Three-quarter chin-up.* Execute chin-up, but beginning with elbows bent at approximately 135 degrees.

   d. *Regular chin-up.* Beginning from a full hanging position, elbows straight.

Fig. 7-23. Chin-up.

20. Pike (Fig. 7-24)

PURPOSE: Strengthen hip flexors and lower abdominals.

EXECUTION: Assume a full hanging position, palms facing either toward or away from body; keeping knees straight, bend at hips until legs are parallel with floor.

Fig. 7-24. Pike.

21. Hanging curl-up (Fig. 7-25)

    PURPOSE: Strengthen hip flexors and abdominals.

    EXECUTION: Assume a full hanging position, palms facing either toward or away from the body; bend the knees and bring them up to the chest.

Fig. 7-25. Hanging curl-up.

22. Sit-up

PURPOSE: Strengthen abdominals.

EXECUTION: Supine (lying on back), bent knees, feet flat on floor, low back flat on floor, hands clasped behind neck, feet supported or unsupported; tuck chin to chest and curl upward, raising trunk to 45 degrees from floor.

NOTE: Some variations of the sit-up are as follows:

a. *Supine.* Feet held by a partner about 2 feet above floor or hooked into stall bars, so that hips and knees are each bent 90 degrees; hands clasped behind head; raise chest upward to thighs.

b. *Supine.* Knees to chest, hands clasped behind head; raise trunk upward to 45 degrees, while extending legs forward simultaneously, keeping feet approximately 1 foot above floor. A V is formed between extended legs and raised trunk. Feet never touch the floor.

c. *Lying on side.* Feet supported by partner, hands clasped behind head; raise trunk laterally from floor about 18 inches; execute from both sides.

23. Push-up

PURPOSE: Strengthen scapular abductors, shoulder flexors, and elbow extensors.

EXECUTION: Prone, hands adjacent to shoulders, toes tucked under; extend arms, raising trunk and legs from floor, keeping body in a straight line between feet and head.

NOTE: An easier method is to execute the push-up with the hands on a low bench or stool, instead of the floor.

24. Back lift

PURPOSE: Strengthen low back, middle back, and upper back (neck) extensors.

EXECUTION: Prone on table or bench, with feet supported and trunk hanging over end of table, hands clasped behind head; lift trunk upward until trunk is slightly higher than table.

NOTE: Avoid raising too high; excessive lift may result in back strain because of lumbar hyperextension and compression of the intervertebral discs.

25. Bench blasts

PURPOSE: Strengthen and improve muscular endurance and power of hip, knee, and ankle extensors.

EXECUTION: Stand in front of a bench 14 to 18 inches high, with one foot on bench. Spring ("blast") upward and, while in the air, execute a scissors step, landing with the opposite feet on the bench and floor. Repeat rapidly, using short but strenuous repeat intervals.

Partner resistive. The next group of strengthening exercises requires the individual to work with maximum effort throughout the entire range of motion for that joint action. The partner provides as much resistance as the person can move against. Too much resistance and the exercise becomes isometric in nature. Too little, and the muscles will not be required to work hard enough. The key is for the individual to put forth maximal effort, with the partner providing just enough resistance so that the person can execute the movement. These exercises will effectively improve strength through the full range of motion if weight-training equipment is not available.

In each case, the name of the exercise denotes the major muscle groups being strengthened.

26. Elbow flexors (Fig. 7-26)

    STARTING POSITION: Standing, arm adjacent to body, elbow extended, palm up.

    EXECUTION: Bend arm upward at elbow as partner applies resistance downward on forearm.

Fig. 7-26. Elbow flexors.

27. Elbow extensors (Fig. 7-27)

STARTING POSITION: Standing, arm adjacent to body, arm bent at elbow, palm up.

EXECUTION: Straighten arm downward at elbow, as partner applies resistance upward on forearm.

Fig. 7-27. Elbow extensors.

28. Shoulder flexors (Fig. 7-28)

STARTING POSITION: Standing, arm at side, palm up.

EXECUTION: Raise arm forward and upward, keeping elbow straight, as partner applies resistance downward on forearm.

Fig. 7-28. Shoulder flexors.

29. Shoulder extensors (Fig. 7-29)

STARTING POSITION: Standing, arm extended forward and upward, elbow straight.

EXECUTION: Lower arm back toward side, as partner applies resistance upward on forearm.

Fig. 7-29. Shoulder extensors.

30. Shoulder abductors (Fig. 7-30)
    STARTING POSITION: Standing, arm at side, elbow straight, palm toward body.
    EXECUTION: Lift arm upward and sideward, as partner applies resistance downward on forearm.

Fig. 7-30. Shoulder abductors.

31. Shoulder adductors (Fig. 7-31)

STARTING POSITION: Standing, arm elevated at side, shoulder height, palm down.

EXECUTION: Lower arm to side, keeping elbow straight, as partner applies upward resistance to forearm.

Fig. 7-31. Shoulder adductors.

32. Scapular upward rotators (Fig. 7-32)
    STARTING POSITION: Seated, legs crossed, bent elbows at sides, palms up.
    EXECUTION: Push arms straight upward to full extension, as partner, standing behind, applies resistance downward on palms.
    NOTE: This exercise also strengthens the shoulder abductors and elbow extensors.

Fig. 7-32. Scapular upward rotators.

33. Scapular downward rotators (Fig. 7-33)

STARTING POSITION: Seated, legs crossed, arms raised upward, fingertips interlocked with partner.

EXECUTION: Pull arms straight downward until hands are shoulder height, as partner applies resistance upward.

NOTE: This exercise also strengthens the shoulder adductors and elbow flexors.

Fig. 7-33. Scapular downward rotators.

34. Scapular abductors (Fig. 7-34)

STARTING POSITION: Standing, feet in a forward-and-backward stride position, elbows bent and close to sides, palms forward at shoulder height.

EXECUTION: Push forward until arms are shoulder height, as partner applies a resistive push toward you with her palms.

NOTE: This exercise also strengthens the shoulder flexors and elbow extensors.

Fig. 7-34. Scapular abductors.

35. Scapular adductors (Fig. 7-35)

STARTING POSITION: Standing, feet in a forward-and-backward stride position, arms extended forward at shoulder height, fingers interlaced with partners

EXECUTION: Pull backward, until elbows are at sides, and partner's arms are completely extended, as partner applies a resistive pull away from you.

NOTE: This exercise also strengthens the shoulder extensors and elbow flexors.

Fig. 7-35. Scapular adductors.

36. Hip extensors (Fig. 7-36)
    STARTING POSITION: Prone, leg straight.
    EXECUTION: Raise entire leg as partner applies resistance downward.

Fig. 7-36. Hip extensors.

37. Hip abductors (Fig. 7-37)
   STARTING POSITION: Lying on side, leg straight.
   EXECUTION: Raise leg as partner applies resistance downward.

Fig. 7-37. Hip abductors.

38. Hip adductors (Fig. 7-38)
   STARTING POSITION: Lying on side, leg straight, raised upward.
   EXECUTION: Lower leg as partner applies resistance upward.

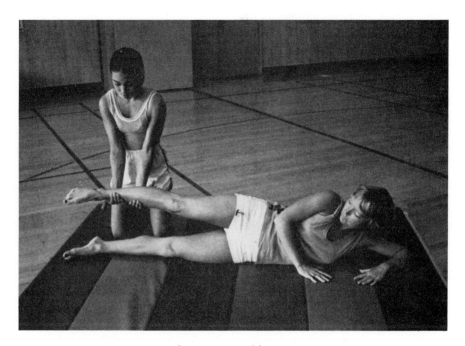

Fig. 7-38. Hip adductors.

39. Knee flexors (Fig. 7-39)

STARTING POSITION: Prone, leg straight.

EXECUTION: Bend knee, raising lower leg, as partner applies resistance downward.

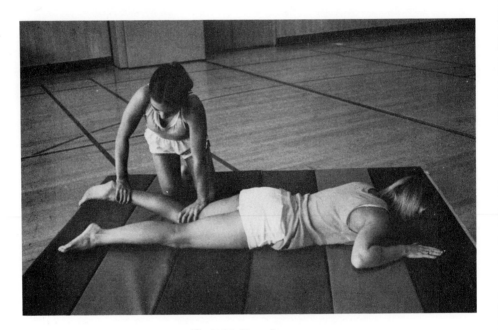

Fig. 7-39. Knee flexors.

40. Knee extensors (Fig. 7-40)
    STARTING POSITION: Seated, knee bent over edge of table or bench.
    EXECUTION: Straighten knee, raising lower leg as partner applies resistance downward.

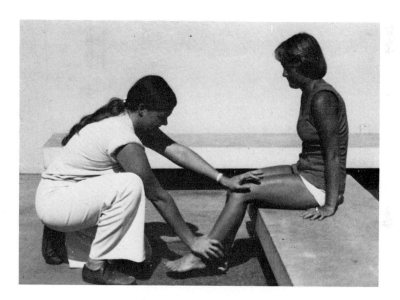

Fig. 7-40. Knee extensors.

Flexibility exercises

1. Posterior and lateral neck
2. Partner's anterior shoulder
3. Anterior shoulder
4. Shoulder towel stretch
5. Partner's lateral trunk
6. Trunk twisting—seated
7. Trunk twisting—standing
8. Low back extensors
9. Hip flexors
10. Hamstrings and low back
11. Hamstrings
12. Quadriceps
13. Hip-thigh adductors
14. Ankle extensors
15. Ankle flexors

Description of flexibility exercises

Stretching exercises to increase flexibility constitute a major part of every athlete's conditioning regimen. One should perform each exercise very slowly, keeping the involved muscle group and connective tissue on stretch for approximately 30 to 60 seconds. By carefully assuming the correct body position, relaxing, and concentrating on the area to be stretched, the tight athlete will find that she can gradually increase the stretched position as the full 30- to 60-second period elapses. The exercises included here are for the major areas of the body that tend to tighten up during muscular work or restrict the athlete's desirable range of motion.

One can often prevent or at least minimize muscle soreness by performing these stretching exercises *preceding* a heavy practice drill or technique workout (during the warm-up period) as well as *after* a workout.

1. Posterior and lateral neck
   STARTING POSITION: Seated, cross-legged, hands clasped behind upper part of head, elbows forward.
   EXECUTION: Pull head forward and down, tucking chin to chest.
   NOTE: To stretch lateral neck, clasp hands along right side of head, above the right ear; pull head down to left, approximating left ear to left shoulder; repeat on other side.
2. Partner's anterior shoulder (Fig. 7-41)
   STARTING POSITION: Seated, cross-legged, hands clasped behind head; partner standing behind, with side of leg supporting the athlete's back.
   EXECUTION: Partner grasps elbows and pulls backward and slightly upward.
   STARTING POSITION: Seated, cross-legged, arms raised overhead; partner standing behind with side of leg supporting the athlete's back.
   EXECUTION: Partner grasps hands and pulls directly backward.
   STARTING POSITION: Seated, cross-legged, arms extended backward; partner kneeling behind.
   EXECUTION: Partner grasps hands and pulls arms together and upward.

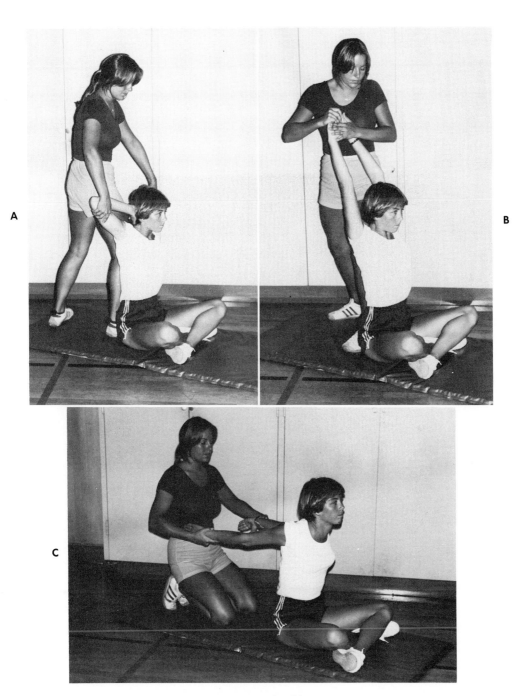

Fig. 7-41. Partner's anterior shoulder. **A** to **C** are variations.

3. Anterior shoulder (Fig. 7-42)
   STARTING POSITION: Seated, knees bent, feet flat, leaning backward on out-
   stretched arms.
   EXECUTION: Slowly slide arms backward until stretching is felt.

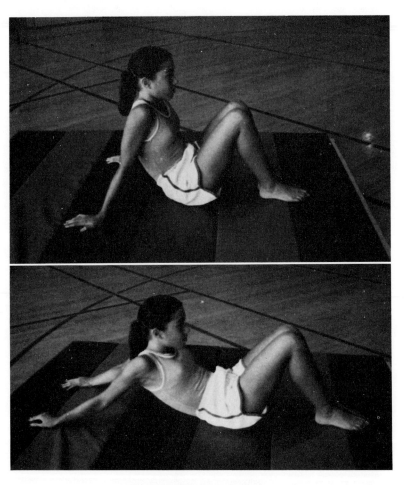

Fig. 7-42. Anterior shoulder.

4. Shoulder towel stretch (Fig. 7-43)
   STARTING POSITION: Seated, cross-legged, towel held behind back.
   EXECUTION: Pull downward on towel with lower hands to stretch shoulder of upper hand; hold and stretch; pull upward on towel with upper hand to stretch other shoulder; hold and stretch; repeat, reversing hand position; gradually attempt to clasp hands behind back.

Fig. 7-43. Shoulder towel stretch.

5. Partner's lateral trunk (Fig. 7-44)

STARTING POSITION: Standing, feet in a side-stride position, arms raised overhead.

EXECUTION: Bend sideward, dropping ear to lower shoulder, and keeping elbow of upper arm close to ear; partner grasps arms and aids in stretch.

NOTE: Keep both feet on floor; avoid twisting trunk or bending at hips.

Fig. 7-44. Partner's lateral trunk.

6. Trunk twisting—seated (Fig. 7-45)
   STARTING POSITION: Left leg bent on floor in front of body; right foot over and outside of left thigh; left hand grasps left ankle.
   EXECUTION: Twist backwards to right; repeat on other side.

Fig. 7-45. Trunk twisting, seated.

7. Trunk twisting—standing (Fig. 7-46)

STARTING POSITION: Stand on right leg, left leg bent, with foot behind right knee; right hand on left knee; left arm extended backward at shoulder height; look back at left arm.

EXECUTION: Twist backward to left; repeat on other side.

Fig. 7-46. Trunk twisting, standing.

8. Low back extensors (Fig. 7-47)

STARTING POSITION: Seated on floor, knees bent, feet flat; each hand goes from inside out and around respective leg and ankle.

EXECUTION: Bend forward, keeping head down; as flexibility increases, slide feet more forward and place forearms on floor.

Fig. 7-47. Low back extensors.

9. Hip flexors (Fig. 7-48)

STARTING POSITION: Lean forward on one knee, extending other leg back with toes tucked under.

EXECUTION: Slide extended leg rearward, stretching front of hip (hip flexors) of extended leg; repeat with other leg.

Fig. 7-48. Hip flexors.

10. Hamstrings and low back (Fig. 7-49)
    STARTING POSITION: Seated, one leg bent, the other leg extended forward.
    EXECUTION: Grasp ankle of extended leg; keeping elbows out, bring chest
    to extended thigh; repeat with other leg.

Fig. 7-49. Hamstrings and low back.

11. Hamstrings (Fig. 7-50)

STARTING POSITION: Supine, one leg extended, with other knee brought to chest.

EXECUTION: Grasp foot of bent leg and extend leg as far as possible; repeat with other leg.

Fig. 7-50. Hamstrings.

12. Quadriceps (Fig. 7-51)
    STARTING POSITION: Leaning forward on one knee, with other knee, extended back, foot upward.
    EXECUTION: Grasp ankle of extended knee and pull forward; repeat with other leg.

Fig. 7-51. Quadriceps.

13. Hip-thigh adductors (Fig. 7-52)
    STARTING POSITION: Seated, feet drawn close to body, soles of feet together.
    EXECUTION: Push downward on inside of knees.

Fig. 7-52. Hip-thigh adductors.

14. Ankle extensors (Fig. 7-53)

  STARTING POSITION: Leaning against wall, body straight, feet pointing directly toward wall, with inner sides of feet touching and heels flat on floor.

  EXECUTION: Keeping heels flat on floor, increase angle of lean by either bending elbows or sliding feet backward.

  NOTE: Avoid arching the back as lean is increased.

Fig. 7-53. Ankle extensors.

15. Ankle flexors (Fig. 7-54)

STARTING POSITION: Assume a push-up position, but with toes extended backward.

EXECUTION: Stretch of anterior ankle flexors is increased by raising of hips.

Fig. 7-54. Ankle flexors.

CONDITIONING PROGRAMS OF WOMEN CHAMPIONS AND SUCCESSFUL COACHES

Although other chapters of this text have been devoted to describing the female athlete and discussing the values and various methods of conditioning, as well as the treatment of common injuries, the ensuing section discusses the reality of conditioning programs in action. The information that follows is the result of extensive personal interviews with numerous national and world-class women athletes and highly successful coaches, covering a broad range of sports.

The focus of each interview is a description of the conditioning program that each athlete is currently using in her particular event. It is apparent that the highly successful female athlete follows a carefully planned comprehensive conditioning regimen designed to bring her to the peak of her performance potential. The persistance, dedication, determination, and willingness to devote hours, days, and months in arduous workouts is a testimony to the deep commitment that these women have made to their sport. Indeed, conditioning and competition comprise their life-style.

BADMINTON

Interview with: Sombat Dhammabusayu, coach
Accomplishments: Represented Thailand in International Competition; coach of the 1977 United States Women's International Badminton Squad.
Interview with: Diana Osterhues, athlete (Fig. 7-55)

Fig. 7-55. Diana Osterhues.

Accomplishments: Member of 1977 United States Women's International Badminton Squad, from which the Uber Cup Team is selected.

Diana, an international caliber player, is also a registered physical therapist, with a background in exercise physiology. She is extremely concerned that the members of the United States Women's International Badminton Squad participate in an organized conditioning program designed to improve the fitness level and subsequent performance of the players. Although other countries have used comprehensive conditioning programs for their players on an organized basis, up till now, the United States players, as a team, have not. In the United States, there is a great variation in fitness levels among individuals. Those who are in best condition are the winners. The top badminton teams in the world are characterized by having players who (1) are superbly conditioned, (2) consequently have excellent lasting power, without fatiguing, (3) have an outstanding mental attitude, and (4) have excellent shot selection and execution.

Diana has formulated a conditioning program for members of the 1977 squad. It stresses the development of muscular strength, flexibility, aerobic and anaerobic capacities. See Table 7-1.

Table 7-1 □ Conditioning program used by United States Women's International Badminton Squad

Stage	Activity	Repetitions per time	Target heart rate	Recommended training schedule
1. Warm-up	*Flexibility* Hamstrings Gastrocnemius, soleus, and Achilles tendon Quadriceps Upper and lower back Shoulder	5 minutes		Build during off season and maintain acquired level
2. Stretching and strengthening exercises		Total time— 10 minutes	120 beats per minute	
	Strength Squat thrusts 3/4 squats Sit-ups Push-ups Pull-ups Fingertip hangs	5 minutes		
3. Aerobic	*Home program*—sustained exercise (running, cycling, jogging, swimming, jump rope)	20 minutes at 3 or 4 times per week	70% to 85% of maximum heart rate	Same as above
	Court program of running using badminton footwork (forward, backward, sidesteps, sidestep reversals)	3 repetitions of 3-minute running and 30-second rest periods for total of 9 minutes; peak exercise time	70% to 85% of maximum heart rate	

	Court pattern drills (with or without racket)—5 suggested patterns Front V's Low laterals or sidesteps Back V's High laterals or sidesteps 2 corner drops (front and back)	each consisting of 30-second periods of pattern work with 2-minute rest periods; total time—20 minutes	1 to 2 months prior to competitive season
5. Cool-down	*Shot practice or cool-down calisthenics, or both*	As needed	Return heart rate as needed down to normal limits
6. Technique	*Selected shot drills with partner* *Games*		As needed, but usually increasing as competitive season nears

BASKETBALL

Interview with: Dr. Frances Schaafsma, coach
Dixie Grimmett, assistant coach

Accomplishments: Frances Schaafsma is Associate Director of Athletics at California State University at Long Beach, as well as Head Basketball Coach. With Dixie Grimmett serving as assistant, this university's basketball program has consistently developed teams that have qualified for the National Championship Play-offs of the Association for Intercollegiate Athletics for Women (A.I.A.W.). Their fine leadership and coaching attracts high-caliber players of all-American and Olympic status.

The demands of basketball are similar in many ways to volleyball. Both demand a good aerobic base, upon which to develop high anaerobic capacity; although basketball does require more running, it is also a game of fast starts, stops, and short sprints. Each game also requires good leg strength and endurance for continuous jumping. Consequently, the conditioning program used by these coaches in basketball closely parallels that used by Dixie in volleyball. The one major difference is in the repeat-interval running program. In volleyball, the maximum distance is 110 yards, whereas in basketball repeats are done at 110 yards as well as 220 yards, because of the longer distances run by players up and down court.

DIVING

Interview with: Pat McCormick, athlete (Fig. 7-56)

Accomplishments: Winner of four Olympic gold medals in diving; two in 1952 at Helsinki for springboard and platform and two in 1956 at

Fig. 7-56. Pat McCormick.

Melbourne for the same events. Winner of twenty-seven national titles, more than double the number won by any other American diver. Since retiring from competitive diving, among many other activities, she directs a sports camp for aspiring young athletes at Webb School in Claremont, California.

Pat firmly believes in the importance of good conditioning in order to be a successful athlete. In her summer sports camp, youngsters participate in a daily regimen of conditioning activities, particularly stressing the improvement of aerobic capacity. This is in addition to the expert coaching that they receive in their selected sport.

According to Pat, in diving, board work contributes 90% to the effectiveness of a dive, with the mechanics of the dive itself, that is, movements executed after leaving the board and entry, contributing only 10%. If the diver cannot get off the board at the proper angle and attain optimum height, then she cannot execute the dive properly.

Strength work

Hurdle. The diver needs good strength in both lower extremities to provide the power for a good hurdle and board spring to attain optimum height off the board. This would involve strengthening the extensor muscle groups of the ankle, knee, and hip. In addition to weight training, she recommends stairjumping, using both legs, along with stair hopping on the hurdle leg.

Dive. Hip flexors need to be strong to quickly execute the pike. Strong abdominals provide power in bending the trunk into the pike, in stabilizing the trunk (along with the back extensors) in the layout position, and in executing rotating maneuvers.

Entry. A clean entry requires the entire body to be well stabilized. Antagonistic muscle groups on the front and back of the lower extremities and trunk all need to be strong to hold the body in vertical alignment. In a headfirst entry, especially in platform diving, the shoulder muscles and elbow extensors (triceps) must be very strong to withstand the force of impact with the water.

Flexibility

Flexibility is extremely important in diving. A good range of motion is required throughout the body so that one may assume the various body positions unique to each dive. The pike position probably demands the greatest flexibility. Pointing the toes well depends on the muscles in front of the ankle being very flexible. To get the forehead and chest down to touch the thighs, one needs good flexibility in the knee flexors (hamstrings) and back extensors. The flexibility needs of the dive are similar to those of the gymnast.

Pat indicates that one of the problem areas for the diver is the low back, because of the arched-back position that many dives require, as well as because of accidental hyperextension as a result of poor technique. Keeping the low back well stretched out may help to minimize the possibility of these overworked muscles from going into spasm.

Aerobic capacity

Pat believes that cardiorespiratory endurance provides the diver with a good fitness base and includes jogging and other aerobic work in the conditioning program for her young divers.

FIELD SPORTS, FIELD HOCKEY, LACROSSE, SOCCER

Interview with: Barbara Longstreth, coach
Accomplishments: Barbara's coaching knowledge is based upon years of experience in field hockey and lacrosse in national and international team play. She is a former member of both the United States field hockey and lacrosse teams. In field hockey, she coached the Philadelphia Sectional Team to a national championship in 1974 and in 1976 coached the Pacific Southwest Sectional Team to second place in the national championships. In lacrosse, she coaches the Philadelphia District Team to national championships in 1975 and 1976. After 2 years on the faculty at California State University at Long Beach, Barbara is continuing to bring quality coaching to the West at Stanford University.

Barbara recommends that her collegiate field hockey players begin their individual preseason conditioning program in July, working out four times weekly and expanding this to six times a week in August. Competitive games usually begin in mid-September, with formal team practice beginning around the first of September. Her suggested 8-week program emphasizes the development of aerobic capacity, anaerobic capacity, strength, flexibility, speed, and stick work.

Flexibility, strength, and speed work

Activities that the athletes should perform daily include stretching exercises for the entire body; strengthening exercises, mainly sit-ups and push-ups; and speed work. The following speed drill is suggested:

Measure out distances of 10, 15, and 20 yards.
Sprint to the 10-yard mark and back using the pivot.
Sprint to the 15-yard mark and back using the pivot.
Sprint to the 20-yard mark and back using the pivot.
Rest 1 minute.
Repeat the circuit, followed by a 30-second rest.
Repeat the circuit.

Running work

Athletes should do distance running of at least 2 miles; on alternate days, they should do interval running. She suggests that the individual run around the perimeter of a field hocky or football field, if available. One circuit consists of jogging along the sideline, sprinting across the end line, jog down the other sideline, and then sprint across the other end line. The athlete should complete one circuit, rest 30 seconds; complete two circuits, rest 30 seconds; complete three circuits, rest 1 minute. Repeat the entire combination two more times, for a total of three.

Stick work

Stick work includes a variety of ball-control drills, dribbling, ball-juggling, passing, and receiving.

GYMNASTICS

Interview with: Jim Fountaine, coach (Fig. 7-57)

Accomplishments: Jim has been coach of the Kips Gymnastic Team of Southern California since 1967. The Kips competitive team is one of the largest in the United States, involving 75 girls in 11 categories of competition. In addition to the

Fig. 7-57. Coach Jim Fountaine spots nationally ranked Donna Turnbow in a complex routine.

team, Jim works with 210 other girls in recreational-instructional classes.

The Kips have dominated California and Region I of the United States Gymnastic Federation (U.S.G.F.) since 1971. In 1974 and 1975, Jim's younger athletes won back-to-back titles in the U.S.G.F. Junior Nationals. In 1977, the Kips took second place in the U.S.G.F. Senior Nationals and the Independent Clubs Nationals. Jim was selected as assistant coach for the 1972 and 1976 Women's Olympic Gymnastic teams. Prominent talented gymnasts on the Kips include *Donna Turnbow,* national champion and number one ranked gymnast in the United States in 1977; *Debbie Fike,* alternate on the 1972 Olympic Team and member of the 1974 World Games Team; *Patti Mirtich,* who placed third in the 1977 Collegiate Nationals; *Shari Smith,* who ranked tenth nationally and is a member of the 1977 United States National Team; and *Susan Archer,* who placed second on the beam in the 1977 Collegiate Nationals, as a freshman at the University of Southern California.

Although a comprehensive strenuous gymnastics workout involving all-out effort will contribute greatly to improving and maintaining the gymnast's fitness level, workouts need to be supplemented with a planned conditioning program for the athlete to achieve her optimum performance level. Gains in strength and flexibility can be attained through progressively designed workouts. As gymnastics does not inherently involve much cardiovascular stress, improvement in aerobic capacity can be achieved by including repeat tumbling routines, for example, 15 in a row, with good spotting provided.

Optimum levels of strength, flexibility, and endurance are important to the gymnast for at least two significant reasons. First, of course, good fitness is required to properly execute the various performance skills involved. Second, perhaps in no other sport is the athlete's safety so dependent on it. Attempting an element that requires more strength than the athlete possesses can easily result in a fall. Good strength, flexibility, and endurance assures the gymnast of good body control, especially when learning new elements. And loss of body control in gymnastics can often result in injury to the athlete, even with good spotting.

Endurance

The Kips members jog daily for approximately 1 mile. They are encouraged to bike-ride and do rope jumping on their own. Jim believes that swimming would also be an excellent way for gymnasts to improve their aerobic capacity.

Strength

Strength improvement is achieved through calisthenics and weight training.

Calisthenics. Exercises include chin-ups; leg-raises to a pike position, while hanging from a bar; chin-ups with a pull-over; bar dips; sit-ups; and jackknives.

Weight training. Weights are particularly helpful in developing upper body strength, which is so essential in gymnastics. Conditioning workouts include the military press, bench press, and latissimus bar pull-downs. Jim has found the girls to be especially weak in the triceps; so the bench press and bar dips are emphasized. Good triceps strength is required in performing the front support on the bar and in free exercise, executing the hip shoot to a headstand.

Flexibility

The importance of good total body flexibility in gymnastics is obvious. The ability to assume the body positions involved in executing the various elements of a routine is largely dependent on excellent range of motion in *all* the major areas of the body. Good flexibility is *especially* important, however, in the shoulder, low back, hamstrings, and hip adductors.

Optimum body weight

Good fitness for the gymnast also involves maintaining an optimum weight in relation to her strength. A weight gain of 10 pounds of fat significantly increases the difficulty of handling the body well. So, maintaining a proper weight in gymnastics is important for more than athletic reasons alone. The quality of her performance and her personal safety are also involved.

Conditioning and workout schedule

The Kips team members who are of national and world-class caliber work out for approximately 6 hours daily. On the day preceding a home meet, the team usually has a light workout lasting only a couple of hours. Time constraints involved on "away" meets usually prohibit a workout on the day preceding the event.

MARATHON RUNNING

Interview with: Miki Gorman, athlete (Fig. 7-58)

                      Jacki Hansen, athlete (Fig. 7-59)

                      Laszlo Tabori, coach

Accomplishments: Miki is a premier distance runner, having won the Women's Boston Marathon in 1974 (2:47:11) and 1977 (2:48:44). She is also a former world record holder in the Women's Marathon. In the summer of 1977, she was the overall winner in the cross-country and marathon at the World Masters Track and Field Championships in Sweden.

Jacki is the former world record holder in the Women's Marathon, with a time of 2:38:17, set in October 1975. She held this record until May, 1977 when it was broken by Chantal Langlace of France with a time of 2:35:18. As the marathon is 26 miles, 325 yards in distance, the runner must maintain a pace of 6 minutes per mile, for the 26-mile event, to achieve these remarkable running times.

Laszlo Tabori was the 1955 world record holder in the 1,500 meters (3:40:8), a 1956 Olympian in the 1,500- and 5,000-meter events, and the third runner in history to break the barrier of the 4-minute mile. He coaches world-class marathoners, Miki Gorman, Jacki Hansen, and the Los Angeles Valley Community College Distance Runners, winners of numerous cross-country championships, 1-mile, 2-mile, and distance-medley relay events.

Fig. 7-58. Miki Gorman, on left, works out with fellow runner.

Jacki and Coach Tabori were interviewed at Los Angeles Valley College during a regular workout in the San Fernando Valley (California), on a July afternoon when the temperature was registering 105 degrees. She began running when she was 22 and entered her first road race in 1972.

She works out 6 days a week, alternating distance running with interval training every other day, with one 20-mile run weekly. She averages approximately 100 miles of running each week.

Laszlo firmly believes in the value of interval training for improving both the runner's speed and endurance. Each athlete's program is highly individualized, with appropriate changes being made as the individual improves in daily workouts. A planned workout on any particular day might be modified according to the runner's individual talent, the weather, how the person feels and is performing that day, and the upcoming competitive schedule.

Interval training workout

A typical interval training workout for Jack and Miki might include the following:

Fig. 7-59. Jacki Hansen.

Warm-up
1. 20 minutes of easy jogging.
2. 15 minutes of stretching.
3. 15 wind sprints, each of which consists of running a length of the football field, followed by a rest interval of a 25-yard jog (along the end line) between each sprint.

Interval training workout
1. 220 yards, 10 minutes, with a 100-yard jog-walk rest interval between each.
2. 2 easy laps.
3. 2½ laps, 4 times.
4. 165 yards, 10 times, with a 55-yard jog-rest interval between each. This track drill is initiated on the middle of the curve, consists of running the rest of the curve and the straightaway, and then jogging the first half of the next curve. The tempo is fairly fast.
5. 2 easy recovery laps.
6. 15 to 20 laps covered by repeat intervals (running followed by jog rest) of varying distances.

Distance workout

After warming up, including stretching, the marathoner will run for 1½ to 2 hours at a pace averaging 7 to 8 minutes per mile. This consists of continuous motion, fartlek type of running, in which the running speed is varied. Total distance of the workout will vary from 10 to 15 miles, again depending on how the runner feels and the competitive schedule.

Recommendations

Team approach. Jacki is a firm believer in the value of using a team approach in conditioning and training athletes, as do those in the European countries. Each athlete could benefit highly and perform closer to her actual potential if a variety of experts would pool their resources toward helping the competitor. Experts would include, besides the coach, a medical doctor, podiatrist (a doctor of foot and lower-extremity problems), a biomechanist, a nutritionist, and a psychologist.

Nutrition. She practices carbohydrate loading before a major distance race to build up muscle-glycogen stores. During a race, she drinks ERG (Electrolyte Replacement with Glucose) to replace water and electrolytes every 3 to 5 miles, depending on the heat.

Proper shoes. When Jacki began running, she suffered from painful foot conditions and sciatica, a syndrome characterized by pain resulting from a stressed low back. (The sciatic nerve originates in the lumbar spine and innervates the leg. When this nerve becomes inflamed from improper movement of a disc, the pain can be felt all the way down the leg.) These serious problems were solved for Jacki by a prominent distance runner and podiatrist, John Pagliano. Jacki's problems stemmed from the fact that she had severely pronated feet (ankles turn inward with excessive weight being borne on the inner side of the foot), a relatively common condition known as varus foot. Dr. Pagliano designed an orthotic device for Jacki's shoes that allows the feet to bear the body weight properly, thereby solving her medical problems. Without this help, it is doubtful that she could have continued her running career.

Miki Gorman's training program differs somewhat from Jacki's. She runs approximately 60 to 70 miles per week and does not include quite so much interval speed training as Jacki does. She peaks about twice a year for a major marathon event. Two of her favorites are the New York City Marathon, usually held in the fall, and the Boston Marathon, in the spring. She begins peaking about 2 months prior to competition by gradually increasing her mileage until she is putting in about 120 miles each week.

MARATHON SWIMMING

Interview with: Siga Albrecht, coach (Fig. 7-61)
                      Penny Dean, athlete (Fig. 7-60)
                      Cindy Cleveland, athlete (Fig. 7-61)

Accomplishments: Siga Albrecht coaches for the Lakewood Aquatics in addition to her successful coaching of men and women distance swimmers. Two of her eight marathon athletes, Penny Dean and John York, are record holders in the Catalina Channel distance event.

Penny Dean is the current world record holder for swimming the 18-mile Catalina Channel. (September 1, 1976; 7 hours, 15 minutes, and 50 seconds). She also holds the world record for swimming 36,000 meters in a pool and won the Amateur Athletic Union Long-Distance Nationals in 1971. Penny had an outstanding swimming career at Pomona College, serving as captain of the women's swim team for all four of her undergraduate years. She competed at three A.I.A.W. Nationals, holds 10 league records, and holds 20 out of 24 of Pomona's Women's Varsity swimming records. She was honored as a collegiate all-American in 1977. Penny's diligent training regimen contributed to her setting a new world record when she became the second person ever to complete

Fig. 7-60. Penny Dean.

a *double crossing* of the Catalina Channel in September 1977. Her time of 20 hours, 3 minutes, and 17 seconds shattered the existing record of 26 hours and 53 minutes, set by Greta Anderson in 1958. On the same crossing, Penny also established a new one-way world record by swimming from Catalina to the mainland in 8 hours, 33 minutes, and 15 seconds.

Cindy Cleveland is an experienced distance swimmer who came within 17 minutes of breaking the women's record for swimming from Catalina to the mainland in 1976. In 1977, she joined the ranks of the very few by completing a *double crossing* of the Catalina Channel in 24 hours, 39 minutes, and 24 seconds. In addition to marathon swimming, Cindy competes for the California State University at Long Beach Women's Swim Team.

Fig. 7-61. Cindy Cleveland, on the left, with another marathon swimmer and coach Siga Albrecht, on the right, after a 10-mile ocean race.

Conditioning and workout schedule

Conditioning for distance swimming is a yearlong process involving a minimum of 6 hours daily in the fall, increasing to approximately 10 hours a day, in late summer, for 6 days a week. The conditioning program is designed to bring the swimmers to their peak in late August in preparation for swimming the Catalina Channel in early September and October. This major event involves an 18 to 21-mile swim between Catalina Island and the southern California mainland. But if a swimmer is going to attempt a *double* crossing, the distance might range from 36 to 40 miles! Other competitive events in August serve as a warm-up for the channel swim. These include the Annual Seal Beach Rough Water Swim, a distance of some 10 miles, and the Annual Catalina Classic, a race of approximately 15 miles, from the isthmus at the west end to Avalon, at the east end, on Catalina Island.

Early fall. In September, marathon swimmers begin training with two pool workouts daily and an ocean workout. Pool work includes kicking and pulling drills and swimming intervals, with concentration on technique and pacing. The morning workout lasts from 1 to 3 hours and the afternoon workout about 2 hours. At first ocean swimming is done only once a week, then twice weekly, and subsequently three times weekly, with distances ranging from 2 to 6 miles. An exercise program is followed, consisting of sit-ups, push-ups, daily extensive stretching exercises for all of the major body areas to prevent muscle soreness, and jogging 3 to 5 miles several times a week.

Winter and spring. The double pool workouts continue each day. Ocean workouts are also conducted on a daily basis, 6 days a week, at slightly longer distances.

Early summer. The frequency of the pool workouts is dropped to only one daily, for 3 hours. The ocean workouts are extended to 8 to 9 miles daily, which require about 4¹/₂ hours to complete.

Midsummer. The daily pool workout is shortened to 1 to 2 hours. The distance of the daily ocean swim is extended to 14 to 18 miles. During these workouts, Penny is concentrating on maintaining a pace of 23 to 24 minutes per mile, whereas Cindy holds a pace of 28 to 29 minutes per mile. As the time for the channel swim draws near, on certain days the pool workout is eliminated as swimmers do an all-day ocean swim of approximately 25 to 30 miles.

Role of the coach

Siga continues to be impressed with the determination and toughness displayed by her women swimmers, in comparison with the men. The close communication with her swimmers that occurs between these lengthy 6- to 7-hour ocean workouts is extremely important to the success of the athlete. Siga has a close relationship with each person and has an intimate knowledge of their personal lives, jobs, interests, and problems. It is important for the coach to be sensitive to their needs, as these factors all influence the swimmer's workouts and progress. She endeavors to help each person to identify the mental as well as the physical requirements involved and to set realistic goals in an atmosphere of confidence and support.

Typical distance workout

A typical ocean-swimming workout of 16 miles might consist of the following:

Mile 1. Warm-up; slow pace, emphasizing stroke technique.

Mile 2. Swim 30 hard strokes, or "bursts," followed by 30 slower strokes, concentrating on technique. Continue alternating between 30 bursts and 30 technique strokes.

Mile 3. A pacing mile; try to swim the mile at a designated pace, for example, a 24-minute mile.

Mile 4. Swim the mile *at least* 1 minute faster than the preceding pace mile.

Miles 5-16. Continue alternating, swimming a pace mile on the *odd-numbered* mile and swimming the next *even-numbered* mile at least 1 minute faster.

Breathing. Most swimmers breathe alternately on each side. Some breathe every three strokes; others might breathe after each six or seven strokes.

Kicking. Marathon swimming involves the upper body mainly, with the legs being used very little. However, use of the legs is encouraged during these distance workouts for the following reasons: (1) On a long swim if the legs are allowed to do nothing, circulation becomes poor and the swimmer will suffer from cold legs; (2) in an ocean race, the swimmer is sometimes caught in an unfavorable current. In this situation, the best course of action is to go into a sprint to get through the current area as quickly as possible. This necessitates a strong kick.

Technique. Good stroke execution is essential in ocean swimming. The swimmer's body position in the water must minimize drag. A higher arm recovery then normal is required because of the ocean chop, which can be severe.

Proper rest and nutrition. The daily physical demands required of the distance swimmer throughout the year make it imperative that she gets 8 to 9 hours of sleep each day and that she maintains a well-balanced diet. Interestingly enough, despite their year-round vigorous conditioning schedules, marathon swimmers are amazingly healthy athletes, rarely suffering a cold!

Channel crossing

A major goal among marathon swimmers is the opportunity to attempt swimming across the Catalina Channel, an 18-mile stretch between Catalina Island and the mainland. Only 30 swimmers through 1976 have officially completed this swim, which was initiated by chewing-gum magnate William Wrigley in 1927.

For a crossing to be declared official, the swimmer must start from dry land and walk at least three steps beyond the waterline upon completing the swim, have no physical contact with anyone or anything while in the water, use no artificial buoyancy aids of any kind, and have official timers.

Support team. A number of people with special skills are involved in contributing toward a successful crossing. A support boat must be available to accompany the swimmer and be in charge of navigation. The skipper must be particularly knowledgeable of the channel, and the vagaries of weather, wind, and currents, as well as tides. The swimmer and coach rely on the skipper's expertise in deciding when to attempt the crossing, including the exact date and time of day for initiating the swim. Most swims begin shortly after midnight.

In addition to the support boat, the swimmer is accompanied by two expert surfboard paddlers, one on each side of the swimmer. The boat sets the course while the paddlers follow the boat and guide the swimmers through the water.

Nutrition. Siga Albrecht's marathon ocean swimmers all use carbohydrate loading before the crossing, to accumulate extra stores of energy, in the form of glycogen, in their muscle tissue. About 1 week before the swim, an exceptionally heavy workout is conducted to deplete muscle-glycogen stores. For the next 2 days, athletes further deplete their muscle glycogen by restricting their diet to fats and proteins. Then, about 4 days before the crossing, swimmers convert to a diet that is almost totally carbohydrate. This procedure brings about the "overshoot phenomenon," which means that the muscles are able to store greater amounts of glycogen than usual in preparation for the lengthy and strenuous work involved in attempting the crossing.

During the crossing itself, swimmers are allowed to bring anything they think they may want to eat along the way. In actuality, they rarely eat much of what they bring, perhaps a few cookies, to get rid of the salty taste of the ocean water.

Fluid intake during the swim is very important, as swimmers become quite thirsty. A fluid-electrolyte drink such as ERG (Electrolyte Replacement with Glucose) has worked well on recent crossings.

Quick recovery. The fast recovery of marathon swimmers after a recent channel crossing is indicative of their excellent physical condition. It is also an index of the good coaching that they receive under Siga Albrecht's guidance. Within 1 to 2 days after the swim, these fine athletes were back again at their distance workouts with positive attitudes and without any residual muscle soreness!

ROWING

Interview with: Joan Lind, athlete (Fig. 7-62)
Accomplishments: Silver Medalist, Single Sculls, 1976 Olympics world-class rower

World-class rower Joan Lind follows an intensive year-round conditioning program geared toward peaking for maximum performance in June, when national competition is regularly held, along with trials for membership on the United States National Team. World team competition between teams from various nations usually occurs in August of each year.

Rowing workouts

During the fall and winter months, from September through January, Joan rows daily beginning at 6:15 A.M. for 6 to 12 miles. Three times a week, after warming up, she rows two races, each 2½ miles in length, *for time,* with a short rest period in between. On alternate days, she rows 10 to 12 miles of *distance training,* to develop a good cardiovascular endurance base. On Sunday, she either runs 4 to 6 miles or rides her bike.

In the spring, the distance work is eliminated, as she begins to concentrate on middle-distance workouts and sprints. Three times a week, she will row two 17-minute middle-distance workouts. On the alternate days, she concentrates on sprints, rowing two 500-meter intensive repeats, with 3-minute rest intervals be-

Fig. 7-62. Joan Lind.

tween each repeat. On Sunday, she adds three to four repeats of hill running to her regular running or cycling schedule.

Weight training

Joan includes weight training in her conditioning program the entire year-round, working out three times per week. Because rowing requires a great deal of strength in every major muscle group of the body, her training program is intensive and comprehensive.

Lower extremities. Exercises to increase leg, thigh, and hip strength include heel raises, leg presses, and knee curls.

Trunk. Exercises include sit-ups; leg raising and lowering on a slantboard, with the low back kept flat.

Upper extremities. Shoulder and upper back exercise included using barbells and performing dead lifts, cleans, back extensions over the end of a table, and rowing. She also performed pull-ups.

She eliminated weight-training work for 2 weeks immediately before any major competition.

Flexibility

Her stretching routine included every major muscle group and joint in the body, as follows:

Leg. Front and back muscle groups
Thigh. Front and back muscle groups
Hip. Front
Trunk. Low back, lateral trunk
Shoulders. Front
Neck. All sides

She is particularly careful to keep the low back stretched, as rowing tends to cause this area to become especially tight.

Endurance

Physiological testing conducted on male rowers at the United States National Training Camp, over a several-year period, showed that national-class rowers had high oxygen-uptake capacities ($\dot{V}_{O_2}$ max.) similar to those of other endurance athletes. It was also shown that in rowing, aerobic metabolic pathways contribute 75% of the energy, with the remaining 25% being supplied by anaerobic pathways. Average absolute $\dot{V}_{O_2}$ values of 5.8 liters per minute were demonstrated by many oarsmen. When Joan was tested in the Human Performance Laboratory at California State University at Long Beach, her $\dot{V}_{O_2}$ max. was 4.1 liters per minute. The difference in $\dot{V}_{O_2}$ max. values between the male rowers and Joan can be accounted for by the larger body size of the men. When this figure is divided by the athlete's body weight, the oxygen uptake in milliliters per kilogram of body weight can be calculated, and athletes of varying sizes can be compared. On this basis, Joan's value of 60 ml./kg./min. compares quite favorably with those of the men, which ranged from 58 to 66 ml./kg./min. Apparently Joan's endurance-training program is working well for her in this most demanding sport.

TENNIS

Interview with: Dr. Joan Johnson, coach
Accomplishments: Selected as coach of the United States Women's Tennis Team for the 1977 World University Games in Bulgaria. Dr. Johnson is also chairman of the Department of Physical Education at California State University at Los Angeles.

The Women's Tennis Team at California State University at Los Angeles begins its preseason conditioning program approximately 3 weeks prior to the beginning of competition. Conditioning workouts are held daily, 5 days per week, for approximately 30 minutes, followed immediately by court-work drills and practice.

Conditioning exercises are included for the development of aerobic capacity, strength, and flexibility. Team members jog about 1 mile each day, on grass as a precautionary measure to avoid possible shin splints. Calisthenics for strength development include sit-ups and push-ups. Heavy emphasis is placed on a variety of stretching exercises. Good flexibility is especially important in tennis because of the many positions of stretch that the player is forced into during a game. Stretching exercises are performed for the Achilles tendon (calf), front of the ankle, thigh adductors, hamstrings, quadriceps, hip flexors, anterior shoulder, and lateral trunk. Leg stretching is also done after jogging. In addition to these conditioning exercises, many on-court drills develop agility and anaerobic capacity, also essential to successful performance.

SKIING

Interview with: Georgene Bihlman, athlete, certified ski instructor (Fig. 7-63)

Accomplishments: Georgene epitomizes the true lifetime athlete, having participated in competitive skiing over a twenty-five year span. She has won over 30 United States Ski Association Gold Medals and has been the holder of a United States Senior National Championship in the downhill, slalom, grand slalom, or combined events, almost annually since 1961. After a major illness and extensive abdominal surgery in 1975, Georgene came back the very next year to take a first in the National Senior grand slalom and a third in the downhill. In the 1977 Senior Nationals, she was second in combined, slalom, and grand slalom and fourth in the downhill at Copper Mountain, Colorado. She is a Certified Ski Instructor at June Mountain, California, and a professor of Physical Education at Bakersfield Community College, California.

Whenever possible, Georgene likes to incorporate skiing technique into her conditioning exercises, thereby involving the same muscle groups that are used while racing. This might include, for example, having the individual perform double-unweighting exercises while on skiis (unweighting both skiis simultaneously), or perhaps doing running on uneven terrain and around trees.

Good muscular strength is important in ski racing. Strong abdominals and

Fig. 7-63. Georgene Bihlman.

back extensors provide stability to the trunk and upper body, allowing the racer to achieve good angulation and maintain balance. She recommends weight training along with calisthenics for strength development.

Racers need to take good care of their knees. Georgene avoids deep knee bends and believes that bicycling up and down hills might be preferable over running as a means of developing cardiorespiratory endurance.

Stretching exercises for the major muscle groups should be included in the skiier's conditioning program, as the racer is often forced to assume extreme body positions to maintain control while maneuvering through the race course.

Because it is much easier to *stay* in condition than it is to *get* into condition, Georgene recommends that the serious racer, if possible, should race the entire year by following the snow in the summer (Chile, New Zealand).

If this is not possible, the racer should continue to maintain a program and participate regularly in vigorous sport activities during the off season. When not racing, Georgene's favorite sports are surfboarding, water-skiing, and beach volleyball.

SOFTBALL

Interview with:	Mickey Davis, professional athlete
	Johnna Moore, former athlete and club owner
Accomplishments:	Mickey Davis

Mickey played amateur softball for 7 years before joining the women's professional ranks. She has been an outfielder for the women's professional Santa Ana Lionettes for the past 2 years. She has been selected five times to the National All-Star Team (all-American) and has played on two teams that won the National Amateur Championship. She also participated in world competition in Osaka, Japan, with her team finishing second.

Accomplishments: Johnna Moore

Johnna is a veteran of 23 years' experience as an outfielder in triple A amateur softball. She formerly owned the Orange Lionettes (now the professional Santa Ana Lionettes). She was named all-American as an outfielder in 1954.

Spring training for the women's professional Santa Ana Lionettes begins April 15, approximately 1 month prior to the start of the competitive season. Conditioning and practice sessions are held four times per week and include exercises to improve aerobic capacity, flexibility, and strength. Each workout lasts 3 hours. Players should already be in fairly good physical condition before reporting.

Aerobic capacity

Most players include jogging in their regular workouts, running approximately three fourths of a mile to maintain a minimum aerobic base. This also contributes to maintaining leg strength and endurance.

Strength

Strength development is achieved through various calisthenics, including sit-ups, push-ups, and some partner-resistive exercises for the arms and shoulders. No formal weight-training program is followed because of a lack of these facilities, but players are encouraged to work out with weights on an individual basis if and when they are able to avail themselves of the equipment. Good strength development of the legs, arms, and shoulders are emphasized for improved running and throwing. As these skills also require good trunk stabilization, abdominal- and back-strengthening exercises are also important.

Flexibility

A good deal of emphasis is put on stretching the major areas of the body, including the calf, low back, hamstrings, quadriceps, hip flexors and adductors, lateral trunk, shoulder, and neck. All players are tested on flexibility at the beginning of spring training to identify any areas of tightness that might require special stretching work.

There is a good deal of variation in the conditioning programs followed by each player. A certain core of exercises is performed on a group basis. But time is also made available for players to do certain exercises that they feel they particularly need to stress.

Unlike the amateurs, the professional Lionettes have the services of an athletic trainer and a team orthopedist. Injured players now receive proper diagnosis and treatment. This has resulted in a faster and more complete recovery. In the past, an injured player would often play "hurt," causing herself further damage and a subsequent prolonged recovery. Having a trainer gives players a feeling of security and confidence by the knowledge that any injuries they might incur will receive proper care.

SWIMMING

Interview with: L. "Pokey" Watson Richardson, coach

Accomplishments: Pokey is coach of the women's swimming team at the University of Southern California. She is also Sports Information Director for Women's Athletics. She has been selected as coach for the 1977 World University Games in Bulgaria. She began her swimming career with the Santa Clara Swim Club and is a double Olympian. In 1964, she was a gold medal winner in the 400-meter freestyle relay. In 1968, she repeated winning another gold medal in the 200-meter backstroke.

To attain the caliber required of a national-level swimmer, the athlete must condition and train 11 months of the year. The indoor competitive season is from October to April; outdoor competition begins in May and lasts through August. This allows September for "active rest"!

At the University of Southern California, men and women swimmers work out together, beginning in September. The preseason conditioning program consists of two phases, early and late.

Early preseason conditioning

The preseason conditioning program gets underway in September, with afternoon workouts scheduled four times per week. Each workout lasts approximately 1¹⁄₂ hours. Calisthenics include a variety of stretching and strengthening exercises. During pool work swimmers concentrate on loosening up, stroke drills, and technique.

Strength development. Both calisthenics and weight training are employed to develop strength in the major muscle groups used in swimming. These are as follows: (1) *arms and shoulders*—latissimus, pectorals, deltoids, and triceps; (2) *trunk*—abdominals and back extensors; (3) *hip*—hip flexors and extensors; (4) *thigh and leg*—quadriceps, hamstrings, and calfs.

Calisthenics include jumping jacks, bench stepping, half squats, running in place, double jumps, ankle and leg raises and flutters from a prone position, sit-ups with variations, and push-ups.

The weight-training exercises are performed to develop strength and muscular endurance. Three sets are executed at each station, with a 10-pound weight increment in each set, as follows:

> *Set 1.* 18 repetitions at first weight for warm-up value
> *Set 2.* 12 repetitions at second weight for endurance value
> *Set 3.* 6 repetitions at third weight for strength value

Sprinters perform their weight-training exercises somewhat differently:

> *Set 1.* 12 repetitions
> *Set 2.* 12 repetitions
> *Set 3.* 6 repetitions twice

As soon as the last weight can be handled proficiently, each set is increased by 10 pounds.

Exercises include dips; leg curls; leg lifts; sit-ups on the incline bench; leg press; pullies, performing specific strokes; latissimus bar pullthroughs; triceps pushes on pulley latissimus bar; pull-overs and arm rotators on barbells.

Work on the Mini-Gym equipment is done in the pool area and includes (1) latissimus pulls, (2) bench pulls (specific strokes), (3) triceps pulls, (4) pushthroughs, and (5) leg presses.

Flexibility. Stretching exercises are performed in a slow, controlled manner and include the following areas: (1) anterior and posterior shoulder, (2) trunk, (3) hip adductors, (4) hamstrings, (5) calf (ankle plantar flexors), and (6) ankle dorsiflexors.

Late preseason conditioning

During the last half of the preseason conditioning program an early morning workout is added to the schedule and the afternoon workout is modified.

Early morning workout. Initially, the early morning workout consists totally of overdistance work in the pool, with stress on the development of a "feel" for the water, stroke mechanics, and improved strength and endurance. This involves swimming, kicking, and pulling drills. The progression for pulling consists of, first, pulling only with the hands, with the feet hanging free; second, pulling with hand paddles, adding distance daily; third, adding resistance to the pull by means of an inflated tube around the ankle to increase drag. A styrofoam pull-buoy between the thighs helps the swimmer maintain a good body position. Such a planned progression in pulling work is important to avoid placing too great a load on the shoulder joint too soon, which might result in shoulder joint injury.

Afternoon workout. At this time, the organized weight training program and calisthenics are eliminated from the afternoon workout. Swimmers are encouraged to continue these exercises, including the Mini-Gym, on an individual basis. Facilities are made available for this purpose. Thus the afternoon period becomes strictly a water workout, with swimmers performing carefully planned schedules of repeat intervals at specified times and distances.

In-season conditioning

The general pattern is for the athlete to continue two-a-day workouts, tapering off before a meet. If it is an especially important meet, no workout is held, but swimmers might take a few laps. If it is a relatively minor meet, a light workout might be conducted on the morning of the meet.

SWIMMING

Interview with: Mona Plummer, coach

Accomplishments: Coach of Arizona State University's highly successful women's swimming team, Mona has established and maintained a winning tradition, attracting top-level swimmers from throughout the United States. Over one particular period, her teams won four out of five national collegiate titles.

The conditioning program at Arizona State University employs weight training for strength development, including the Universal Gym and Nautilus equipment. Men and women swimmers work out together. The program consists of a circuit with 20 to 36 stations. Heavy emphasis is also placed on increasing flexibility of the major areas of the body.

TRACK AND FIELD—JUMPERS, HURDLERS, AND SPRINTERS

Interview with: Dave Rodda, coach

Accomplishments: Dave has coached women's track and field for 17 years, including the Long Beach Comets and the Lakewood Internationals. He has also served as the women's coach for the Junior International Amateur Athletic Union Track and Field Team in 1973, the Pan-American Team in 1975, and the 1976 U.S.A. Dual Meet Team against Russia. In 1977, he coached the United States World Cup Team, including such world-class athletes as (1) *Martha Watson* (Fig. 7-64), four-time Olympian and former American record holder, long jump, and former world record holder, 60-meter dash; (2) *Joni Huntley* (Fig. 7-65), 1977 American record holder, high jump; (3) *Kim Attlesey,* Junior American record holder, long jump; and (4) *Pat Donnelly,* 1976 Olympian, 100-meter hurdles.

The conditioning program of the Lakewood International Women's Track and Field Team is a carefully designed yearlong program consisting of three major phases: foundation, preparation, and competition. Fig. 7-66 highlights the purpose and essential elements of each phase.

Fig. 7-64. Martha Watson. (Photo by William Stuart, Huntington Beach, Calif.)

Fig. 7-65. Joni Huntley. (Photo by William Stuart, Huntington Beach, Calif.)

TRACK-AND-FIELD THROWING EVENTS

Interview with: Les Berman, coach

Accomplishments: Coach of the Lakewood International Track and Field Team for thirteen years, including the following Olympians: *Sherry Calvert,* two-time Olympian, 1972 and 1976, javelin; *Karin Smith* (Fig. 7-67), 1972 Olympian, javelin; *Sandi Tyler* (Fig. 7-68), 1972 Olympian, high jump; *Emily Dole* (Fig. 7-69), member of the Junior and Senior United States International Team, shot put; *Vivian Turner,* member of United States International Team, discus. Also Les has served as coach of the United States International Track and Field Team in 1972 and 1976.

The weight of throwing events consist of the shop-put, javelin, and discus. In all three, the four most important factors to be developed, in addition to technique are (1) speed, (2) strength, (3) flexibility, and (4) endurance.

Strength

These events are referred to as "power events," requiring explosive force and speed of motion. This force, in turn, demands a great deal of strength. Regular weight-training techniques, emphasizing heavy resistance and few repetitions and executed at top speed should be emphasized. In addition to weights, strength-training devices such as the Exer-Genie and the Mini-Gym can allow

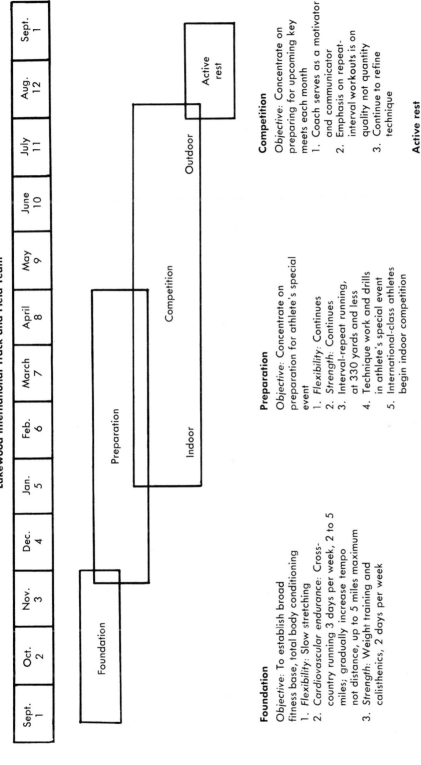

Yearlong conditioning program
Lakewood International Track and Field Team

Sept. 1	Oct. 2	Nov. 3	Dec. 4	Jan. 5	Feb. 6	March 7	April 8	May 9	June 10	July 11	Aug. 12	Sept. 1

Foundation

Preparation

Indoor Competition Outdoor

Active rest

Foundation

Objective: To establish broad fitness base, total body conditioning
1. *Flexibility:* Slow stretching
2. *Cardiovascular endurance:* Cross-country running 3 days per week, 2 to 5 miles; gradually increase tempo not distance, up to 5 miles maximum
3. *Strength:* Weight training and calisthenics, 2 days per week

Preparation

Objective: Concentrate on preparation for athlete's special event
1. *Flexibility:* Continues
2. *Strength:* Continues
3. Interval-repeat running, at 330 yards and less
4. Technique work and drills in athlete's special event
5. International-class athletes begin indoor competition

Competition

Objective: Concentrate on preparing for upcoming key meets each month
1. Coach serves as a motivator and communicator
2. Emphasis on repeat-interval workouts is on quality not quantity
3. Continue to refine technique

Active rest

Objective: Change of pace but maintain fitness level Participate in favorite active recreational sport

Fig. 7-66. Yearlong conditioning program, Lakewood Internationals, Lakewood, California.

the athlete to develop strength while performing the identical movement pattern that she employs in the event.

Ankle, knee, and hip extensors need to be well developed, along with the abdominals, which provide additional power from the trunk and hip rotation, in all three skills. Strong abdominals also serve to stabilize and block (stop the motion) of the nonthrowing side of the body as the throwing side rotates quickly forward. The shoulder, upper back, and arm muscles also require good strength. A good strength development program also helps to minimize muscle injuries caused by imbalance in strength between opposing muscle groups.

Weight training

Coach Berman recommends that weight training should begin in the fall and that work should be concentrated on the major muscle groups of the body as follows:

Lower extremities. Heel raises, leg press, hamstring curls, half squats with weights.

Trunk. Sit-ups on incline board, with weights behind head; sit-ups with a twist, crossing elbow to opposite knee; back extensions, face lying over the end of a table but avoiding arching of the back.

Upper extremities. Bench press; bent-over rowing, elbow curls; bar dips (triceps).

Flexibility

Good flexibility is important in order to assume the best wind-up position, to put the power muscles on stretch, and to add to the distance and time of the power buildup. The need for good hip and trunk flexibility is especially apparent in the javelin throw, which requires the upper body and throwing arm to be twisted back, while the hips and legs are being carried forward during the approach run. This also demands excellent flexibility of the throwing shoulder.

JAVELIN

Interview with: Karin Smith, athlete (Fig. 7-67)
Accomplishments: Member 1976 Olympic Track and Field Team, javelin,
        Member of 1976 Amateur Athletic Union National Team
        Member of 1976 United States National Collegiate Track and
        Field Team.

Karin's off-season workouts extend for 6 months beginning in September and tapering off in February in preparation for the competitive season lasting from March through August.

Off-season conditioning workouts

Major features of Karin's off-season conditioning consist of (1) heavier implement-throwing techniques; (2) anaerobic work, emphasizing starts, sprints, and jumping; (3) weight-training; and (4) stretching. She works out three times weekly.

Heavier implement throwing. These drills, always preceded by a warm-up of vigorous activity and stretching, require the person to throw an implement

Fig. 7-67. Karin Smith.

heavier than a javelin and against a wall or fence. Sometimes both arms are used in the throw; otherwise the regular javelin throwing technique is used. This will consist of 5 sets of 10 standing throws, followed by 5 sets of running and throws. Karin jogs and sprints between each set.

In the early season, she throws a medicine ball, using both arms. She then progresses to a 4 to 5-pound ball such as an indoor shot; several weeks later, within the same workout, she might do 5 sets of 10 each standing throws and 5 sets of 10 each running throws using a 3-pound weight; she then repeats some sets using a 2-pound weight. Eventually, she progresses to throwing a light-weight bamboo pole (running throws). The basic purpose of these progressive drills is to develop strength and speed of motion using the same muscle groups and movement patterns that she utilizes in the javelin throw itself.

Fig. 7-68. Sandi Tyler. (Photo by William Stuart, Huntington Beach, Calif.)

Anaerobic capacity drills. Her workouts also include jumping and running activities. These serve to increase leg strength, speed, and muscular and anaerobic endurance. She will execute, for example, 15 standing jumps; 15 jumps down from a bench and then to the pit; and 5 to 10 triple-jump types of bounding. Her running work often includes approximately 7 sets of 30-yard wind sprints, from starting blocks, in addition to doing 80- to 100-yard runs interspersed between her jumping drills.

Weight training. Karin uses a combination of weight-training exercises and calisthenics in her strength-development program. Her weight work routine consists of approximately 10 exercises of 2 to 3 sets each. She performs a 50-yard jog between each. The following is her program:

1. *Trunk rotations*. 95-pound barbell across back of shoulders, with trunk twisting

2. *Trunk extensions.* 95-pound barbell, across back of shoulders, standing; bend forward from waist and then return to erect position; 12 repetitions
3. *Arm rotations.* Same weight and position as in 2; rotate arms in a crawl arm stroke (figure-eight motion); 12 repetitions
4. *Twist and bend.* Same weight and position as in 2 and 3; bend forward at hips, bringing right arm down and forward to the right, and return to stand; repeat to left side; 6 repetitions each side
5. *Rowing.* 95 pounds; 12 repetitions
6. *Snatches*
7. *Cleans*
8. *Squat jumps.* 45 pounds; 5 sets of 10 repetitions with a 40-yard run in between each set.

Other strengthening exercises include the following:

1. *Bar handing:* 1 arm; 2 arms; 1 arm with a twist
2. *Sit-ups:* Supine, with trunk extended over a table edge; 25-pound weight held behind the neck; feet supported; 3 sets of 10 repetitions
3. *Back extension.* Prone, with a 25-pound weight held behind neck, lift trunk upward; 3 sets of 10 repetitions

Stretching. Stretching is included in every workout, prior to performance of weight work. Most major muscle groups are covered.

In-season conditioning workouts

During the competitive season, she works out daily but limits her weight training to twice weekly. She performs the following drills for a distance of 30 to 40 yards each:

1. Jogging, with emphasis on a high rearward kick
2. Lunge walking
3. Crossover-step agility drill
4. Walk on toes; return on heels
5. Bounding, landing with both feet, and then jumping as a kangaroo jumps
6. One-legged hop; return using other leg
7. Skipping
8. Sideward leaps
9. Jumping, bringing knees to chest

SHOT PUT

Interview with: Emily Manuma Dole, athlete (Fig. 7-69)
Accomplishments: Member of the Junior and Senior United States Intercollegiate Track and Field Teams.

Emily follows a daily weight-training program, emphasizing heavy resistance and few repetitions. Her conditioning workouts also include stretching and endurance activities.

Weight training

She performs 3 sets of five repetitions each, at each exercise station. Included on p. 192 are samples of her workouts. The number in the parentheses indicates her maximum lift in pounds for a single repetition.

Fig. 7-69. Emily Dole. (Photo by William Stuart, Huntington Beach, Calif.)

1. Bench press   (235)   2 sets of 190 × 5
                                                         1 set of 200 × 5
2. Behind-the-neck press   (220)   2 sets of 180 × 5
                                                         1 set of 185 × 5
3. Military incline press   (215)   1 set of 175 × 5
                                                         2 sets of 180 × 5
4. Upper body rotation: Olympic bar   3 sets of 45 × 20
5. Dead lift   (415)   1 set of 350 × 5
                                                         1 set of 360 × 5
                                                         1 set of 365 × 5
6. Clean   1 set of 175 × 5
                                                          1 set of 180 × 5
                                                          1 set of 185 × 5

7. Clean and snatch	(210)	1 set of 170 × 5
		1 set of 175 × 5
		1 set of 180 × 5
8. Clean and jerk	(200)	1 set of 165 × 5
		1 set of 170 × 5
		1 set of 175 × 5
9. Half squat	(500)	3 sets of 400 × 5
10. Sit-ups on incline board		5 sets × 20

Aerobic capacity and flexibility

Prior to her weight-training workout, Emily jogs for approximately 1 mile and performs a variety of stretching exercises before and after each lifting. She includes the hurdle-stretch (posterior thigh [hamstrings]), low back stretch, side-bending, and "windmills" of the outstretched arms, among others.

Anaerobic capacity

She also includes interval-training wind sprints, daily. A typical running workout might consist of the following:

$$5 × 30 \text{ yards}$$
$$5 × 40 \text{ yards} \quad or \quad 10 × 50 \text{ yards}$$
$$5 × 50 \text{ yards} \qquad\qquad 5 × 25 \text{ yards}$$

MIDDLE DISTANCE RUNNING

Interview with: Francie Larrieu Lutz, athlete (Fig. 7-70)

Accomplishments: Francie has held, and presently holds, so many records that it will not be possible to enumerate all of them. Some of her more notable achievements are as follows: (1) was two-time Olympian in the 1,500-meter event (1972, Munich; 1976, Montreal); (2) world record holder, indoor mile; (3) was national record holder in the indoor mile, 1,500-meter and 3,000-meter events; (4) regained the national record in the outdoor mile during the summer of 1977 in 4:28:2; (5) in 1977, was declared the outstanding woman athlete at the National Amateur Athletic Union Indoor Championships, winning both the mile and two-mile, both events being run within 35 minutes of each other; (6) also in 1977, by virtue of her continued successes, won a berth on the United States National Team to the World Games.

Francie began her running career when she was 13. She attributes much of her present success to her first coach during what she refers to as her "molding years" when she was between 15 to 19 years of age. She learned the meaning of personal discipline; she enjoyed the training atmosphere and the feelings of fellowship, understanding, and support that she received from her family, coach, and teammates. The running experience gave her a place to go and provided for her an opportunity not found elsewhere. She found that although the program made her work very hard, it was still within a fun atmosphere.

Fig. 7-70. Francie Larrieu Lutz, on right, in one of her many first-place finishes. (Photo by William Stuart, Huntington Beach, Calif.)

This earlier running period provided her with an exceptionally good conditioning base, which she has continued to maintain over the years. This allows her now to concentrate more fully on improving speed through better technique. She believes that her performance reached a plateau during the years 1972 to 1975, without being able to show continued improvement. She credits her present coach, Preston Davis, with helping her break through this barrier, through technique work (sprint form, arm action, and knee lifts), to achieve some of her best performance times in recent years.

Off-season training

Francie's off-season training consists of two workouts daily, 5 days a week, with one workout each on Saturday and Sunday. Her daily early morning workout consists of running an "easy" 3 to 5 miles in neighborhood parks and the beach.

During her afternoon workouts on Monday, Wednesday, and Friday, she concentrates on interval work, doing 4 to 12 repeats of 200 to 800 meters (the longer the distance, the fewer the repeats). The relief interval consists of a 110-yard jog or a distance equal to that of the work interval. On alternate afternoons, she distance-runs for 4 to 10 miles.

In-season training

During the competitive season, she adjusts her conditioning schedule according to her competitive schedule. She tapers off her workouts 2 days prior to a meet. On the day preceding a meet she will do an easy morning run; in the evening she performs a racing warm-up, including strides and a couple of fast 50 to 150-yard sprints, depending on how she feels.

Flexibility

Francie believes that maintaining flexibility can be a real help to the middle distance–distance runner, who often is relatively tight. She includes anterior hip (hip flexors), posterior thigh (hamstrings), and low back and posterior neck stretches in her flexibility-exercise program.

Strength

She became quite aware of the importance of arm strength in running on the day she set the American record in the mile. It was particularly hard-to-forget race with a close finish, and it left her arms totally exhausted and tingling. This experience convinced her of the need for upper body strength.

Although at first she was not able to do a single push-up, she worked up to performing 50, twice daily. Now on a maintenance program, she includes 15 to 25 standard push-ups and 25 to 50 bent-knee sit-ups in her workouts.

Francie admits that she is inconsistent in using weight training but believes that any added strength can only help the woman runner. She has included the military press, bench press, arm curls, and bar dips in her program.

VOLLEYBALL

Interview with: Dixie Grimmett, coach
Accomplishments: Selected Coach, World University Games, 1975; Head Volleyball Coach, California State University at Long Beach; winner of the A.I.A.W. National Championships in 1972 and 1973.

Dixie strongly believes in the importance of a preseason conditioning program for her volleyball players. During the summer, each potential team member is expected to participate in a carefully structured conditioning program in order to be at a fairly high fitness level when official team workouts begin in the fall. Conditioning activities consist of six components: (1) aerobic base, (2) anaerobic capacity, (3) weight training, (4) flexibility exercise, (5) ball-handling practice, and (6) jumping activities.

Testing

Before embarking on the 12-week program that she has devised, each athlete measures herself on height, body weight, and circumference of thighs, hips, calf of legs, and biceps. She also tests herself on a standing jump-reach test. These measurements are reported to Coach Grimmett on the first day of practice and are used for comparison when the same tests are repeated later during the season.

Preseason conditioning program

Aerobic base. This consists of jogging for 2 miles, 6 days per week. Tempo should progressively be increased until the athlete can run the 2 miles in approximately 16 minutes or less.

Anaerobic capacity. Repeat interval running is initiated after 7 to 10 days of jogging. (The 2-mile jogging program is also continued.) Interval running is done three times per week, alternating with the weight-training program. Included below are the distances and target times at various phases within the 12-week program.

Week	Distance (yards)	Number of repetitions	Time (seconds)	Rest between repetitions (minutes)	Total distance (yards)
1	55	10	9	$^1/_2$-1	550
	110	6	17	1-2	660
4	55	12	8.8	$^1/_2$-1	660
	110	8	16.8	1-2	880
8	55	16	8.4	$^1/_2$-1	880
	110	12	15.2	1-2	1,320
12	55	20	8.1	$^1/_2$-1	1,100
	110	14	14.6	1-2	1,540

As can be seen, one can obtain a progression by increasing the number of repeats and decreasing the target time (increasing the speed).

Weight training. Weight training is done 3 days per week, alternating with interval running. Two sets of 8 to 10 repetitions are performed at each exercise station. Some of the exercises are as follows:

1. Parallel squats
2. Supine bent-elbow pull-overs
3. Seated, triceps, extension, behind the back
4. Knee curl
5. Upright rowing
6. Bench press
7. Latissimus pull-downs
8. Wrist curls
9. Dead lift
10. Quadriceps lift (knee extensions)
11. Heel raises

In addition, 3 sets of 30 repetitions each of sit-ups are performed, and as many bar dips and chins as possible are done at each workout.

The value of these strengthening exercises (along with running) in improving the athlete's performance has been made readily apparent, since most players experience a gain in jumping heights ranging from 2 to 6 inches in test and retest comparisons.

Flexibility. Stretching exercises are performed daily and include most major muscle groups of the body: (1) calf, (2) hamstrings, (3) quadriceps, (4) hip flexors, (5) hip adductors, (6) low back, (7) lateral trunk, and (8) shoulders.

Ball handling. Athletes are encouraged to practice in passing and volley techniques. Setters should try to set from 150 to 200 balls per day, 5 or 6 days per week.

Jumping ability. Jumping drills should be performed every other day, simulating the spike approach, take-off, and arm swing, as well as blocking maneuvers.

In-season conditioning program

During the competitive season, weight-training is conducted on an individual basis, twice weekly, on nongame days. Interval running (anaerobic work) is incorporated into specific court drills during practice. Stretching exercises are performed as part of the warm-up, preceding daily practice. Practice is held five times per week for 2 1/2 hours each day.

Interview with: Marilyn McReavy and Mary Jo Peppler

Accomplishments: Both Marilyn and Mary Jo are former Olympians. In 1972, they formed the E Pluribus Unum team, winning the national title in 1972 and 1973. Together, they coached the first professional volleyball team to be coached fully by women, with Mary Jo being voted coach of the year in the International Volleyball Association in 1976. Both are now coaching the women's Intercollegiate Volleyball team at Utah State University.

Volleyball has been undergoing rapid changes within the last decade. Today's game is much more highly competitive, aggressive, and strenuous, requiring players to be in top condition if they are to perform at their best and achieve success.

One of the main reasons for its being more physically demanding is the changeover of the United States Volleyball Association (U.S.V.B.A.) to international rules. Under international play, only one substitution is allowed per game per player or a total of six per game. This more limited substitution will profoundly affect the amateur game in at least two ways. Players will have to develop all-around skills, both offense and defense; also players will have to be in excellent condition, especially in strength and anaerobic capacity because of fewer rest periods and subsequent prolonged playing time. An international match can last from 3 to 5 hours, requiring players to be continuously diving, hitting, and jumping for every set on their side and block against every spike on the other.

The Association for Intercollegiate Athletics for Women (A.I.A.W.) will be changing to international rules, beginning with the fall of 1977, but with easier substitution rules, allowing twelve substitutions per game. But both Marilyn and Mary Jo feel that the trend toward more limited substitutions requiring players to develop both offensive and defensive skills and greater stamina will eventually filter down to colleges and universities and then to high schools and younger age groups.

The three major aspects of their conditioning program are weight training, jumping, and running. Although some stretching exercises are included, they do not stress flexibility so much as the Japanese teams do.

Weight training

Weight training is done three times weekly. The athletes have use of Nautilus equipment and include work on the following muscle groups and body areas:
1. Back and hip extensor strength
2. Knee extensors
3. Toe raises for calf strength
4. Pull-overs for shoulder and arm extensor strength

They exclude dips and the bench press to minimize the possibility of overloading the shoulder and elbow joints. They use wall pulleys to develop strength in the muscles used in the serving motion, as well as pull-ups. Some rope-skipping is also included.

Jumping

A variety of jumping drills are performed: the approach and jump; continuous double-leg jumping; and hopping on one leg for a number of times and then alternating to the other leg.

Running

Athletes participate in running intervals, three times per week, on an individual basis. Shorter distances, not exceeding 440 yards are run, with the emphasis on increase speed. After a warm-up jog, a player might run 5 repeats of 50 to 100 yards, with short rest periods in between.

In addition to the above activities, much conditioning work is incorporated into the regular workouts and skill practice sessions. This includes repetitive rolls, dig and dives, and "pepper." Each drill is performed at a rapid pace for 20 to 30 minutes.

Year-round schedule

The main phases of the year-round volleyball workout schedule is generally as follows:

Spring. Conditioning and skill practice.

Fall. Competitive season for intercollegiate volleyball; conditioning continues but is decreased in scope; more emphasis on technique and strategy.

Spring. Amateur league volleyball (U.S.V.B.A.).

Summer. National team competition for top players; others maintain fitness through an appropriate individual conditioning program, summer softball, and swimming.

CONDITIONING FOR RUNNING

In addition to being a sport in and of itself, running is an essential part of most athletic events played on land; it is also one of the best activities contributing to improved aerobic capacity. George Leonard said it well:

"If infantry is the queen of battle, running is the queen of athletics. It is the essence of most sports played on dry land, both the conventional and the new. Basketball, soccer, football, rugby, baseball, cricket, field hockey, various forms of tag, Frisbee, earth ball—all of these, it might be said, are complicated exercises for running. Pole vaulting, javelin throwing and broad jumping begin with and depend upon running. Tennis is a series of short, dancing sprints, as are handball and other racket, net and wall games. Dance explores the aesthetic possibilities of the run and the leap. And gymnastics without the brief preparatory dash would lose much of its variety and sparkle."[7]

Sprint events

Sprint events of short duration such as the 100 and 200 meters, depend entirely on anaerobic processes for energy. Successful performance is largely a function of the runner's speed, which in turn is mainly dependent on strength. To increase running speed, the athlete must improve either (1) length of stride, (2) leg speed, or (3) a combination of these factors. Increasing the power of the muscles of the hips and legs, by increasing their strength, assists in attaining faster running speed.[5]

Training programs for sprinters are aimed at developing speed and usually involve running a series of fairly strenuous repeat intervals at race pace or faster and jogging or walking during a brief rest interval. Arduous interval training of this type, however, should only be introduced after a solid endurance base has been developed.

Middle distances

Middle-distance events including the 400, 800, and 1500 meters depend on energy obtained by a combination of anaerobic and aerobic processes. Training regimens typically include methods used by sprinters as well as those employed by distance-event athletes.

Distance events

Distance-running events lasting 3 minutes or longer, including the 3,000 meters, cross-country, and marathon, are endurance events that depend almost solely on aerobic processes for energy. This involves efficient functioning of the cardiovascular and respiratory systems. Even sprinters and athletes whose sports are largely anaerobic in nature need a good endurance base upon which to build their anaerobic capacity and to improve their ability to recover quickly between successive anaerobic events, or spurt type of movements.

Endurance is best developed by long, continuous running to give a good total mileage each week. The beginning runner should slowly progress up to running 2 to 3 miles daily. At this time, a weekly "long jog" of about twice the average daily distance should be added to the training schedule if she wishes to specialize in distance running.[13]

Premier marathoners like Jacki Hansen and Miki Gorman use a combination of long aerobic runs and high mileage (about 100 miles weekly) to develop their endurance. On alternate days, their workouts consist of highly strenuous interval training to develop speed and racing technique.

Women in distance running

For many years until just recently, the prevailing medical opinion held that distance running was completely beyond the woman's physiological capacity and thus could be harmful to her. In 1976, the longest Olympic running event for women was 1,500 meters, which is less than a mile. Female runners were prohibited from running the marathon in the United States until 1972 when the American Athletic Union finally endorsed all distances for women runners. Until then, only the mile and the cross-country events had been sanctioned.[13]

Interest in distance running among women athletes is growing rapidly. As more women begin to participate in this sport, performance times continue to improve. During the 10-year span from 1967 to 1977, the world record for the women's marathon changed hands fourteen different times! In 1971, 3 hours was considered the impossible barrier for women in the marathon. In 1975 alone, 27 women ran under that time, and 2:30 has now become the new impossible barrier.[13]

Injury problems in runners

Whether an individual is interested in becoming a runner or wishes to employ running as a means of developing aerobic capacity for use in another sport, certain precautions should be followed when initiating a running program.

The act of running places of great deal of stress on the various weight-bearing joints of the body, especially the foot and knee. A variety of injuries, often referred to as overuse syndromes, can result unless these precautions are taken.

Proper progression. The body is a remarkably adaptable instrument and will respond favorably to the demands put upon it. But sufficient time must be allowed for these changes to occur. If too much stress, too soon, is placed upon muscles, tendons, ligaments, fasciae, and joint capsules, these overused tissues will become irritated and inflamed. One should begin the running program at a relatively slow pace and short distance, giving these tissues time to gradually adapt to more stress. As improvement occurs, distance and tempo can gradually be increased.

Proper conditioning. The act of running itself will help strengthen the weak muscles, tendons, and connective tissues that are involved in propelling the body and stabilizing joints. Strengthening exercises for the ankle, knee, and hips can further aid this process. Strengthening exercises are also of value in minimizing muscle imbalance between antagonistic muscle groups.

Running requires good mobility of the ankle joint and flexibility of the muscles, tendons, and fasciae of the entire lower extremity. If these structures are too tight, they will be subjected to repeated overstretching while running, which can result in inflammation and pain. Running also tends to cause the low back muscles and hamstrings (knee flexors) to tighten up. Consequently, the runner's training program should include stretching exercises for all these body areas.

Biomechanical and structural problems. Most human feet have been subjected to such longtime abuse that they no longer function efficiently in weight bearing and in propulsion. The added stress imposed by running can result in inflammation of ligaments and musculotendinous units and subsequent pain. A common example is excessive ankle pronation, or *varus*. Uneven leg length or a

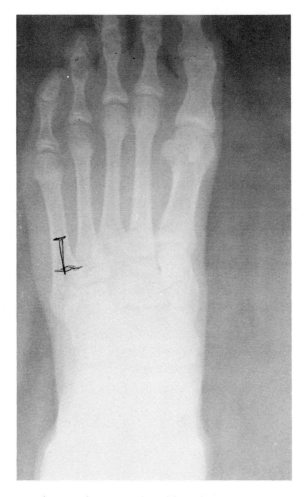

Fig. 7-71. Morton's syndrome. This x-ray film of foot shows first metatarsal (on right) to be shorter than second metatarsal. This condition often causes biomechanical imbalances within the foot, with subsequent foot problems. This and other conditions can be alleviated by competent podiatrists specializing in sports medicine.

longer second metatarsal bone in the foot (Morton's syndrome, Fig. 7-71) may also predispose the runner to painful conditions. Podiatrists with a special interest in sports medicine can often alleviate these problems through the use of an orthotic insert in the shoe that allows the foot to bear weight and function properly.[9]

Common overuse injuries

Some common overuse injuries occurring in running include shin splints, tendonitis, plantar fasciitis, stress fractures, and chondromalacia.

Shin splints. Various types of leg pain along the front or back of the tibia is referred to as the shin-splint syndrome and is usually described as a musculotendinous inflammation.[4] The anterior muscles of the leg are particularly susceptible when they are overused to compensate for forefoot imbalance or when heel contact is made on hard surfaces. At heel contact on a hard surface, the anterior muscle group contracts to aid in decelerating the foot as it contacts the ground. Overuse of these muscles causes irritation and edema. The pressure of this fluid pushes against the confining fascia resulting in reduced blood flow and subsequent pain in the anterior compartment.

Another factor contributing to this condition may be muscular imbalance between the weaker anterior muscles and the stronger, tight posterior muscle group leading to anterior muscle group overuse. Subotnick recommends the use of ice massage, functional orthotics, and strengthening and flexibility exercises as effective treatment. Additionally, the runner should use a shoe with good shock absorption and limit running to softer surfaces such as grass.

A posterior-compartment shin splint often involves inflammation of the posterior tibialis muscle just behind the medial malleolus of the tibia. The runner who has an excessively mobile pronated foot is particularly susceptible, since this causes the muscle to be overstressed during the stance phase of the run. Treatment is similar to that recommended for anterior-compartment shin splints.

Jackson[4] indicates that another type of shin pain is attributable to a stress reaction of the distal posteromedial part of the tibia itself, as differentiated from pain caused by soft-tissue inflammation. An incipient stress fracture may be involved. Rest seems to be the best treatment for this syndrome.

Tendinitis. Tendinitis is inflammation of a tendon. Inflammation of the anterior tibialis or posterior tibialis tendons is associated with shin splints. In runners, it is exceptionally important to keep the Achilles tendon and the hamstring tendons well stretched. If not, they can become subjected to overstretching and subsequent injury. Or, the irritation may be caused by overuse. This injury is often slow in healing and has a tendency to reoccur. Subotnick[12] recommends ice massage, rest, and elevation for the first 24 to 48 hours to diminish swelling. Gradually, stretching exercises should be introduced, and the athlete should use a heel lift in her shoes to relieve the tendon of excessive tension. Klafs and Arnheim[6] recommend ultrasound as an effective therapeutic modality.

Plantar fasciitis. Plantar fasciitis refers to an inflammation of the broad, flat band of fascia that connects somewhat like a bowstring, from the calcaneus to the metatarsal heads. Running on hard surfaces or increasing running tempo or distances too quickly can irritate this tissue, resulting in pain on the medial plantar aspect of the foot, just anterior to the calcaneus. A pronated foot predisposes a runner to this condition.

Stress fracture. A stress fracture consists of an incomplete fracture (a localized area of numerous microfractures) of presumably normal bone and usually confined to the lower extremities. Like metal, bone tissue can experience fatigue failure if it is repeatedly subjected to compressive overloading (Table 7-2).

Compressive overloading can result from poor shock absorption or from improper distribution of compressive forces throughout the foot or leg when running.

Poor or inadequate shock absorption occurs in several ways:

1. If the running surface is too hard, or the shoes do not cushion shock sufficiently.

2. If the calf muscles (ankle extensors) do not perform adequately in absorbing shock because of fatigue.

Causes of improper distribution of force include the following:
1. Muscular fatigue causes an alteration in normally good gait, leading to abnormal loading patterns.
2. Biomechanical imbalances within the foot, such as a short first metatarsal (Morton's syndrome) or excessive pronation (varus) (Fig. 7-71).

Common sites of stress fractures include the metatarsal bones, the calcaneus, the distal tibia and fibula (runners), and the proximal tibia (jumpers).

A stress fracture may be suspected when the athlete experiences pain simultaneously with foot contact while running; the site is also painful upon palpation. There is edema. This may occur after an unusually heavy running workout, or if the individual has been pacing her training progression too rapidly. The condition is not associated with any sudden trauma.

Follow-up x-ray films should be taken at 2-week intervals with suspected stress fractures, since the initial x-ray examination frequently appears normal. Radioisotope scans will show a microfracture site sooner than will an x-ray film.[4]

Healing may require from 2 to 6 weeks, during which time the athlete must *not* run. Running can be resumed only after an adequate healing time has been given, the fracture site is pain free to palpation, and a test run is also found to be pain free.

The following precautions are suggested in preventing stress fractures:
1. Biomechanical imbalances of the foot (excessive pronation, short first metatarsal, and so forth) should be corrected by use of an orthotic insert worn in the running shoes. This can be provided by a podiatrist.
2. Running on hard surfaces should be avoided.
3. Running shoes with good shock-absorption capability and arch and heel support should be worn.
4. Intensity and duration of running workouts should be increased slowly enough for the musculoskeletal system to adapt to the stresses being imposed.
5. Workouts should include stretching exercises for the anterior and posterior muscles of the ankle (ankle flexors and extensors) to maintain good range of motion.

Table 7-2 □ Pathomechanics of stress fracture

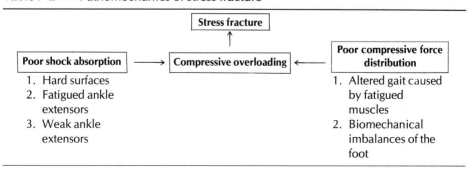

6. Workouts should include strengthening exercises for these same muscle groups.[2,8,11]

Chondromalacia. Chondromalacia of the knee (runner's knee) refers to a degeneration of the cartilage of the undersurface of the patella and is associated with running activities.[12] The symptoms of this condition include chronic pain, weakness, crepitation on movement of the patella, mild swelling, and tenderness.[4]

Good patellar stability is dependent on both dynamic and static factors. Dynamic stabilization is mainly provided by an equalized pulling on its superior border by the quadriceps tendons (much like pulling on a horse's reins). If a strength imbalance exists, the patella may be forced out of its femoral groove during knee extension (frequently laterally) causing excessive friction and wearing on its undersurface. This also occurs if the tibial tubercle of the lower leg is not in vertical alignment with the femur. Excessive ankle pronation will often cause the leg (and tubercle) to rotate medially in relation to the femur above. This will also predispose the patella to be displaced laterally, when the quadriceps contracts in knee extension. A similar problem may occur if the runner has an excessively wide pelvis, thereby causing the quadriceps to exert a lateral pull on the patella. This may lead to patellar subluxation (partial dislocation) and chondromalacia.

These problems can be alleviated by strengthening exercises for the quadriceps and the use of an orthotic insert in the shoes to regain normal foot balance and alignment of the lower leg, in case of ankle pronation.[12]

Importance of good shoes

A good running shoe can often spell the difference between running joyfully or having to experience the pain associated with overuse injuries. A well-constructed shoe, with a good fit, provides proper support for the foot, helps to absorb shock, and protects the foot from being cut or bruised, a situation that could occur if one attempts to run barefoot. Barefoot running is to be avoided altogether.

Support. With regard to support, a good-fitting shoe provides lateral stability to the heel and some support to the medial arch. This can minimize the biomechanical imbalances that exist in many persons' feet, by restricting the tendency of the heel to turn inward and the arch to collapse medially when running. This tendency toward pronation, if excessive and not controlled, predisposes the foot to overstress injuries such as tendinitis of the Achilles tendon, plantar fasciitis, shin splints, and chondromalacia.

Shock absorption. A good shoe minimizes shock absorption in two important ways. First, it is constructed of materials that absorb force. Second, when a shoe helps the foot to remain in a balanced, neutral position (minimizing pronation mainly), the muscles of the front and back of the ankle are better able to perform their shock-absorbing function, with minimal stress and fatigue.

Shoe construction.[1,10] The various components of an athletic shoe are as follows (Fig. 7-72):

Last. Basic mold around which the shoe is manufactured.

Sole. Bottom part of the shoe and, in a running shoe, composed of three layers.

OUTER SOLE. Layer that makes contact with the ground, provides protection,

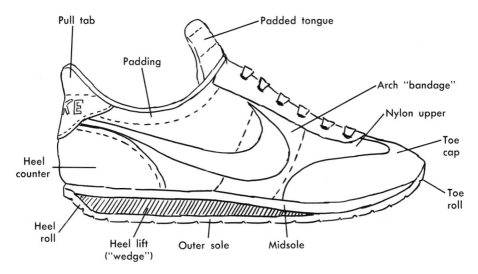

Fig. 7-72. Anatomy of a running shoe. (Artwork Margaret Miller, Long Beach, Calif.)

traction, and force absorption; the most common types are the waffle, ripple, and transverse cut

MIDSOLE. Part between the outer and inner sole and often wedge shaped; gives shock absorption and provides heel lift

INNER SOLE. Layer that makes contact with the foot and can be composed of leather, canvas, terry cloth, or Spenco

Foxing. Rubber or leather that gives added lateral and medial support to the shoe.

Toe cap. Foxing at the toe area to prevent scuffing and allow toe room

Heel counter. The inflexible material that surrounds the heel area and provides stability to the foot by reducing the tendency of the heel to pronate at foot contact

Pull tab. Allows the shoe to be pulled on easily and with padding reduces pressure against the Achilles tendon

Upper. The material composing the upper part of the shoe, with nylon being preferred

Arch "bandage." Supports and stiffens the side panels; adds lateral support

Considerations in shoe selection. When choosing a running shoe, one should look for the following characteristics:

1. The *outer sole* should be flexible enough to allow the foot to bend easily at push-off and should be tough but soft enough to provide cushioning (Fig. 7-73).
2. The *midsole* should also be flexible and provide shock absorption. Look for its wedge shape, which provides heel lift and minimizes overstretching of the Achilles tendon.
3. The *heel counter* is one of the most important aspects of the shoe. It should be rigid to minimize the tendency of the heel to pronate, which predisposes to soft-tissue injuries.
4. The *box toe* should be adequately roomy in vertical height, length and

Fig. 7-73. Good shoe flexibility. (Courtesy Nike Co., Beaverton, Oregon.)

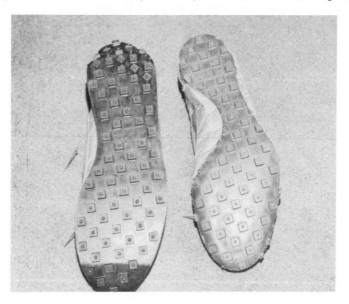

Fig. 7-74. Waffle-sole design in a training shoe, left, and a racing shoe, right.

width. Good vertical clearance minimizes abrasion with the top of the toes. Adequate length prevents jamming of the toes. (See discussion below on proper fit.)

5. A *nylon upper composition* is essential for a running shoe. It is less abrasive than leather and does not take on the shape of the foot as does leather. It is more comfortable, retains less moisture, and dries faster than does leather.

6. *Other considerations* include the composition of the inner sole, tread, shoe weight, and sock selection. The best material for the inner sole is Spenco, a nitrogen-impregnated neoprene. It has excellent shock-absorping qualities and is soft and nonabrasive. Cloth insoles should be avoided as they tend to irritate. Tread design is a matter of preference, but the waffle tread may have some advantage in allowing the foot to undergo torque at push-off (Fig. 7-74). Regarding weight, the lightweight shoe may give the runner a slight advantage in speed, but it provides less protection than does the heavier one. A cotton sock should always be used for running, since it adds cushioning and absorbs perspiration. Nylon, on the other hand, retains heat and moisture.[10]

Proper fit. The shoe should fit well in terms of overall length, width across the ball of the foot, and a snug heel (Fig. 7-75). The best time to shop for shoes is later in the day, when the feet are larger. Always measure the foot while standing. The total length should be approximately 1/4 inch longer than the longest toe since the foot will expand by about one full size when running. The lasts used by various manufacturers differ in width across the ball of the foot and in the heel. Find a brand that provides widths that suit your particular type of foot. Only recently have some manufacturers designed shoe lasts more suitable for the female foot, which tends to be more narrow than that of boys and men. The toe box should allow free movement of the toes. Corns and cramping can lead to hammer-toe deformities.

Shoe modifications. If a runner has some particular biomechanical problem, such as excessive pronation or a tendency to tendinitis, shin splints, or other overstress injuries, she should consult a podiatrist. This specialist can design

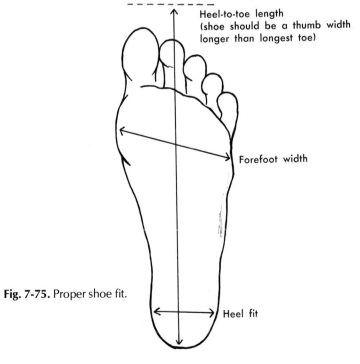

Heel-to-toe length
(shoe should be a thumb width
longer than longest toe)

Forefoot width

Heel fit

Fig. 7-75. Proper shoe fit.

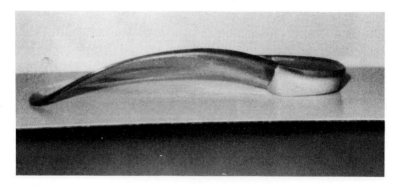

Fig. 7-76. Orthotic insert.

wedges and other orthotic inserts (Fig. 7-76) for the shoes that can minimize and often ameliorate these difficulties.[10]

Bra support

Most women find it necessary to wear a good bra support while running. Comfort depends on good support with minimal chafing. A recent study indicates that few athletes were satisfied with the bras that they were wearing during athletic competition. It was found that a well-fitted bra could minimize vertical and lateral excursions of the breasts in running and jumping, providing much comfort for the players. It was theorized that soreness and tenderness of the breasts reported by numerous female athletes could be minimized by the regular wearing of a well-fitted supportive bra during sports practice and competition, particularly for women with moderate to full-sized breasts.[3]

REFERENCES

1. Farris, N.: New trends in athletic shoe design and construction. Paper presented to Podiatric Sports Medicine Seminar, Costa Mesa, California, March 6, 1976.
2. Gilbert, R.: Stress fractures in runners. Paper presented to Podiatric Sports Medicine Seminar, Costa Mesa, California, March 6, 1976.
3. Haycock, C. E., and Gillette, J.: Female athletes need good bras, Physician Sportsmed. **5:**15, August 1977.
4. Jackson, D. W., and Bailey, D.: Shin splints in the young athlete: a non-specific diagnosis, Physician Sportsmed. **3:**45, March 1975.
5. Jensen, C. R., and Schultz, G. W.: Applied kinesiology, New York, 1977, McGraw-Hill Book Co., Inc.
6. Klafs, C. E., and Arnheim, D. D.: Modern principles of athletic training, ed. 4, St. Louis, 1977, The C. V. Mosby Co.
7. Leonard, G.: The ultimate athlete, New York, 1975, The Viking Press.
8. Mack, R., et al.: Symposium on stress fractures, American College of Sports Medicine, Anaheim, California, May 6, 1976.
9. Pagliano, J.: Foot problems in runners. Paper presented to Seminar in Conditioning for Women's Athletics, California State University at Long Beach, October 1976.
10. Pagliano, J.: Construction, selection and fit of the running shoe. Paper presented to Podiatric Sports Medicine Seminar, Tucson, Arizona, March 26, 1977.
11. Shuster, R. O.: Prevention of stress fractures. Paper presented to Fourth Annual Sports Medicine Seminar, American Academy of Podiatric Sports Medicine, San Francisco, California, May 1, 1976.
12. Subotnick, S.: Podiatric sports medicine, Mount Kisco, New York, 1975, Futura Publishing Co.
13. Ullyot, J.: Women's running, Mountain View, California, 1976, World Publications.

PART FOUR

Sports training

8 □ Anthropometric factors in injury

IMPORTANCE OF INJURY PREVENTION

Enthusiasm in espousing the many values that can accrue to the individual through participation in competitive sports must be tempered with the knowledge that the risk of injury to the athlete is also inherent in any physical activity. The risk of becoming injured varies greatly between sports, as we well know. Football and other collision sports can be classified as being high risk and downright dangerous. In others, such as golf and archery, the chances of injury to the athlete are relatively low, as far as acute traumas are concerned. But even in non-collision sports, where the risk of acute injuries is not so great, such as tennis or badminton, the active athlete subjects her body, muscles, and joints to repetitive physical stresses involving *compression* (pushing together of weight-bearing joints, such as occurs when one lands from a jump), *tension* (pulling apart or stretching of muscle fascia and ligamentous tissue as body parts are put into extreme positions), *torsion* (excessive twisting movements at the joints), and *friction* (the wearing and sliding past each other of bone, ligaments, and muscle-tendon tissues) among others. In these cases, the body can experience a series of microtraumas, any one of which is not serious, but the accumulative effect of which can result in painful inflammatory conditions including bursitis, myositis, tendinitis, and arthritis.

Whether the athlete suffers an acute injury of sudden onset, such as a severe sprain, or has a condition that develops over a period of time before becoming symptomatic, such an injury can well lead to arthritic problems during middle age. Many former high school and collegiate athletes as they approach their 40s and 50s begin to suffer knee problems (such as chondromalacia, or torn cartilage) or low back pain (degenerative disc disease) that are partially a result of their earlier athletic careers.

Persons charged with the responsibility for administering athletic programs are obligated to make the competitive experience as safe as possible for the young athlete. Probably the two most important factors contributing to the athlete's safety are quality coaching (so that techniques are executed properly and efficiently) and the athlete's being well conditioned prior to engaging in competition. Other factors include proper equipment, well-maintained facilities, and excellent medical care, including a preparticipation physical examination, prompt treatment by a sports medicine specialist, and thorough rehabilitation programs when injury does occur.

RELATION OF INJURY TO ANTHROPOMETRIC CHARACTERISTICS

Although there is a considerable amount of scientific research available today that is devoted to the physiological implications concerning the female in sports activities, little research has been conducted on the anatomic aspects. It must be assumed, therefore, that because of the relatively slight differences in skeletal muscle structure, the mechanisms that produce certain types of injury in the male are also responsible for similar injury in the female. Well-trained women coaches and trainers, in our opinion, would materially reduce injuries, since most well-conditioned, well-trained individuals can undergo strenuous competitive programs without injury, whereas the poorly conditioned person is prone to a multitude of ills and injuries.

Injury predisposal

Bone formation and growth are influenced by functional stresses as well as by nutrition, heredity, biochemical influences, and vascular conditions.[6] Bone strength develops with use. The well-conditioned athlete will have strong healthy bones, which are able to withstand stresses, torques, and shocks. The musculature of the body, in addition to providing the motive force for the skeleton, acts as a cushioning pad to protect the bones against trauma. Only a few parts of the body are unprotected, such as the skull, the anterior aspect of the tibia (shinbone), and the dorsal aspects of the hands and feet. The areas of the body are usually protected by gloves, pads, shoes, or other devices in those activities where they are particularly vulnerable to injury.

The muscles serve not only as a means for movement and protection, but they also enable the body to project itself or to impact force to extraneous objects. The strength of the musculature serves an additional protective function in that it permits the development of counterforces in contact activities. Thus the development of strength in a training program takes on a twofold importance—sufficient strength to perform a desired activity competently and sufficient strength to withstand or counteract the physical shock attendant to performance. As muscles are developed, the strength of the ligaments and tendons develops concomitantly, thus permitting the joints to function more effectively both in terms of performance and protection.

The body build (somatotype) of an athlete may make her susceptible to certain kinds of injuries.[4] Certain mechanical factors such as the angle of pull, the position of the body or its parts, the application of force or torque, and speed may also set the stage for injury. Not to be overlooked is the posture of the individual; postural deviations may make an athlete particularly prone to a specific type of injury.[4] The well-trained coach or trainer should be familiar with various postural deviations that may lead to injury and then take the necessary steps to either ameliorate or correct them.

If the initial or preseason physical examination reveals that a girl is injury prone, she should be counseled to give up a particular sport if it is ascertained that corrective or preventive measures cannot be successfully undertaken. On the other hand, if the condition seems remediable, steps should be taken to set up a training program that will achieve the desired results.

Growth, particularly during adolescence, which is the period of greatest physical growth, is an extremely important factor in predisposition to injury. Growth in all anatomic factors does not proceed at a common constant rate. For example, closure of the epiphyseal seal, the growth center of the limbs, does not occur until the termination of puberty (although because of the earlier maturation of the female the epiphyses will ossify and cease growth about 3 years prior to those of the male).[6] These centers are especially vulnerable to trauma. Such trauma can and often does result in osteochondritis, a serious degenerative joint disease that usually attacks the weight-bearing joints. Osteochondritis is characterized by destruction of the articular cartilage with lipping and spurring of the bone, resulting in impaired function. Such epiphyseal injuries seem to be much more common among male high school athletes than among athletes in their very early teens. Since girls do not as yet compete as extensively in some of the contact sports that often produce such injuries, it is difficult to draw any conclusions as to how serious the implications may be for female athletes. However, girls and women do compete in track and field and in gymnastics, two sports that do involve considerable stress upon the joints in a variety of ways. It would seem that in general that which applies to the male athlete must surely within certain limits apply to the female.

Some common injuries of the female athlete

The discussion that follows deals with some of the more common injuries of female athletes.

Overstrain. Overstrain injuries appear to be as prevalent among female athletes as among males.

Foot injuries. Foot injuries in particular seem to have a high incidence rate. Common overstrain injuries of the foot include second metatarsal strain, metatarsal fascial strain (the result of continual pounding of the unprotected foot on a hard surface, often found among dancers and gymnasts), longitudinal arch strain, and stress fractures of the metacarpals and phalanges (Fig. 8-1).

Ankle and knee joint injuries. These injuries involve trauma to the bursae, periosteal trauma, and inflammation of the tendons and tendon sheaths, etc. Many of these injuries occur because of the employment of poor mechanics in walking and in running. If not corrected, chronic conditions can result. Many girls have difficulty in running because they have developed poor locomotor habits. The broader pelvis of the female causes the femur to articulate at a more acute angle, thus inducing a decided lateral sway of the body when running, although recent studies seem to indicate that this motion has little or no relationship to the velocity of the run.[1, 5, 7] Runners should be taught to develop a good knee lift on the forward carry of the free leg and avoid "casting," or flinging the lower leg and foot out to the side when executing the swing phase. This action of casting causes an inward rotation of the femur and results in more than normal stress being imparted to the medial aspect of the knee joint when the foot is planted on the ground at the end of the swing phase. If the runner suffers from valgus knees (knock-knees), the resulting trauma can cause considerable joint injury over a period of time.[4] This condition can also make the individual more prone to an acute injury as well. Proper foot placement and good leg elevation on the swing phase, coupled with a straight leg carry, will produce better results in terms of performance and will materially reduce the possibility of ankle and knee joint injury (Fig. 8-2).

Severe torsion of the joints usually results in considerable tissue damage and can incapacitate an athlete for a considerable period of time. The flexed knee is

Fig. 8-1. A, The dancer and gymnast are particularly susceptible to foot injuries. **B,** Repetitive lumbar hyperextension can result in painful trauma to the low back.

Fig. 8-2. Finger sprains, ankle-joint sprains, and knee-joint trauma are special hazards to the volleyball player.

particularly vulnerable, since force that is projected to either side of the knee and produces either a forced abduction or an external rotation is capable of causing a rupture of the medial collateral ligament, a chipping or fracturing of either meniscus (semilunar cartilage discs), or dislocation. Often tears of either the anterior or posterior cruciate ligaments (or of both) may accompany the medial collateral ligament injury. Ligamentous injury can occur with or without injury to the menisci.

Lumbar spine. Certain sport activities place particular stress on the lumbar spine. One study showed that young female gymnasts engaging in strenuous training and competition displayed an incidence of pars interarticularis defects an affectation of the vertebra) that was four times higher than that of the nonathletic population. This problem is believed to be caused by repeated microtraumas associated with sports requiring repetitive hyperextension of the lumbar spine. This condition is seen in young male and female athletes participating in karate, football, gymnastics, hurdling, pole vaulting, high jump, and other jarring sports. The incidence of pars interarticularis defects in the female athlete appears similar to that of males performing similar activities.[2]

Shoulder and elbow joint injuries. Although not so common as injuries to the lower extremities, shoulder and elbow joint injuries nonetheless pose some problem for the female athlete. As previously indicated, the angle of the arm in support activities is somewhat unfavorable and subjects the arm to some strain. The narrower shoulder breadth, often coupled with hyperextension and outward angling of the forearm, creates problems in arm-force movements such as arm circling or rotation and throwing, often exposing the arm joints to unusual strain with resul-

Fig. 8-3. Professional pitcher Nancy Welborn shows the unusual stresses that pitching places on the upper extremities. (Photo by Phyllis Stevens, Anaheim, Calif.)

tant injury. Throwing movements, particularly those employing rapid, jerky movements, as in throwing a javelin, often result in a sprain because of overstretching the joint capsule. Either acute or chronic trauma may cause injury to the bursae (tiny fluid sacs adjacent to joints whose purpose is to reduce friction within the joint), thus inducing bursitis, an inflammatory condition of the bursa.

Strains and sprains to the elbow joint often occur after a fall upon the outstretched hand with the elbow in complete extension. The elbow is forced into *hyperextension* that results in a tearing of the capsular and tendinous tissues anterior to the joint. Throwing movements that are accompanied by a sudden and forceful supination or pronation also subject the elbow joint to severe strain. The whipping type of throw, involving supination or pronation, often causes a severe trauma identified as medial epicondyle avulsion, more commonly known as "tennis," "golfer's," or "Little League" elbow (Fig. 8-3).

Fig. 8-4. Both competitor and coach incur the risk of injury during the execution of the more difficult gymnastic moves.

Splints. The term "splint" refers to trauma that one induces by performing on a hard nonabsorbent surface. Splints affect either the forearm or the anterior aspect of the tibia (commonly known as the shin). It is distinctly an overuse syndrome. *Forearm splints* occur when there is inflammation and tenderness, particularly of the brachioradialis, the flexor pollicis longus, and the supinator muscles. There may also be some damage to the periosteum of the radius. Activities involving support or forceful landing on the hands such as performing on the uneven parallel bars, vaulting, tumbling, and free exercises appear to be the chief causes of this condition (Fig. 8-4). *Shin splints* occur when the anterior tibialis is subjected to unusual and continued stress, as in sprinting, playing a game on a hard or unyielding surface, or the takeoff phase of a jump. They are characterized by pain, heat, tenderness, and some swelling. Both of these conditions require careful diagnosis since they frequently mask more severe injuries such as periostitis, tenosynovitis, or myositis.[3]

SUMMARY

The anatomic differences between the sexes generally favor the male in sports performance. Although maturation of the female is accelerated, the longer, slower growing period experienced by the male results in a heavier, larger, and more rugged structure that possesses mechanical and structural advantages, particularly where the upper body is concerned. The longer and heavier bones add to body weight and the longer levers provide a much greater excursion of the moving ends, resulting in greater speed and force, a decided advantage in throwing, striking, and explosive types of events. Conversely, the female is limited in those events by her smaller size. However, because of her body proportions she enjoys advantages in balance, stability, and flexibility. Anthropometric differences indicate that the female should compete only with those of her own sex in activities where strength and power are the principal factors, but she can hold her own against the opposite sex in activities that demand dexterity.

REFERENCES

1. Hettinger, T.: Physiology of strength, Springfield, Ill., 1961, Charles C Thomas, Publisher.
2. Jackson, D. W., Wiltse, L. L., and Cirincoine, R. J.: Spondylolysis in the female gymnast, Clin. Orthop. **117:**68-73, June 1976.
3. Klafs, C. E., and Arnheim, D. D.: Modern principles of athletic training, ed. 4, St. Louis, 1977, The C. V. Mosby Co.
4. Lowman, C. L.: Effects of postural deviations on athletic performance. In Proceedings of the Fourth National Conference on the Medical Aspects of Sports, Chicago, 1962, American Medical Assocation.
5. Oyster, N., and Wooten, E. P.: The influence of selected anthropometric measurements on the ability of college women to perform the 35 yd. dash, J. Am. Coll. Sports Med. **3:**130, 1971.
6. Rasch, P. J., and Burke, R. K.: Kinesiology and applied anatomy, ed. 4, Philadelphia, 1971, Lea & Febiger.
7. Rose, D. L.: The effect of the obliquity of the shaft of the femur upon speed of running and vertical jumping ability. Master's thesis, Pennsylvania State University, 1959.

9 □ Incidence, type, and cause of injury

For many years, prevailing medical opinion indicated that participation in highly vigorous, stressful, competitive sports would be harmful to the female, in view of her smaller, lighter skeletal framework, less ligamentous and muscular strength, and supposedly more delicate breasts and genitalia when compared with the male. Indeed, a survey on injuries incurred by female athletes appeared to support this contention in 1964.[7] Klaus found the overall incidence of athletic injuries in women to be almost double that in men, with the largest percentage of injuries occurring in sports that required explosive efforts such as sprints and the long jump.

The incidence of overstrain injuries, contractures, tendinitis, bursitis, and various foot problems was four times higher for women. Based upon these findings, a well-known exercise physiologist recently concluded that such activities are probably not suited to the female's musculoskeletal system!

To conclude that the higher number of injuries was attributable entirely to the female's generally smaller bone structure and muscle mass was unfortunate indeed, because completely ignored were the two factors that are apparently most responsible in the prevention of injuries of the athlete of either sex—good conditioning and good performance technique, which in turn are dependent on good coaching. It is highly probable that the higher number of injuries among women athletes of almost 15 years ago who comprised the forerunners of the women's athletic revolution was an outgrowth of inadequate conditioning programs and relatively inexperienced coaching and subsequently poorer skills than anything else.

Although a paucity of information still exists regarding injuries in women's sports, the few studies that have been conducted recently indicate that the better conditioned athlete is, indeed, less susceptible to injury; that *among the highly trained athletes*, there is no difference in injury rates between the sexes; and that the types of injuries are the same for men and women athletes engaged in the same sport. Additionally, earlier concerns regarding the female athlete's susceptibility to chest contusions or breast injuries appear unfounded.

Kosek[8] conducted a 2-year injury survey involving 361 schools and 19 sports. Sports reporting the highest number of injuries were basketball, volleyball, field hockey, and gymnastics, whereas those having the fewest injuries included golf, squash, and archery. The most common types of injuries were sprains, strains, tendinitis, contusions, and patellar problems. Injuries sustained by female athletes were essentially no different from those for men, nor were the well-trained (conditioned) women athletes more prone to injury. Kosek, a registered physical therapist and certified trainer, anticipated that the injury rate will decrease as better coaches and trainers become available to women's athletic programs.[3]

J. Garrick, M.D. and former director of the Sports Medicine Clinic of the

Table 9-1 □ Seattle interscholastic athletic injury study

Sex	Sport	Total number of participants	Total number of injuries	Injury rate	Leading type I	Leading type II	Leading location I	Leading location II	Medical doctor seen	Incurred during practice	Time loss (5+ days)
M	Football	309	265	0.86	Sprain (30%)	Strain (28%)	Thigh 19%	Knee 15%	30%	67%	23%
M	Wrestling	125	106	0.85	Strain (37%)	Sprain (33%)	Knee 23%	Shoulder 15%	49%	64%	28%
W	Gymnastics	41	23	0.56	Sprain (48%)	Strain (26%)	Low back 44%	Ankle 9%	17%	83%	30%
M	Track and field	144	50	0.35	Strain (42%)	Sprain (28%)	Thigh 24%	Leg 22%	34%	57%	44%
M	Basketball	136	46	0.34	Sprain (54%)	Strain (15%)	Ankle 52%	Thigh 7%	33%	66%	11%
M	Soccer	52	16	0.31	Contusion (44%)	Sprain (25%)	Ankle 25%	Eye 19%	31%	81%	19%
W	Track and field	111	32	0.29	Strain (34%)	Inflammation (25%)	Leg 31%	Foot 16%	41%	83%	52%
W	Basketball	28	8	0.29	Strain (38%)	Sprain (25%)	Knee 25%	Ankle 25%	50%	63%	29%
M	Baseball	130	30	0.23	Sprain (30%)	Strain (17%)	Fingers 17%	Knee 17%	33%	47%	17%
M	Cross-country	70	16	0.23	Strain (38%)	Chondromalacia (25%)	Knee 44%	Leg 19%	38%	79%	25%
	Total	1146	592	0.52							

*From Garrick, J. C.: Presentation made at American College of Sports Medicine Conference, Anaheim, California, May 6, 1976.

School of Medicine at the University of Washington, studied athletic injuries incurred by boys and girls involved in interscholastic athletics in four Seattle high schools. An injury was defined as any traumatic medical condition arising out of scheduled participation in the athletic activity, characterized by at least one of the following: (1) missing at least one practice, (2) missing at least one game, (3) removal from a game and not being allowed to return, and (4) seeking traditional (family) medical attention.

The top ten interscholastic high school sports, in terms of number of injuries per number of participants or injury rate, is shown in Table 9-1. Of these ten, only three are girls' sports: gymnastics, ranking number three with an injury rating of 0.56, followed by track and field and by basketball, ranked number seven and eight, both with an injury rating of 0.29. Based upon these data, it does not appear that the girls are more injury prone than are boys; indeed, the opposite appears to be the case. Whereas the average injury rate for all athletes in the ten sports was 0.52, the rate for all girls in their three sports combined was 0.35, compared with an injury rating of 0.55 for the boys. When football and wrestling are excluded, the boys' injury rate dropped to 0.30 (Table 9-2).

Although the injury rate for all girls sports combined was lower, a higher percentage of the girls injuries required a time loss of 5 days or more, as shown in Table 9-2. Of the girls' injuries, 37% compared with 24% of the boys' resulted in losing 5 or more days of practice. The extent to which this indicates that the girls' injuries were more serious, or slower to respond to treatment; or attributable in part to sociocultural reasons, sexual differences, involving "playing hurt," or differences in motivation levels; or perhaps in treating similar injuries in girls more conservatively than in boys are questions that remain unanswered. The injury rate for boys' track and field was higher than that for the girls: 0.35 versus 0.29. Time loss caused by injuries in this same sport was slightly higher for the girls with 52% of the injuries requiring a loss of time of 5 days or more, whereas 44% of the boys' injuries resulted in a similar time loss.

The Seattle study clearly demonstrates the similarity in types of injuries incurred by high school boy and girl athletes. Generally, they are of the overuse type

Table 9-2 □ Comparison of injury rates between girls and boys in Seattle interscholastic athletic injury study*

Sex	Total number of participants	Total number of injuries	Injury rate	Average time loss (5+ days)
Girls	180	63	0.35	37%
Boys	966	529	0.55	24%
Boys (excluding football and wrestling)	532	158	0.30	

*From Garrick, J. C.: Presentation made at American College of Sports Medicine Conference, Anaheim, California, May 6, 1976.

affecting the lower extremity and mainly include muscular strains and connective tissue sprains. The high incidence of low back problems in girl gymnasts (44%) and leg inflammation of girls' track and field athletes (25%)—probably shin splints—deserve particular attention.

Albohm[1] conducted a survey of common injuries among high school female athletes involving 240 teams from twelve states in seven sports. Results are shown in Table 9-3. She concluded that any differences in type and frequency patterns are attributable to the different demands in the various sports that they pursue, rather than to any significant structural or physiological differences between the sexes. Also, conditioning programs aimed at achieving the highest levels of strength and endurance would probably provide the female athlete the best defense against injury.

Some interesting insights into the type and incidence of injury incurred by women athletes at the college level were provided by Gillette.[5] She collected data on 361 schools, involving nineteen major sports. The incidence of injury was highest in basketball, volleyball, field hockey, and gymnastics and lowest in golf, synchronized swimming, squash, and archery. She determined the relative risk of injury per sport by dividing the total number of injuries per sport by the number of colleges participating (rather than by the total number of participants), thus determining the average number of injuries per college, for each sport. (See Table 9-4.)

Table 9-3 □ Common injuries among high school female athletes*

Sport	Most frequent type of injury	Site of injury
Basketball	Sprains	Ankle
Golf	Blisters	Hands, feet
Gymnastics	Contusions	Hip
	Dislocations	Elbow
	Blisters	Hands
Swimming	Strains	Shoulder
	Cramps	Legs
Tennis	Strains	Upper body
	Blisters	Feet
Track and field	Strains	Quadriceps
		Hamstrings
		Groin
	Abrasions	Extremities
	Shin splints	Leg
	Sprains	Ankle
Volleyball	Contusions	Knee, elbows
	Sprains	Fingers
	Abrasions	Knee, elbow

*From Albohm, Marge: Physician Sportsmed. **4**:46, Feb. 1976.

The most common types of injuries incurred were ankle sprains, knee injuries, and contusions (Table 9-5). The least common injuries were those to the breast, head, and neck, according to respondents. When the same data was organized into type of major injuries by sport,[6] the most serious injuries, including major fractures, head injuries, and dislocations, were in basketball, field hockey, softball, and gymnastics. (See Tables 9-6 and 9-7.)

Table 9-4 □ Injuries to women in nineteen intercollegiate sports (1974-1974)*

Activity or sport	Number of injuries	Number of colleges participating	Average number of injuries per college
Basketball	1,178	186	4.12
Volleyball	691	251	2.75
Field hockey	668	148	4.51
Gymnastics	453	122	3.71
Track and field	306	105	2.91
Tennis	275	259	1.06
Softball	240	157	1.53
Lacrosse	192	38	5.05
Competitive swimming	128	119	1.08
Badminton	50	70	0.71
Snow skiing	37	33	1.12
Cross-country	36	28	1.29
Fencing	24	44	0.55
Bowling	10	46	0.22
Soccer	8	10	0.08
Synchronized swimming	8	39	0.21
Archery	8	29	0.28
Squash	7	9	0.78
Golf	7	72	0.10

*From Gillette, J.: Physician Sportsmed. **3:**61, May 1975.

Table 9-5 □ Most common injuries to female athletes*

Injury	Number of responses	Percent of responses
Sprained ankles	312	86
Knee injuries	236	65
Contusions	154	43
Low back injuries	50	14
Muscle pulls and strains	26	7
Shin splints	25	7
Hand and finger	13	4
Wrist	6	2
Blisters	3	1

*From Gillette, J.: Physician Sportsmed. **3:**61, May 1975.

Table 9-6 □ Type of major injuries by sport*

	Fractures	Dislocations	Severe sprains and strains	Extensive lacerations	Concussion or skull fracture	Eye injuries	Dental injuries	Tendon tears	Heat exhaustion	Cervical neck injury	Total
Basketball	X	X	X	X	X	X			X		7
Volleyball	X	X	X			X					4
Field hockey	X	X	X	X	X		X				6
Gymnastics	X	X	X		X					X	5
Track and field	X	X						X			3
Tennis			X			X		X			3
Softball	X	X	X	X	X						5
Lacrosse	X	X	X	X							4
Competition swimming			X								1
Badminton			X								1
Snow skiing			X								1
Cross-country skiing			X								1
Fencing				X							1
Bowling			X								1
Soccer			X								1
Synchronized swimming			X								1
Archery											0
Squash			X								1
Golf			X								1

*From Haycock, C. E., and Gillette, J. V.: J. Am. Med. Assoc. **236:**163, July 1976.

Table 9-7 □ Probable causes of injury*

Cause	Number of responses	Percent of responses†
Improper training methods	214	59
Inadequate facilities	81	22
Poor coaching techniques	75	21
Inadequate equipment	50	14
Improper use of equipment	40	11
Other‡	120	33

*From Gillette, J.: Physician Sportsmed. **3:**61, May 1975.
†Total is greater than 100% because respondents often indicated more than one cause.
‡Includes responses related to the above causes but generally of an ambivalent nature.

The respondents felt that improper training methods, including inadequate conditioning prior to entering collegiate sports, along with a lack of modern training techniques were major factors in injuries to women athletes. Inadequate facilities and poor coaching techniques were also listed as factors. Respondents recommended better training (conditioning) techniques, including weight training, and preseason, in-season, and off-season training conditioning programs as the best solution to prevent injuries. They also strongly suggested providing athletic trainers for women's programs.

Further evidence substantiating that any higher incidence of injuries observed in female athletes is attributable to their generally poorer fitness level rather than to a musculoskeletal system that inherently cannot withstand the stresses of sport, is provided by the training records of West Point's first women recruits. In 1975, the President of the United States signed into law a bill directing that women be admitted to America's service academies beginning with the 1976-1977 academic year. The United States Military Academy's Office of Physical Education undertook a preliminary study to determine the extent to which differences between male and female recruits would affect the ability of women cadets to perform within established USMA programs and to determine what adjustments in training programs and procedures might be necessary to accommodate for any performance variances between men and women cadets.[11]

"Project 60" was a 10-week study conducted to investigate the physical capabilities of a group of 63 women volunteers, 16 to 18 years of age. One third of the subjects served as a control group; one third engaged in a 4-day-a-week program of reveille exercises, identical to that taken by regular cadets, and consisting of calesthenics, rifle drill, and running; and one third participated in a 3-day-a-week strength-training program.

Injuries sustained by individuals in the reveille-exercise training group included one ankle sprain, six shin splints, two incidences diagnosed as Achilles or peroneal tendinitis, and two fibular stress fractures. Problems reported in the strength-training group included initial muscle soreness, three muscular strains, and two cases of patellar chondromalacia. Although the incidence of injury was considerably higher for these young women volunteers, as a group, than for male cadets engaged in similar training, *none* of the women who scored highest on the original fitness tests incurred any injuries during the training period. It was obvious that the physical fitness level of the individual affected her susceptibility to injury.

When the first women cadets entered West Point and began their intensive 18-hours-per-day program of cadet basic training during the summer of 1976, their scores on basic physical fitness and performance tests and on the Physical Aptitude Examination (P.A.E.) were much lower than those of male cadets. And the women displayed more injuries during the conditioning and training programs than had been the case in the Project 60 study. Tomasi and Peterson[10] attributed these differences, however, mainly to cultural influences that until recently have encouraged males to be physically active but generally discouraging females to develop their physical potential. In their opinion, our cultural mores have short-changed women in terms of their physical development, with the result that there is a preponderance of young adult women with generally poor fitness levels who really have never been challenged physically.

The Office of Physical Education has been highly impressed with the substantial improvement shown by women cadets in regard to their physical achievements as a result of their vigorous, well-designed conditioning and training program. Whereas, as estimated, less than 1% of the general college-age female population can perform pull-ups, 90% of their women recruits can now perform this test satisfactorily. These same cadets, wearing fatigue dress and army boots, perform the 2-mile run in under 13 minutes. The O.P.E. faculty at West Point is proud of the accomplishments of their female cadets, who have demonstrated their ability to meet the vigorous physical demands of military academy training.

A panel of experts concurred that the American society has not encouraged women to stay in good physical condition, at least not to the same extent as men, and indicated that the female's *lack of conditioning* is what has made her more susceptible to injury, rather than any inherent structural fragility. It was noted that as the experience of the woman skier becomes greater, as she progresses from novice to intermediate to advanced, her injury rate becomes more similar to that of the man, because her conditioning becomes similar. A noted orthopedist in *Sports Medicine,* Dr. Thomas McLaughlin, has observed no difference in stress fractures between men and women. Either the person is out of condition and tries to train too hard too quickly or is highly trained and motivated and suffers an overuse stress fracture from working too hard. The conclusion reached by the panel was that as the number of women participating in athletics increases, the myths about female limitations in sports will decrease. Differences in type and incidence of injuries between men and women are attributed to the lower fitness and conditioning level of the female, a factor that can be improved with appropriate training.[9]

REFERENCES

1. Albohm, Marge: How injuries occur in girls' sports, Physician Sportsmed. **4:**46, Feb. 1976.
2. deVries, H. H.: Physiology of exercise for physical education and athletics, ed. 2, Dubuque, Iowa, 1974, William C. Brown Co., Publishers.
3. Garrick, J. C.: Presentation made at American College of Sports Medicine Conference, Anaheim, California, May 6, 1976.

4. Gillette, J.: What kinds of injuries occur in women's athletics, Scholastic Coach **46:**51, Sept. 1976.
5. Gillette, J.: When and where women are injured in sports, Physician Sportsmed. **3:**61, May 1975.
6. Haycock, C. E., and Gillette, J. V.: Susceptibility of women athletes to injury, J. Am. Med. Assoc. **236:**163, July 1976.
7. Klaus, E. J.: The athletic status of women. In Jokl, E., and Simon E., editors: International research in sport and physical education, Springfield, Ill., 1964, Charles C Thomas, Publisher.
8. Kosek, Sherry: Nature and incidence of traumatic injury to women in sports, Proceedings of the National Sports Safety Congress, 1973.
9. Ryan, A. J., and others: Women in sports—are the problems real? Physician Sportsmed. **3:**49, May 1975.
10. Tomasi, L. F., and Peterson, J. A.: Telephone interview, June 1977.
11. Tomasi, L. F., Peterson, J. H., Pettit, G. P., Vogel, J. V., and Kowal, D. M.: Women's response to army training. Physician Sportsmed. **5:**32, June 1977.

10 □ Prevention, evaluation, and care of injuries

Development of skill and understanding in the practice of athletic training requires considerable specialized education and a great deal of practical experience. The training per se is paramedical; the trainer must be well qualified and competent to work with and under the direction of a medical doctor. Not only is a thorough knowledge of anatomy, physiology, and kinesiology necessary but familiarity with certain aspects of physiology should also be acquired. Knowledge of the prevention of injury and the mechanisms that cause injury along with a thorough understanding of rehabilatory techniques are equally important. Generally a background in the fields of corrective or physical therapy is desirable although not necessarily a requirement. The trainer-coach has the responsibility of preparing herself adequately in all phases of the training and conditioning program. Not only must she learn to quickly identify and intelligently evaluate the nature and the extent of sports injuries but must also be prepared, in the absence of medical advice, to follow through with the decision as to whether continued participation would be detrimental to the athlete. Further, she must be prepared to institute and carry out emergency procedures and first aid when warranted and must be capable of providing follow-up care.

It is not the intent of this book to present the many varied facets of athletic training: the reader who desires such detailed information should refer to a comprehensive text in the field such as *Modern Principles of Athletic Training* by Klafs and Arnheim. Rather, it is our desire to present an overview of those training procedures and principles that are most common to girls' and women's athletics, with the thought of acquainting the reader with the prevention, care, and general rehabilitation techniques dealing with those injuries that the female athlete most often incurs. Information on common injuries, basic bandaging and taping techniques, rehabilitation procedures, and established first-aid techniques are presented. Suggested basic equipment and supplies for instituting and maintaining a training program are presented in the appendix. Bear in mind that this information and material is also useful at the college level.

ROLE OF ADEQUATE CONDITIONING

If athletic training and conditioning are to be approached in a positive manner, the primary focus should be on *injury prevention*. The care and rehabilitation of the athlete after injury become second and third steps when the first has failed. A major if not the prime cause of athletic injury is lack of physical fitness because of poor or inadequate conditioning. The lack of muscular strength or balancing, absence of minimal flexibility, and inadequate ligamentous or tendinous strength are singly or collectively responsible for most injuries. Excessive fatigue or a lack of stamina, faulty or inadequate nutrition, and psychological factors are also contributory. The trainer-coach should plan ample time for preseason conditioning as well as provide sufficient time between competitions to permit her athletes to acquire and maintain an adequate state of physical fitness. Once a high level of fitness is reached, it can be maintained with much less effort. Such fitness provides a strong defense against injury. Players who are well conditioned do not tire so easily and therefore are less susceptible to harm in injury-provoking situations. In addition, the physically fit athlete functions at optimal capacity and thus performs better.

THE TRAINING ROOM

In the last few years there has been a decided growth in the establishment of training programs at the high school level in girls' athletics. Since girls' athletic programs are growing in number, consideration should be given to a girls' training room, an integral part of the properly conducted sports program. Facilities for the prevention, management, and rehabilitation of sports-incurred injuries are of inestimable value.

Unless a new facility for physical education and sports is to be built, most coaches must utilize an existing room, revamping it insofar as feasiblity and funds will permit. Often the room presents a number of disadvantages, most of which can be either eliminated or mitigated to some degree. Any room is better than no room at all; a little work and thought can go a long way in making a limited facility workable. It is often possible to construct or make over equipment to serve the purpose. Bear in mind that it is not necessary to have a great deal of expensive equipment in order to have a good training facility.

A functional training room should be approximately 700 to 1,000 square feet to serve an average-size school. A room 20 by 30 feet would do admirably. The fact that girls usually don't play football, which requires platoons of players, makes it possible to get by with considerably less floor area than the men's program demands. Preferably, the room should be located immediately adjacent to the locker, shower, and toilet rooms and have reasonable access to the sport area. An outside corner room that has natural light and ventilation would be most desirable. The windows should be located at least 6 feet high on the wall to provide a maximum amount of wall space for supply cupboards and for the installation of rehabilitation equipment. Either a concrete or tile floor, with one or more suitably located floor drains that permit easy floor washing, is best. The room should have its own water supply, drainage tiles, and electrical service. The walls should be painted in light pastel colors with ample artificial illumination provided; fluorescent lighting has proved the cheapest operationally and the most satisfactory functionally.

The room should have three specific areas: an area for bandaging, strapping, and general care of athletic injuries; an area for carrying out rehabilitation programs; and a small area for administrative purposes. The latter should contain a desk, a chair, and a file cabinet. Several wall cabinets containing supplies complete this area. The area for general care should comprise about one half of the remaining area; it can be equipped with several 6-foot benches (16 to 18 inches in height) and one or two plinths (treatment tables 30 inches high consisting of a tabletop, approximately 26 by 78 inches, padded with 3/4 to 1 inch of foam rubber

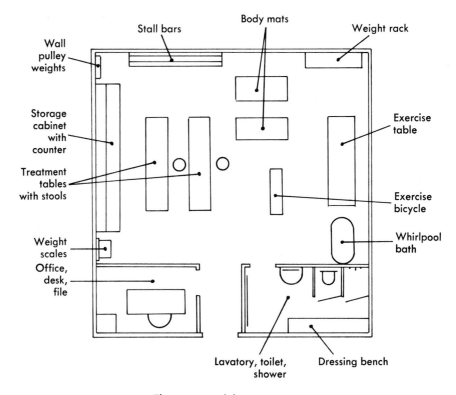

Fig. 10-1. Model training room.

and covered with Naugahyde or plastic). These are simple in design and can be constructed at very little cost. Plinths are used for strapping, bandaging, and for general care.

The rehabilitation area takes up the remainder of the available space. It should be set up with weights for the progressive resistance exercise program, one or more heat lamps, several sponge, plastic-covered body mats, and, if at all possible, a whirlpool bath. Any good text on rehabilitation, training, or corrective physical education will offer suggestions for additional equipment.

More equipment can be added to any area when needed if space and, particularly, the budget permit. Lists of suggested supplies for both the training room and for the field kit are given in the Appendix. A model training room with basic equipment that could be set up at nominal cost is portrayed in Fig. 10-1.

RECOGNIZING AND EVALUATING INJURY

Many schools do not have a physician present at practice or competition because of either budgetary limitations or the general unavailability of medical personnel. This places on the trainer-coach the responsibility of appraising the severity of the injury, deciding whether or not to permit the player to continue, and in the case of severe injury administering first-aid procedures. She must also become familiar with preventive measures that will permit her charges to participate in training or competition with a minimum chance of injury. Preventive measures consist of awareness of the athlete's physical condition, preventive wrapping or strapping, and knowledge of the various injury provoking mechanisms peculiar to the sport. Some knowledge of rehabilitation procedures is also necessary.

Recognizing an injury and its seriousness is not an easy task. Some abnormal conditions tend to be masked by misleading symptoms and, unless a physician is available, identification of the cause can be difficult. In making an evaluation it is better to err on the side of safety by being as cautious as possible. Snap judgments are uncalled for but rapid judgments must frequently be made. There are no substitutes for experience, and the opportunity to work under a qualified doctor or trainer provides the necessary background to enable one to recognize and evaluate injuries. A logical and orderly procedure is necessary. Familiarity with the signs of specific injuries can be gained through study and experience, first, by being aware of the mechanism that produced the injury, and, second, by utilizing specific techniques to methodically and carefully inspect the injury. Use of the ears, eyes, and hands enables one to gain the information needed to recognize and evaluate most injuries with a reasonable degree of accuracy and to ascertain the proper first-aid procedure to be employed.

Examination procedures

Visual inspection. Careful visual examination of the injury may disclose certain distortions, swellings, or discolorations of the skin surface. The trained observer will make a visual comparison with the opposite body part to ascertain if there are significant differences in appearance and size.

Palpation. Careful and gentle probings with the hands can give some clue to the existence of any abnormalities. Again, comparison with the opposite body part, degree of swelling and tautness, sensitivity, and heat are all clues that must be used to get the complete picture. Pain upon palpation is a valued symptom that must not be overlooked.

Auscultation. Sounds often reveal valuable information. A grating or harsh rubbing sound (crepitus) may indicate a fracture. Joint sounds, as the part is moved, may indicate either an arthritic condition or some derangment within the joint structure. The athlete should be carefully questioned as to whether she heard a sound when the injury occurred.

History. Careful questioning during and immediately after the examination often elicits information that is of material assistance in pinpointing the nature and extent of the injury.

Points to follow. In making an on-field examination of an injured athlete one should do the following:

1. Be aware of how the accident happened, either by observation or by questioning the athlete, if she is conscious and able to respond.
2. Observe the position or attitude of the body, which frequently will give a clue as to how the accident occurred and what body part is injured.
3. If the athlete is unconscious, immediately check for respiration and for pulse; if one or both are not apparent, initiate remedial measures immediately.

4. If the athlete is conscious, elicit from her how the accident took place and where the injury is. Reassure her, by talking to her to prevent undue emotional stress.
5. Compare the corresponding part with the injured part, looking for deformities, protrusions, or lacerations. In all head injuries look for bleeding or the extrusion of a pale straw-colored fluid from any of the orifices. Check the pupils for discrepancies.
6. Check for movement ability and pain reaction.
7. Loosen any tight or constricting equipment.
8. Move on down the body, checking each part and gently palpating for abnormalities or deformities.
9. Do not move the athlete unless she is fully conscious and rational. Only when you are satisfied that no serious injury exists should you permit transport. When a lower extremity is injured, do not permit her to "gut it out" by insisting on walking off unaided. Many such injuries are seriously aggravated by a display of bravado. Insist upon suitable transport.
10. In suspected back or neck injuries, because of inherent gravity of spinal injuries, *do not move the athlete unless directed by a physician,* or unless a paramedical team has taken over the situation. In all such transport a spine board must be used.

The initial evaluation is the key to successful immediate care.

These techniques must be employed by the trainer-coach in a careful, sequential, and logical manner if she is to accurately assess the problem and determine the next step. One must bear in mind that these procedures in no way qualify the trainer-coach to take the place of the physician. When a physician is present or immediately available, the physician's diagnosis prevails. Table 10-1 provides a concise reference for the recognition, evaluation, and treatment of the injuries most common to sports participation.

TYPES OF INJURIES

Injuries are usually classified as either *external,* or *exposed,* or *internal,* or *unexposed.* The latter are those injuries that do not break the skin. Injuries may be either *acute* or *chronic* in nature. Acute injuries are preponderant in athletics. These are injuries that are incurred very suddenly and are usually of short duration, whereas the chronic injury is one that results from continued trauma over a long period of time and is slow in response to treatment. Often chronic injuries respond only to radical (surgical) treatment. Reference to Table 10-1 should be made by the student as she reads the following discussion.

Inflammation. Inflammation is defined as a defensive reaction of tissue to irritation. Such irritation may be bacterial, chemical, mechanical, or toxic. It should not be confused with infection, a different condition, although one may arise from the other. Inflammation may result from a mechanical force (blows from a person or from foreign bodies), tissue exposure to chemicals or electricity, thermal agents (heat and cold), and microorganisms. Such causative agents, it is believed, produce a cellular disruption that results in metabolic changes that in turn release certain substances that initiate the inflammatory process. The general symptoms are pain, heat, redness, swelling, and a slight increase in body temperature, often accompanied by a headache. Certain pathological changes take place that result in a concentration of white blood cells at the site of injury followed by extravasation of blood in the tissue area. This in turn leads to repair and eventual healing.

Infection. Infection results when the body is invaded by a pathogenic agent, either a microorganism or a virus, that multiplies and produces deleterious effects. A localized infection is usually accompanied by inflammation. The symptoms are identical to those of inflammation, notably pain, heat, redness, swelling, and disordered function.

Repair and healing. Repair begins with the exudate of the inflammatory process, which contains a number of immature connective tissue cells. These, together with endothelial cells, which line the blood and lymphatic vessels and the heart, form a granular mass that replaces the exudate and gradually forms a loose, highly vascularized connective tissue. As healing progresses, this young connective tissue loses its vascularization and becomes a fibrous, inelastic scar.

Primary healing, or healing by first intention, occurs in an incised wound where the edges or lips of the wound are closely apposed, even, and firm. Approximation, or pulling together, of the lips produces a minimum of granulation and, as a result, very little scarring. *Secondary healing,* or healing by secondary intention, occurs when the wound is gaping with large tissue loss. Such a wound is prone to infection and is difficult to approximate to any degree. This type heals from the bottom upward and is accomplished through the formation of granulation tissues. Usually such healing results in considerable scarring.

Acute conditions

Exposed wounds. Such injuries are usually categorized as abrasions, incisions, lacerations, and puncture wounds. Infection is an ever-present danger in these injuries since the agent producing the wound usually introduces an infective agent into the soft tissue when entry is made.

Abrasions result when the skin is scraped away by a rough surface. Floor burns, which occur as the result of sliding across the floor (a frequent occurrence in basketball), mat burns (often called "strawberries"), and ground scrapes are indicative of this type of injury. Both the epidermis and the dermis are worn away through the scraping contact, resulting in a myriad of small capillaries being torn and exposed; dirt and other foreign matter are introduced into the abraded tissue. If not properly cleaned and debrided (removal of dead tissue,) infection may result. *Incised wounds* are made by a sharp instrument such as a knife that cleanly cuts the surface of the skin. It sometimes occurs when a blow is delivered to the skin that is stretched tightly over a sharp, bony prominence. It is the least serious of the exposed wounds, relatively free of infection, and heals nicely. *Lacerations* involve tearing of the tissue, resulting in a jagged edge to the lips of the wound. As with abrasions, infection is common; the wound must be carefully cleaned and debrided. As previously indicated, this type of wound heals by secondary intention and often results in scars. The many pointed implements and objects used in sports contribute to the high incidence of this type of injury. *Puncture wounds* are extremely dangerous since they are usually caused by the entrance of a sharp, pointed object such as a track-shoe spike that can introduce the tetanus bacillus into the bloodstream. Such a wound, because of the nature of the penetration, has

Text continued on p. 240.

Table 10-1 □ General management of athletic injuries*

Category	Type	Symptoms	Treatment	Rehabilitation
Exposed wounds	Abrasion	Skin abraded or scraped away; capillary bleeding	Debride and cleanse; apply mild antiseptic and sterile gauze pad; secure with adhesive tape strips	
	Incision	Lips of wound sharp and well defined—may tend to gape; often profuse bleeding	Stop bleeding; debride and cleanse; approximate edges and pull together; secure with butterfly bandages; if wound is over 1/2 inch in length (sufficiently deep so that fatty tissue is evident) or gaping in character, refer to physician for treatment to prevent scarring	
	Laceration	Lips of wound jagged and irregular	Stop bleeding; refer to physician for treatment and to prevent scarring	
	Puncture	Visible signs vary from deep open wound to almost indiscernible mark	Because of danger of tetanus, refer immediately to physician for treatment	
Unexposed wounds	Contusion	Pain, swelling, discoloration, and local, subcutaneous hemorrhage usually forming hematoma; occasionally transitory paralysis of part	Stop bleeding, reduce swelling with cold pack and compression bandage; rest	Mild exercise
	Strain (mild)	Local muscle spasm, tenderness, and weakness	Apply pressure bandage and cold pack for 1 to 2 hours; ice message with static stretching of part; if soreness persists for some time use light massage above and below injury; apply mild heat with static stretching	Athlete should maintain a modified workout program

	whirlpool (warm) helpful	
Strain (moderate)	Moderate muscle spasm, swelling, pain, tenderness, and some discoloration	Elevate injured part, apply pressure bandage and cold pack for 24 hours or longer; refer to physician for diagnosis and medication; on second day apply ice massage or cold whirlpool, (60° F.) for 20 minutes; support area with elastic bandage; on third and following day apply moist heat packs, analgesic balm packs, infrared light, etc.; maintain support bandage until full use of part is regained	Throughout treatment athlete should participate in general exercise program and as symptoms decrease, a light program of progressive resistance exercises involving affected part should be instituted; normal sports activity should be restricted for at least 3 weeks
Strain (severe)	Severe muscle spasm, considerable amount of pain, swelling, and hemorrhage with loss of function; on occasion muscle separation, identified by palpation, may occur	Elevate injured part; apply pressure bandage and cold pack for minimum of 48 hours; refer to physician for diagnosis and medication; subsequent treatment from second day on is identical to that for moderate strain	Throughout period of treatment athlete should participate in general exercise program, and as symptoms decrease, progressive resistance exercise program should be instituted for injured part; normal sports activity should be restricted from 3 to 4 weeks
Sprain (mild)	Mild disability, pain, and swelling; some hemorrhage and weakness of injured part	Elevate injured part; apply pressure bandage and cold compress for several hours; encourage movement if it can be done painlessly; apply elastic wrap to obtain mild pressure	Athlete should be able to participate in normal fashion

Continued.

*Adapted from Klafs, C. E., and Arnheim, D. D.: Modern principles of athletic training, ed. 3, St. Louis, 1973, The C. V. Mosby Co.

Table 10-1 □ General management of athletic injuries—cont'd

Category	Type	Symptoms	Treatment	Rehabilitation
Unexposed wounds—cont'd	Sprain (moderate)	Moderately severe sudden pain that persists for some time; swelling, tenderness, pain on movement, and some hemorrhage	Elevate injured part; apply pressure bandage and cold pack; apply cold at intervals for at least 24 hours; employ adhesive strapping to maintain pressure and support; permit no weight bearing (crutches must be used until soreness subsides); attempt to maintain normal movement; on second day continue cold, pressure, and elevation to control swelling and hemorrhage; subsequently use heat therapy from two to three times daily; encourage normal movement but avoid weight bearing until normal function is restored; apply preventive strapping	Restriction from normal sports activity; as pain and swelling subside, use progressive resistance exercises to build up injured part
	Sprain (severe)	Severe, sudden pain and loss of function; tenderness, swelling, considerable hemorrhage, and tearing of ligamentous tissue	Treat for shock if necessary; refer to physician for x-ray examination and diagnosis; elevate injured part and apply pressure and cold at intervals; if no fracture is present, apply constant pressure and support with strapping; permit no weight bearing; crutches may be used later; on second day, treatment is identical; on third day utilize ice massage	Complete recovery may take from 3 or 4 weeks to a full season; follow-up treatment should duplicate that for mild sprain

			and 20 minutes in 36°F. whirlpool if available and permit limited movement; subsequent treatment should utilize superficial heat and massage above and below injured site so not to disturb clot; deep therapeutic heat should now be applied
Hemorrhage	Capillary	Small, fairly slow flow or oozing of blood	Place sterile compress over cleansed wound and apply gentle pressure; hold compress in place with elastic or roller gauze bandage (bleeding stops in a matter of minutes)
	Venous	Steady flow of dark blood; fair volume of bleeding occurs	Apply compress and secure with elastic bandage; elevate injured part (pressure prevents flow and permits clotting)
	Arterial	Bright red blood ejected in spurts corresponding to heart rate	Delay in controlling bleeding is dangerous and may prove fatal; *prompt action is necessary*; apply firm digital pressure directly over arterial pressure point or compress bandage directly over hemorrhage site; if necessary to use tourniquet, loosen every 10 minutes to prevent gangrene; secure medical aid as quickly as possible; hospitalization may be necessary

Continued.

Table 10-1 □ General management of athletic injuries—cont'd

Category	Type	Symptoms	Treatment	Rehabilitation
Shock		Drop in body temperature, blood pressure, and pulse rate; respiration shallow and rapid; color, ashen gray; cold perspiration; at times, loss of consciousness; if conscious, may be very thirsty, sometimes appears to be very drowsy	Control any bleeding; keep trunk and head level, with legs slightly raised; reestablish normal body temperature by covering subject; apply heat if available; if unconscious, turn head to one side so that mucus or saliva can drain out; give oxygen if available; replace fluids if necessary with water, salt, or glucose; refer to physician	Variable
Dislocation	Subluxation	Loss of function, deformity, swelling, hemorrhage, pain and tenderness, and muscle spasm (splinting of area)	Treatment for both types is same; *make no attempt to reduce the injury since additional soft-tissue damage may be incurred;* place injured limb in support sling or splint, depending on site of injury, and transport patient to physician by ambulance if hip, leg, knee, or ankle involved; suspected spinal dislocations—make subject as comfortable and warm as possible; *above all, do not move the subject;* phone for medical aid; if necessary, treat for shock and control	After reduction and use of medical prescription, program of progressive resistance exercises should be established; recovery time runs from a few weeks to several months
	Luxation	Symptoms same as for subluxation except that deformity is obvious and separation of bones comprising joint usually discernible		

| Fracture | Loss of function, false joint, deformity, swelling, pain, and crepitus; in a compound fracture there may be hemorrhaging | *Administer first aid only; make no attempt to reduce the fracture since additional soft-tissue damage may be incurred; if there is injury to neck or spine, do not move the subject; secure immediate medical help; control hemorrhaging and treat for shock; splint the limb as it is; it may be necessary to straighten limb somewhat to permit splinting; when hemorrhaging is present, stop bleeding and do not splint; in all instances secure immediate medical help* | Recovery period varies according to type, nature, and severity of fracture; rehabilitation procedures should be carried out under medical supervision; they involve general physical conditioning and pregressive resistance exercises |

a nasty habit of partially sealing itself after withdrawal of the causative agent, making cleansing and sterilization of the wound difficult. There is an ever-present danger of lockjaw from a puncture wound, and the athlete should be immediately referred to a physician for a tetanus shot or a booster shot. This procedure should be carried out in the case of a severe laceration as well.

Unexposed wounds. Wounds called unexposed do not break or penetrate the epidermal layer of the skin and are classified as contusions, muscle strains, joint sprains, and fractures. They require a period of rehabilitation after the injury; the degree to which proper care is provided quite often determines how prolonged such rehabilitation will be.

Contusions or bruises. These wounds result from traumatic blows to the tissue; the symptoms are pain, swelling, and discoloration. Blood and lymph flow into the injured area and form a hematoma, or blood tumor. The application of a pressure bandage and cold packs to the area will minimize the hemorrhaging and reduce the possibility of scar tissue, which can occur as the result of clot formation. Contusions of the bone such as a heel bruise (commonly called a "stone" bruise) can also occur. Palpation usually reveals a hard area (the result of hemorrhage), pain, and at times a brief period of paralysis of the injured part because of sensorimotor impairment.

Strains. Strains involve the muscle tissue and accompanying fascial, tendinous, or ligamentous structures, any one or all of which may be involved. According to common usage, a strain is a muscle "pull." It is usually a tear in the body of the muscle proper or in the adjacent tissues. Unequal development of opposing muscle groups seems to be a common factor in the predispostion to strains. The athlete frequently overdevelops the quadriceps group of muscles on the anterior aspect of the thigh, while failing to develop the antagonistic hamstring muscle group on the posterior aspect. A sudden violent contraction of the quadriceps, as encountered in sprinting, overwhelms in a sense the ability of the hamstrings to react reciprocally, resulting in the belly of one or more muscles or their accompanying colloidal tissues being torn. Often the athlete hears a snap or a popping sound when the injury occurs. There is immediate pain, loss of function, and weakness of the affected part. In severe strains a depression in the muscle may be palpated at the site of injury, indicating that the tissues have parted. At times she may have had muscle fatigue or spasms shortly prior to the incident.

Sprains. The sprain is a serious injury and one of the most common disabling injuries encountered in athletics. It results from a violent traumatic or twisting force that disrupts the joint by forcing it beyond its normal range of movement, tearing and stretching the ligaments and tendons surrounding and investing the joint. Often there is injury to the articular capsule and the synovial membrane. After the initial shock there is extravasation of blood and synovial fluid into the joint cavity. The usual signs of inflammation appear—tenderness, heat, swelling, and somewhat later ecchymosis (the resultant blue and black color, later changing to greenish yellow, which appears as a result of extravasation of blood into the skin or mucous membrane). Sprains are usually classified as *first, second,* or *third* degree, depending on the extent and severity of the trauma. Joints that are most subject to spraining are the ankle, knee, and shoulder, whereas the wrist and elbow are the least often injured. Again, since internal hemorrhage is present, a pressure bandage and the application of cold packs to the area is advised.

Dislocations. Dislocations are defined as the displacement of bony surfaces that comprise a joint and are the result of forcing the joint beyond its normal anatomic limits. They are often complicated by an accompanying fracture of one or more bones. Generally, dislocations are dichotomized as *subluxations,* which are partial or incomplete separations between the articulating bone surfaces, and *luxations,* which are total or complete separations. Identifiable symptoms are joint deformity, pain, swelling, loss of limb function, and shock. In evaluating a possible dislocation, gently palpate the joint to determine the degree of change or loss of normal body contour and visually compare the injured joint with its normal counterpart. *Above all, do not attempt to reduce the dislocation!* Manipulating the limb can have serious consequences. The physician will take an x-ray film of the injury to determine the extent and degree of internal damage before attempting any restoration or treatment. Immediate first-aid procedures involve the application of an elastic pressure bandage and cold packs to the injured area to reduce hemorrhage and swelling; then a supportive bandage or splint is applied to prevent further strain on the injured part and to enable the patient to be transported for medical treatment. Bear in mind that fractures often accompany a dislocation; therefore treat every subluxation or luxation as a fracture.

Fractures. When a bone is broken, a fracture is said to have occurred. Fractures may be caused by direct violence, when force is transmitted to the bone itself and the break occurs at the point of force application, or by indirect violence, as in falling on an outstretched hand and arm with the elbow fixed so that the force is transmitted along the limb and the clavicle fractured, or by muscular contraction in which there is a sudden violent contraction of a muscle group of such magnitude that a bone is broken.

Fractures are generally categorized as *simple* when there is a break in the bone but no external wound is apparent and *compound* when the skin is broken and one or more portions of the fractured bone extrude through the skin, resulting in an external wound. Fractures must be carefully handled since further injury to muscles, nerves, and blood vessels can easily occur. Recognition of the gross signs is important so that the patient may be given proper emergency care and transporated to a physician as expeditiously as possible. Only by x-ray examination can the extent, severity, and accessory involvements of the injury be assessed. When a fracture is suspected, the following steps should be taken:

1. Determine the mechanism of the injury.
2. Make an inspection of the area involved using visual and tactile techniques. Look for the following:
   a. Deformity
   b. Swelling
   c. Site tenderness
   d. Crepitus (a grating or rubbing sound heard on movement of the ends of a broken bone)
   e. Discoloration
   f. Shock

If the limb must be moved to accomplish first aid, it should be done with great care, keeping it well supported at all times. Extension (by gently drawing the limb downward while being careful to maintain the natural line of the limb) may be necessary so that the limb can be adequately splinted. The patient should not be moved until the limb has been splinted and properly supported. In the case of severe compound fracture, particularly when there is hemorrhaging, it is safer to attempt to stop the bleeding, treat the patient for shock, and make no attempt to splint. An immediate call for emergency medical help should be placed while the trainer-coach administers first aid. The patient should be left where she is and made as comfortable as possible until professional help arrives. It is inadvisable to attempt to clean a wound or to extend the limb in this instance because of the risk of carrying the infection inward. Usually a broken bone that is properly set heals completely with little or no complications.

Splinting. Splinting is the application of an appliance, generally of metal or wood, to fix and immobilize a body part, particularly a fracture, and to prevent further damage to the part. Splints are applied after injury when it is necessary to transport the individual; they are often used after surgery or during rehabilitation procedures when it is desirable to keep a part firmly fixated until healing has progressed. After a severe strain, splints may be used as a temporary support or to limit movement. Should it become necessary to utilize splinting, the following procedures should be used:

1. Fixate the injured site by applying the splints and then, using a square knot, fasten the securing bandage be placed directly over the fracture, since complications can ensue.
2. Always include the joints above and below the fracture site when splinting; for example, a fracture of the tibia would require immobilization of both the knee and the ankle joints.
3. Pad the splint well to prevent further injury or tissue damage.
4. Always splint the fracture at the scene of the injury before transporting the athlete.
5. Avoid drawing bandage ties too tight since normal circulation must be maintained at all times.

Recently splints of the inflatable type have found favor since they give firm yet gentle support, are easily applied, and are compact when deflated.

Chronic conditions

A chronic condition results when an injury that is not properly cared for does not respond to treatment but is persistent and recurrent. An accumulation of microtrauma over a long period of time will often result in a condition of long duration as well. Inflammation is generally present, although the classic syndromes of heat, pain, redness, and swelling do not appear. The presence of a consistent low-grade inflammation usually leads to cellular changes that terminate in generalized connective tissue scarring. Recurrent injury to a part often produces a chronic condition.

The general care for a chronic condition is basically the same as the care for acute conditions. Such care stresses rest and, if necessary, some supportive strapping. The use of heat in some form such as diathermy, whirlpool bath, or ultrasound is usually advisable under prescription and medical direction.

SOME COMMON INJURIES AND PROBLEMS

Charley horse. This term applies to the contusion of the thigh muscle. The condition results from a forceful blow to the quadriceps area resulting in a forceful impingement of the muscle on the femur. The injury is classified by the degree of severity as mild, moderate, or severe. Pain is quite severe and there is loss of function with considerable swelling and capillary effusion at the site of injury. Compression and the application of cold packs are commonly used to control hemorrhage. Rehabilitation employs rest and the use of hydrotherapy and electrotherapy combined with mild stretching. On occasion some coaches advise the athlete to "run off" a charley horse; this is extremely unwise and can only lead to further tissue damage. In situations involving a mild charley horse or if rehabilitation has been effected but added protection to the injury is desired, the thigh can be properly strapped so as to permit normal use.

Stitch in the side. This phenomenon, frequently encountered by the poorly trained or untrained athlete, is identified by a sudden, sharp, violent pain in the mid-or lateral thorax so severe as to double up the athlete and deter her from continuing her performance. The exact cause is not known, but investigators have theorized that the phenomenon is attributable to ischemia, a lack of blood flow to the diaphragm brought about by a time lag in the redistribution of blood caused by the necessity of the respiratory muscles to work anaerobically during the initial phases of heavy exercise. The condition is transitory in nature and ceasing activity leads to almost immediate relief in most instances. With adequate training this distressing problem disappears completely.

Muscle cramps. A cramp is a muscle spasm. There are many causes of cramps—lack of adequate circulation to the particular muscle or muscle group, exposure to cold or heat, dietary deficiencies, vitamin deficiencies, and a lack of calcium or salt, to mention the more common ones. The best immediate treatment is to place the muscle or muscles involved in a position of static stretch, holding the position until the cramp releases. Some residual soreness usually persists but heat and massage tend to eliminate such discomfort. A cramp in the calf of the leg may be relieved by placing the foot in a position of dorsiflexion (raising the foot toward the shin as far as possible) and maintaining this position until the spasm is alleviated. Even more effective is to position oneself approximately 30 to 36 inches away from a perpendicular surface and, with both feet maintained flat on the floor and the back straight, incline forward and, placing the palms of the hands flat against the surface, bend the arms until the position of extreme stretch of the calf muscles is attained. Hold this position until relief is obtained. The common use of forceful walking as a palliative is not only extremely painful but usually proves ineffective. In addition, there is always some danger of tissue damage. Should cramps persist over a period of time, it might be well to attempt to determine the underlying cause, in some instances a dietary or mineral deficiency, which when identified and properly treated obviates further trouble.

Muscle soreness. Muscle soreness is usually the result of early-season or unaccustomed strenuous activity. As a rule, soreness appears some 4 to 8 hours after exercise and is of relatively short duration. This is a general soreness, followed by a localized soreness (myositis) some 8 to 24 hours after exercise that persists for several days before gradually disappearing. It has been postulated that such myositis results from tissue damage, principally the tearing of minute muscle fibers accompanied by a resultant capillary hemorrhage. Such muscle soreness may be caused, at least in part, by tonic muscle spasm. As indicated previously, static stretching seems to give relief from pain and discomfort, whereas light exercise coupled with message and heat assists in reducing the attendant stiffness. The resulting circulatory increase hastens recovery.

Breast protection. Although breast injuries incurred in sports are relatively infrequent, there are times when the breasts must be protected because of either previous trauma or possible future trauma. Cumulative trauma can result in serious complications. Painful blows to the breast that result incontusions and hemorrhages into the loose fatty tissue do, on occasion, occur and can result in fat necrosis, which is clinically difficult to differentiate from carcinoma. Inasmuch as the current trend seems to be toward more contact sports, many of which are extremely physical (such as karate football), a protective device that will reduce or eliminate breast injuries, in certain instances, may be indicated.

Protection can be provided by any one of the various lightweight plastic cup brassieres that are commercially available. Such devices are worn over the regular brassiere and provide a full measure of protection without in any way encumbering the wearer. They are quite reasonable in cost and merit consideration.

Activity during menstruation. The avoidance of strenuous activity may be advisable for the first day or two after the onset of menstrual flow. At this time the organs are engorged with blood and somewhat heavier; hence activities involving jarring or sudden starting or stopping and those movements involving twisting may well be avoided. It appears that the problem of whether to participate or not during premenstrual, menstrual, or postmenstrual periods is primarily a matter of whether the specific individual feels up to it. One must remember that psychogenic factors are involved, and although an athlete may be able to participate physiologically, her mental and emotional set at such times may militate against such participation. A sharp drop in performance deserves investigation. As a general rule, those who participate during the menses at the same level of intensity as they do between periods appear to benefit by participation. For a more detailed discussion regarding menstruation and physical performance, refer to Chapter 3.

CARE OF THE FEET

There is an old adage in sports circles that states, "An athlete is only as good as her feet." This is indeed a truism. Many a victory has been forfeited and many a victory gained because of the condition of an athlete's feet. Attempting to participate in training or competition when troubled by any of several foot problems is not only uncomfortable or painful but continued trauma can lead to more serious conditions. Many athletes have structural deviations in the body that bring about foot problems; others have structural problems within the foot itself. Faulty bone alignment, improper foot-placement habits, and weak ligaments all interfere greatly with good locomotion, limiting the athlete's performance. Participation in sports makes severe demands upon the feet and the legs. This in itself should make the trainer-coach cognizant of the need for proper care and protection of the feet. A short talk during training periods in which foot care is stressed should make athletes more conscious of the need for such care.

One of the major causes of foot problems is the wearing of improper footgear. Socks or "pushers" that are too short or too tight or that crimp up within the shoe can cause blisters. Wearing shoes that are not large or long enough to permit normal foot expansion or the wearing of socks can cause a variety of problems such as bunions, corns, or even stress fractures of the phalanges or metatarsal bones. It is best to fit shoes so that when the wearer is standing, there is from 1/4 to 1/2 inch of freedom at the toes and sides to permit the toes to move. It should be possible to wear pairs of two socks, a thin cotton pair and the competitive socks or pushers. The use of a skin toughener or zinc talcum powder also aids in reducing friction and prevents chafing and subsequent blistering or irritation. Wearing a new pair of shoes for practice or competition can sometimes prove disastrous. New shoes should be carefully and slowly broken in; at the first sign of irritation, preventive measures should be instituted. Some of the more common foot problems and some suggestions for their care and treatment follow.

Blisters. When unaccustomed or excessive friction is produced between the skin and the sock or shoe, the epidermis is pulled away from the dermis and fluid fills the resulting space. Normally an ordinary blister is no cause for alarm. However, untreated or improperly treated blisters are prone to infection, which can develop into a septicemic condition. Treatment should be as follows:
1. Cleanse the blister and the surrounding area with soap and water and dry thoroughly. Cleanse the area with alcohol applied with sterile cotton or a sterile swab.
2. If the blister is intact, perforate it at its perimeter base *with a sterilized needle* and permit it to drain. If necessary, mild pressure can be applied to the area with a sterile pad.
3. If the encapsulating skin has been torn away and the injury is open, carefully cut away the torn tissue with *sterile scissors,* following the perimeter. Apply a sterile dressing with a bland ointment and treat as a wound.
4. If the blister is intact and has been drained, apply a sterile pad covered with a bland healing ointment or use an impregnated sterile pad; secure in place with adhesive tape. After treatment the athlete should eliminate the cause and establish a daily ritual of painting the feet with a skin toughener such as benzoin and using a foot powder. It may be necessary to protect the injured area from further pressure by the use of a felt or sponge doughnut pad.

Corns. Probably because of female adherence to fashion, which more often than not decrees footwear in terms of what is considered stylish, the prevalence of corns appears to be far greater among females than among males. Corns are the result of either poorly fitted footgear or certain pathological conditions such as a hammertoe. Corns are classified as either soft or hard. Soft corns develop as the result of pressure exerted by an ill-fitted shoe coupled with an excessive amount of perspiration and usually develop on the fourth or fifth toe. The symptoms are pain and tenderness accompanied by inflammation. A thickened circular area of skin forms. Treatment involves keeping the affected area clean and dry by a change of socks daily or oftener and use of a keratolytic agent such as salicylic acid applied with a lamb's wool pad or with a soft rubber pad.

The hard corn results either from a deformity of a toe, for example, a hammertoe, or from pressure. This condition is more serious. The symptoms are again pain, tenderness, and inflammation. Some degree of disability may be present. This condition is chronic and results in the buildup of a large horny epidermal layer. Treatment is best carried out by a physician or a podiatrist. The trainer-coach can assist by seeing to it that the athlete has properly fitting shoes and having the athlete soak her feet daily in warm, soapy water to help soften the corn. The use of a commercial doughnut-shaped felt corn pad or the construction of a small soft-rubber doughnut can provide protection.

Hyperhidrosis. This condition is the production of excessive foot perspiration, which keeps the skin moist and sets up a ready stage for skin irritation. Dusting the feet both before and after practice and competition as well as before putting on street shoes can help alleviate this condition. Wiping the feet with alcohol and then air drying them and applying either powdered alum or boric acid seems to aid in controlling such perspiration. Dusting street and sports shoes with talcum powder before putting them on is also advisable.

Athlete's foot. This affection is a fungus infection of the feet. Proper foot hygiene by the athlete and the maintenance of hygienic conditions in the shower and the locker rooms are the best preventives. Various antifungal preparations are available and such agents should be used according to directions. The continued maintenance of good foot hygiene is absolutely essential.

SUGGESTED READINGS

American National Red Cross: First aid textbook, ed. 4, New York, 1957, Doubleday & Co., Inc.

Anderson, W. A. D., and Scotti, T. M.: Synopsis of pathology, ed. 9, St. Louis, 1976, The C. V. Mosby Co.

Belilios, A. D., Mulvaney, D. K., and Armstrong, J. F.: A handbook of first aid and bandaging, London, 1962, Baillière, Tindall & Cox, Ltd.

Erdelyi, G. J.: Gynecological survey of female athletes, J. Sports Med. Phys. Fitness **2:**174, 1962.

Gendel, E.: Pregnancy, fitness, and sports. In Proceedings of the Seventh National Conference on the Medical Aspects of Sports, Chicago, 1965, American Medical Association, pp. 43-46.

Klafs, C. E., and Arnheim, D. D.: Modern principles of athletic training, ed. 4, St. Louis, 1977, The C. V. Mosby Co.

Mills, L. C., and Moyer, J. F., editors: Inflammation and diseases of connective tissue, Philadelphia, 1961, W. B. Saunders Co.

Raney, R. B., Sr., Brashear, H. R., Jr., and Shands, A. R., Jr.: Handbook of orthopaedic surgery, ed. 8, St. Louis, 1971, The C. V. Mosby Co.

Stimson, B. B.: A manual of fractures and dislocations, Philadelphia, 1956, Lea & Febiger.

11 □ Bandaging and strapping

A basic knowledge of bandaging and strapping is essential to the trainer or trainer-coach if she is to function intelligently and effectively. These two areas are brought into action as either preventive measures or as means to assist and speed up the physical restoration of the athlete after an injury. Preventive bandaging or strapping should be used only when an inherent weakness or a chronic condition exists and the affected site needs protection and reinforcement. Muscle or joint weakness is a corollary of injury, and one frequently needs to bandage or strap the area either to immobilize it or to restrict movement until complete healing has taken place. In situations wherein a relatively mild degree of injury is present, it may be bandaged or strapped to permit the athlete to continue sports participation. It is wise, in such instances, to secure medical opinion as to the advisability of continued participation.

The following techniques are basic to injury prevention and management but offer, by no means, a comprehensive selection. They do, however, present those techniques most commonly used and generally applicable to the situations usually encountered in high school and college athletic and sports programs.

BANDAGING

Bandages are designed to hold dressings in place over surface wounds, to create pressure in order to control hemorrhage, to secure splints, and to provide either support, restriction, or immobilization for injured parts. Athletic bandages usually consist of gauze, cotton cloth, or elastic cloth, each having a specific use. Gauze is used principally for externally exposed wounds, whereas cotton cloth is used primarily for ankle wrapping or for the triangular or cravat type of bandage. The elastic bandage is used either for compression or for giving support and stability to a given part without impairing mobility. The following résumé of bandaging and strapping procedures is by no means comprehensive; only the basic types most necessary in girls' and women's sports are discussed. For a more comprehensive presentation, refer to Klafs and Arnheim's *Modern Principles of Athletic Training*.

Triangular bandage

This bandage, generally used in first aid, is a triangular piece of either muslin or cotton cloth, approximately 40 to 44 inches wide on each side. It is an extremely versatile bandage since it can be used unfolded or folded to form a broad or a narrow bandage, depending on what is required. It is easy to apply and in an emergency can be improvised from any number of materials. It can be used in cases where the roller type of bandage is not satisfactory, for example, in making a sling. It can also be used to fix splints and to secure pads or compresses. The bandage is usually identified as having a base, two sides, and an apex or point (Fig. 11-1). It is secured by means of the reef or square knot.

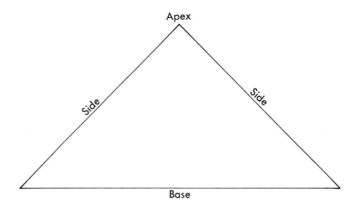

Fig. 11-1. Triangular bandage.

Fig. 11-2. Cervical arm sling.

Cervical arm sling (Fig. 11-2)

Purpose. To support the hand, wrist, and forearm.

Materials. One triangular bandage and one large safety pin.

Procedure

1. Place bandage under injured arm, apex toward elbow.
2. Carrry end of triangle nearest body up over shoulder of injured arm.
3. Pull free end over shoulder of uninjured side.
4. Tie the two ends behind the neck with a square knot, taking care to position the knot somewhat to the side of the neck where it is comfortable to the patient.
5. Bring the apex around to the front of the elbow and fasten it with the safety pin.

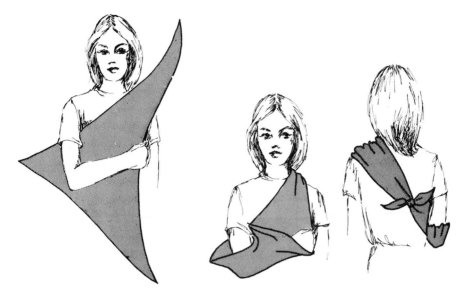

Fig. 11-3. Shoulder arm sling.

Shoulder arm sling (Fig. 11-3)

Purpose. To support the hand, wrist, and forearm when there is injury to the shoulder girdle or when the cervical arm sling is annoying to the patient.

Materials. One triangular bandage and one large safety pin.

Procedure

1. With the injured arm held at a position of 70 degrees, place the upper end of the shoulder sling over the *uninjured* shoulder side.
2. Bring the lower end of the triangle over the forearm and pull it up between the upper arm and the body and then up over the back toward the opposite shoulder to meet the other end. Secure the two ends with a square knot.
3. Bring the apex around to the front of the elbow and fasten it with the safety pin.

Roller bandages

Roller bandages have many uses in athletics—to support or immobilize, to secure dressings, and to apply pressure for hemorrhage control. Roller bandages come in different widths and lengths and thus are versatile when it comes to conforming the bandage to the body part: The 2-inch width by 6-yard length is best for hand, finger, toe, and head bandages; the 3-inch by 10-yard length for the extremities; and the 4-inch by 10 yard length for bandaging thighs, groins, or the trunk. The bandage comes rolled in a cylinder and is unrolled as it is applied, hence the name "roller" bandage.

Points to remember

1. Hold bandage with the loose end placed so as to unwind from the bottom of the roll. The free hand holds the end of the bandage in place on the part to be bandaged.

2. The roll is then unwound around the area to be bandaged, alternating the roll from hand to hand as the part is encircled.
3. Anchor the bandage with two or three turns, one over the other, before proceeding into the bandage pattern.
4. Use moderate tension.
5. Be certain that the turns lie flat. Wrinkling can cause blisters or severe skin irritation.
6. Lock the bandage at its termination by applying adhesive tape or by pinning the bandage after two or three terminal turns, each overlaying the preceding turn.
7. Avoid too much tension. Be sure that there is adequate circulation to the bandaged part. Cyanotic signs (darkish or bluish tinge) of the body portion or of the extremity's surface distal to the bandage indicate that the bandage was applied too tightly. When freedom of movement for the body part is desired, apply the bandage while the part is maintained in a position of maximum muscle contraction so as to ensure normal circulation.

Circular bandage (Fig. 11-4)

Purpose. To anchor other types of bandages or to support the wrist, ankle, or other cylindric body parts.

Material. A 2-inch roller bandage.

Procedure

1. Take one turn around the part at a slight angle.
2. A small triangle of bandage is exposed by this turn.
3. Bend the triangle back over the initial turn and follow with several more turns over the turned-down portion.
4. Fasten the bandage securely at a point away from the injury or at a place where it will not interfere with movement.

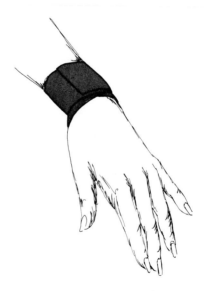

Fig. 11-4. Circular bandage.

Spiral bandage (Fig. 11-5)

Purpose. To cover a wider area than the circular bandage (for example, the forearm or the lower leg).

Materials. A 3-inch roller bandage and adhesive tape for anchoring.

Procedure

1. Fold two 6-inch lengths of adhesive tape lengthwise. These will be placed on either side of the bandage to prevent it from slipping.
2. Anchor the bandage by taking several turns at the smallest circumference of the wrist.
3. Continue encircling the forearm, moving upward in a spiral fashion with each successive turn overlapping the preceding turn by approximately one third its width.
4. Terminate the windings just below the elbow by taking several circular turns. Secure the bandage with adhesive tape.

Ankle and foot spica bandage (Fig. 11-6)

Purpose. Primarily to compress new injuries and to hold analgesic heat packs in place.

Materials. A 3-inch roller bandage and adhesive tape.

Procedure

1. Anchor the bandage by taking a couple of turns around the foot near the metatarsal arch.
2. Bring the bandage across the instep and then around the heel and back to the starting point.
3. Continue overlapping each succeeding revolution approximately three fourths the width of the preceding one, progressing upward on the foot and the ankle.
4. Use two turns to lock the bandage immediately above the ankle and secure with tape.

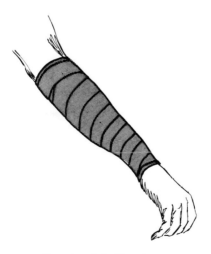

Fig. 11-5. Spiral bandage.

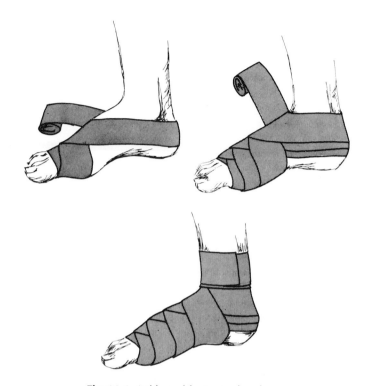

Fig. 11-6. Ankle and foot spica bandage.

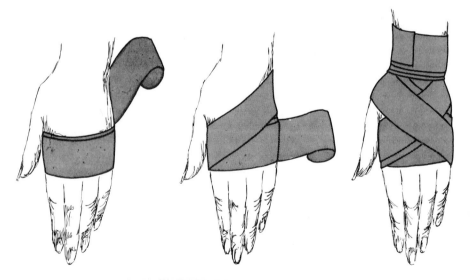

Fig. 11-7. Hand and wrist figure-eight bandage.

Hand and wrist figure-eight bandage (Fig. 11-7)

Purpose. To hold dressings in place and expecially good to support hand and wrist.

Materials. A 3-inch roller bandage and adhesive tape.

Procedure

1. Anchor the bandage by taking several turns around the palm of the hand immediately above the thumb junction.
2. Carry the roll obliquely across either the palmar or dorsal aspect of the hand, depending on the relative position of the wound to the wrist, encircle the wrist, and return to the anchor position.
3. Continue the pattern until as many figures as are required are completed; then lock with two turns around the wrist, securing with a strip of adhesive tape.

Cloth ankle wrap (Fig. 11-8)

Purpose. To give added support to the ankle insofar as protection against medial and lateral motions is concerned.

Materials. A 2- or 3-inch cloth or elastic bandage and adhesive tape.

Procedure. The bandage is applied with the leg in an extended position, preferably with the athlete seated on a bench or table with the lower half of the calf extending beyond the edge of the bench. The foot should be in a normal position.

1. Start by taking the initial wrap high up on the instep, crossing obliquely at an acute angle to the inside of the foot. Continue under the arch, moving up on the outside of the foot, crossing at the initial point, continuing around the ankle, and hooking around the heel.

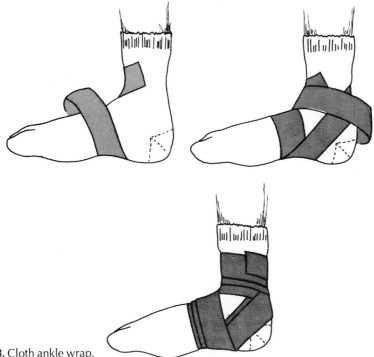

Fig. 11-8. Cloth ankle wrap.

2. Continue up the inside, over the instep, around the ankle, and hook the opposite side of the heel, thus completing a series of the wrap.
3. Repeat a second series with the remaining material, encircling the ankle, and secure or lock with adhesive tape.

   NOTE: One bandage is approximately 96 inches long. If such length is too bulky, cut down on the overall length. There may be instances where it is more desirable to use adhesive tape instead of the cloth wrap, particularly when more support is needed. See the following discussion regarding strapping with tape.

ADHESIVE STRAPPING

The use of adhesive strapping for various strapping techniques offers a support medium that is superior to bandage wrappings, although some slight disadvantages are encountered. To protect the skin as well as to offer a good adhering base, a tincture of benzoin compound or other commercial spray adherent should be applied. The former has a color and odor that some women seem to believe is objectionable. However, several new colorless and virtually odorless spray adherents are now obtainable. The adherent serves a dual function —that of protecting the skin from irritation and that of offering a base for the adhesive surface of the tape. In the case of ankle strapping, it is usually best to pull an orthopedic sock over the foot and ankle as protection against skin irritation, thus eliminating the necessity of an adherent.

Points to remember

1. Whenever tape is to be applied, cleanse the body surface well. Remove all dirt and perspiration from the skin by bathing the area with mild soap and water.
2. Remove any body hair that is present by shaving or using a depilatory.
3. If additional surface preparation is required apply a base adherent.
4. Select the proper width of tape for the strapping to be done—$1/2$- to 1-inch tape for hands and feet, $1^1/2$-inch tape for ankles, and 2- to 3-inch tape for larger skin areas such as thighs or back.
5. If strapping a joint for stability, place the joint in the position that is desired before strapping and maintain the integrity of that position during strapping.
6. Overlap each succeeding strip by one half of the preceding layer.
7. Avoid strapping with one continuous length since this often results in impeded circulation. Make one turn at a time, tear the tape, and then overlap the starting end by approximately 1 inch.
8. Keep the layers smooth to avoid irritation.
9. As with bandaging, start with an "anchor" and end with a "lock."
10. In removing tape, exert the pulling force parallel to the surface of the body rather than exerting a forceful outward wrench. The use of a tape scissors or a tape solvent will make the task easier.

Metatarsal arch support strapping (Fig. 11-9)

Purpose. To assist in maintaining the integrity of the metatarsal arch when the arch is weak or painful. The strap can be employed with or without a felt or sponge rubber pad and fitted and placed under the arch of the foot.

Fig. 11-9. Metatarsal arch support strapping.

Material. A roll of 1- or 1¹/₂-inch adhesive tape.

Procedure

1. Start the tape at the top of the foot and in line with the distal aspect of the little toe, moving toward the lateral (outside) aspect of the foot. Continue around under the foot and arch (medial side) to the top of the foot, and tear the tape so that a 1- to 1¹/₂-inch overlap is obtained.
2. Repeat successive overlaps, each overlapping the preceding one by one half to one third. Continue this procedure to a point approximately 1 inch in front of the anklebone.
3. Apply from three to four half-wraps, the beginning and end of each being applied on a line just under the anklebone.

Game strapping (Fig. 11-10)

Purpose. To provide maximum support for weak ankles.

Materials. A roll of 1¹/₂-inch of adhesive tape, adherent spray, or an orthopedic stocking.

Procedure. Have the athlete sit on a table or bench with the leg to be bandaged extended over the edge and the foot held in a position of 90 degrees.

1. Place a single anchor strip around the ankle about 3 inches from the malleolus (round projecting part of the anklebone).
2. Apply three stirrup strips, each being applied from the anchor strip, down the side of the leg and ankle, under the instep, and back up the other side, terminating on the anchor strip. Each stirrup strip should overlap the preceding strip by approximately one half its width.
3. Apply six circular strips, commencing at the anchor strip and moving downward until the malleolus is completely covered. Apply each strip slightly to the left or right of the center of the anterior aspect of the lower leg and ankle and terminate with about a 1-inch overlay.
4. Apply three strips around the arch.
5. Terminate by applying a heel lock. Start the tape strip high on the instep, carry it along the ankle at a slight angle, then under the heel and arch, and up over the other side, and terminate at the initial starting point. After tearing the tape, repeat the entire procedure in reverse.

Shin splint strapping (Fig. 11-11)

Purpose. To relieve the strain put on the anterior lower leg muscles. Shin splints result early in training, particularly when the athlete has been running

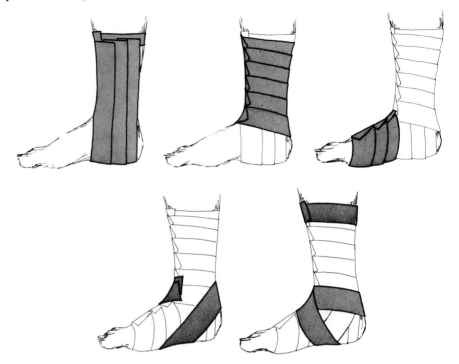

Fig. 11-10. Game strapping.

and jumping on a hard surface. It is a painful condition, resulting particularly from straining the anterior tibialis muscle. This type of strapping reduces pain and discomfort to a great degree. It is believed that the longitudinal arch may also come into the picture in shin splints, hence the additional taping of the arch to provide more support and thus ease some of the tibial pull.

Materials. A roll of 1½-inch adhesive tape and a strip of foam rubber 1½ inches wide and from 6 to 8 inches long.

Procedure. Complete relaxation of the leg during strapping is imperative. Have the athlete sit on a bench or table with the knee flexed, foot flat on the floor, and lower leg and foot thoroughly relaxed.

1. Apply a stirrup strip beginning halfway up the medial aspect of the leg, crossing over the medial malleolus, under the arch, and terminating opposite the starting point.
2. Lay the strip of foam rubber lengthwise directly over the muscle area that is painful and have the athlete hold it firmly in place while you apply a series of circular strips, beginning at the top level of the stirrup strip. Each strip should overlap the preceding one approximately one third of its width until the sponge rubber is completely covered. Start each strip on the medial aspect, bringing it around the back of the leg and terminating it with a 1-inch overlap. Strips must be applied firmly.
3. Apply the metatarsal arch wrap and, if desired, terminate with a heel lock.

Knee strapping (Arnheim technique) (Fig. 11-12)

Purpose. To give support and stability to the knee. This strapping will prevent the knee from hyperextending, assist the cruciate ligaments, and may also be

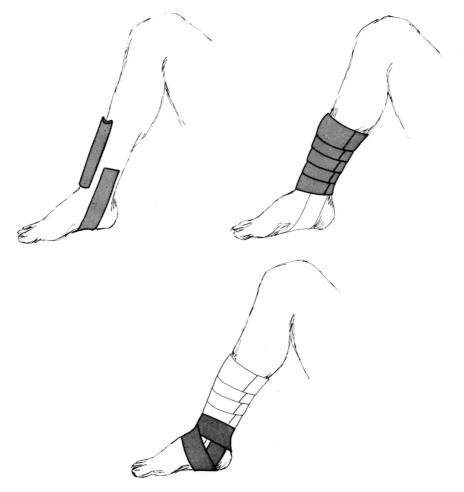

Fig. 11-11. Shin splint strapping.

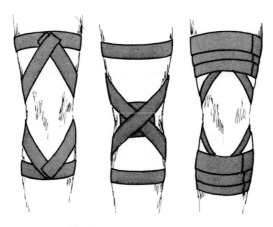

Fig. 11-12. Knee strapping.

employed for the support strained hamstring tendons. There are numerous other strapping procedures frequently used that are complex in their application.

Materials. A roll of 1½-inch adhesive tape, a 4- by 6-inch pad of felt, cotton, or gauze, and a 2-inch heel lift.

Procedure. All superfluous hair must be removed from 6 inches above the knee to 6 inches below. Application of a tape adherent is advisable.

1. To facilitate the individual applying the wrap, it is suggested that the subject stand on a table or a bench approximately 3 feet high. The 2-inch heel lift is placed under the heel of the injured leg, permitting the leg to become slightly flexed and relaxed.
2. Apply two anchor strips, one approximately 6 inches above the knee and the other some 6 inches below the knee. Do not apply these firmly since they are applied directly over muscles that will expand during exercise.
3. Place the gauze pad in the popliteal space (directly in back of the knee between the hamstring tendons) to protect the nerves and the blood vessels from constriction by the tape.
4. Beginning on the outside anterior aspect of the leg anchor, apply a strip of tape upward and diagonally across the popliteal space, anchoring the pad, continuing upward around the thigh, and terminating on the thigh anchor strip on its anterior aspect.
5. Apply a second strip, starting at the same place as the first. However, carry it upward diagonally on the medial aspect, across the posterior aspect over the popliteal space, continuing upward and then around the thigh, finishing on the anterior aspect of the thigh anchor strip. There is now a crisscross over the gauze pad.
6. Overlay the first strip by two thirds with another strip of tape, following the same pattern as the first. Repeat the second pattern by overlaying the second strip. If the athlete is heavily muscled or has considerable adiposity of the leg and thigh, apply additional strips using the same alternating pattern.
7. Secure the supporting strips by applying three overlapping strips over the original anchor strips at the leg and thigh.

Hamstring strapping (Fig. 11-13)

Purpose. To help alleviate the hamstring pull by stabilizing the contused muscles.

Materials. A roll of 1½-inch adhesive tape, an elastic Ace bandage, a 6- by 8-inch piece of nonsterile cotton or ½-inch soft foam rubber, and a 2-inch heel lift.

Procedure. Have the subject stand on a 3-foot high bench or table with the heel lift placed under the heel of the injured leg.

1. Place the pad over the injury and secure it with three encircling strips, one strip 1 inch below the top, one strip around the middle, and one strip 1 inch from the bottom. Do not apply the tape tightly; its function is merely to position the pad.
2. Beginning just above the knee, anchor the elastic bandage by taking several turns and then proceed spirally up the leg to cover the pad. When the pad has been covered, wind the wrap spirally downward to cover the preceding series in place.

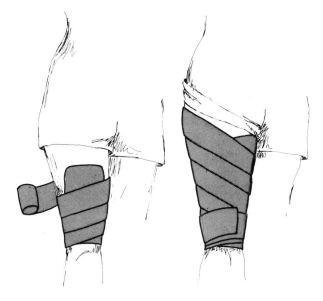

Fig. 11-13. Hamstring strapping.

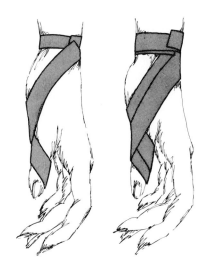

Fig. 11-14. Thumb strapping.

3. Lock the wrap in place by securing it with adhesive tape. Apply the bandage with moderate tightness.

Thumb strapping (Fig. 11-14)

Purpose. To give support and stability to the thumb while permitting its use.

Materials. A roll of 1-inch adhesive tape. If additional stability is required, a 2-inch roller gauze bandage can reinforce the strapping.

Procedure. The hand should be held relaxed with the palm up and the arm slightly flexed at the elbow.

1. Apply a strip of tape around the wrist, carrying the strip under, around, and over the thumb and back to the wrist.
2. Apply a second strip that overlaps the preceding strip by one half its width, starting slightly above the wrist strip and halfway up the preceding strip.
3. Continue, using as many additional strips as are needed to adequately support the thumb. Secure the wrist wraps by applying two or three locking strips. If additional stability seems desirable, apply the roller bandage by anchoring it with several turns about the wrist and then, following the strapping pattern, around the thumb and back to the wrist. Apply no more than two complete wraps. Secure with one or two turns around the wrist and then lock with adhesive tape.

Wrist strapping (Fig. 11-15)

Purpose. To give stability and support to the wrist.

NOTE: When a mild strain or sprain is encountered and it is desirable to have the sportswoman continue participation, a simple series of tape wraps can be applied as follows:

Using 1-inch tape and adherent, apply a series of three or four wraps, each overlapping the preceding one by one half its width. Start just above the hand, on palm side, and place each wrap completely around both sides of the wrist, terminating on the back of the wrist. This type of wrap will give adequate support, yet permit free movement (Fig. 11-15).

Materials. One roll of 1-inch tape and tape adherent. The following strapping should be used for a severely injured wrist where support, protection, and limitation of movement are desired.

Procedure. For any wrist-taping procedure it is advisable to have the patient's wrist flexed toward the injured side, with the fingers slightly spread so as not to restrict circulation or impinge upon nerves.

1. Place an anchor strip approximately 3 inches above the wrist, completely encircling it.
2. Place a second anchor completely around the center of the hand, crossing just below the articulation of the fingers with the hand.
3. Carry a strip of tape diagonally upward across the wrist joint, starting at the little finger side of the lower anchor and terminating on the thumb side of the upper anchor.
4. Carry a second strip diagonally across the wrist from the thumb side to the little finger side, again starting on the lower anchor and terminating on the upper anchor.
5. Repeat steps 3 and 4 four more times, overlapping each preceding strip about one third its width, moving progressively toward the lateral aspects of the hand and wrist.
6. Apply a series of figure-eight taping over the preceding applications by encircling the wrist, carrying the tape over the back of the hand diagonally to the hand, which is then encircled twice. The tape strip is now carried up diagonally across the hand to where the figure eight started. Repeat the entire figure-eight pattern several more times.

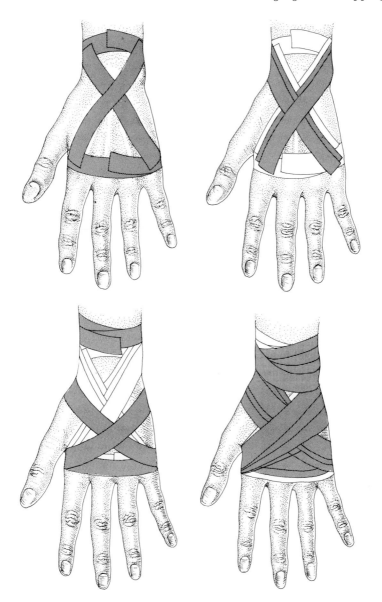

Fig. 11-15. Injured-wrist strapping.

Shoulder spica bandage (Fig. 11-16)

Purpose. To be used for support or for keeping a dressing or an analgesic pack in place.

Materials. One roll of 3- or 4-inch elastic roller bandage and adhesive tape.

Procedure. The armpit (axilla) should be protected with a pad to prevent skin irritation and circulatory constriction.

1. Anchor the bandage with one turn around the affected arm.

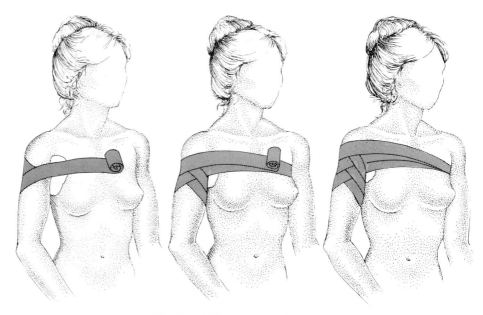

Fig. 11-16. Shoulder spica bandage.

2. After the bandage is anchored, securely carry it around the back, under the opposite arm, across the chest,* and back to the injured arm.
3. Repeat the procedure by wrapping around the arm, across the back and chest, overlapping the first wrap by one half its width.
4. Continue the progressively upward (by one half each preceding wrap width) pattern of the figure eight, anchoring the terminal end of the wrap with one or two strips of adhesive tape.

Hip spica bandage (Fig. 11-17)

Purpose. To support the injured hip flexors or hip adductors. It is also used for keeping a wound dressing or an analgesic pack in place.

Materials. One roll of 3- or 4-inch elastic bandage and adhesive tape.

Procedure

1. Starting at the upper end of the thigh, encircle the thigh and the groin, bringing the bandage back to and crossing the starting end to anchor it.
2. Continue the wrap, carrying it around across the back just above waist level and bringing it above the point of the hip (iliac crest), across the abdomen, and down to the groin level.
3. Repeat the previous wrap in its entirety, overlapping the initial wrap approximately one half its width.
4. Secure the terminal end of the bandage with one or two strips of adhesive tape.

---

*When the patient has small breasts, the wrap can be carried over the breast on the unaffected side. Where large or pendulous breasts are encountered, the bandage is more secure if passed under the breast. The nipple should be protected by a small gauze pad.

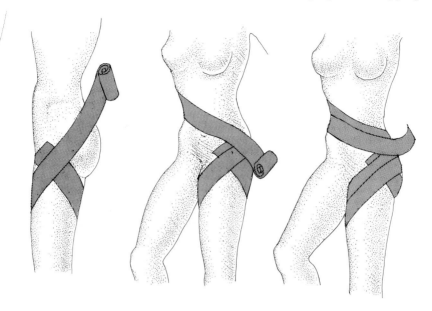

Fig. 11-17. Hip spica bandage.

NOTE: If a groin injury has been incurred and it is desired to restrict leg movement to some degree, reverse the entire wrap; that is, encircle the groin and thigh in the opposite direction and then carry across the abdomen and back in that order.

Quadriceps strapping (Fig. 11-18)

Purpose. To assist the quadriceps muscles against the pull of gravity and to give protection and support when moderate or severe quadriceps contusions or strains are present.

Materials. One roll of 2-inch adhesive tape, a roll of 3-inch elastic tape, a 6-inch elastic bandage, a 2-inch heel lift, and shin toughener.

Procedure. Have the patient stand on a training table with the 2-inch lift under the heel of the injured relaxed leg. The weight is completely supported by the normal leg. The trainer stands facing the front of the injured thigh.

1. Using the 2-inch adhesive tape, place an anchor strip, approximately 8 to 9-inches long, on the center of the inner aspect of the thigh starting just above the medial femoral condyle of the knee.
2. Using two strips of tape form an X on the front of the thigh, place the lower end of each piece about 2 inches above the kneecap and starting and finishing on the respective anchors.
3. Continue to apply strips of tape moving upward, with each succeeding X overlapping the previous one by one half its width, finishing the series when approximately three fourths the thigh length and the quadriceps are completely covered. As the successive strips are applied, they should always be pulled diagonally upward so that the quadriceps group is pulled upward to counteract gravitational pull.

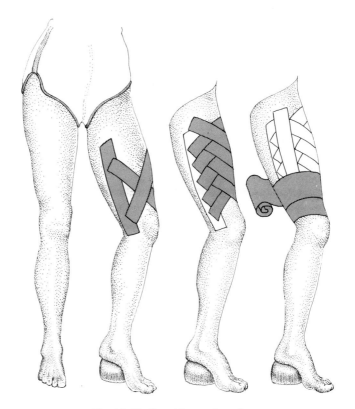

Fig. 11-18. Quadriceps strapping.

4. Place a locking strip of adhesive tape lengthwise over the ends of the diagonal strips, one lock on the inner aspect, the other on the outer aspect of the thigh.
5. To further stabilize the quadriceps, apply either the 3-inch elastic tape or the 6-inch elastic roller bandage, encircling the thigh.

Injured ankle strapping (Fig. 11-19)

Purpose. To stabilize a newly sprained ankle and usually for a lateral sprain.

Materials. Tape adherent, a roll of 1¹/₂-inch adhesive tape.

Procedure. Patient is seated on a table, leg extended with foot held at a right angle during the taping. The trainer stands facing the sole of the patient's foot. Apply tape adherent to the foot, ankle, and leg to within 6 inches of the knee. It may be necessary to remove superfluous hair from the leg prior to adherent application.

1. Place an anchor strip of tape around the ankle, approximately 2 to 3 inches above the malleolus (round projection of the anklebone) and just below the belly of the gastrocnemius muscle.
2. Place a second anchor strip around the lower portion of the instep, posterior to the head of the fifth metatarsal (little-toe side).
3. Place a stirrup strip immediately behind the malleolus, starting on the in-

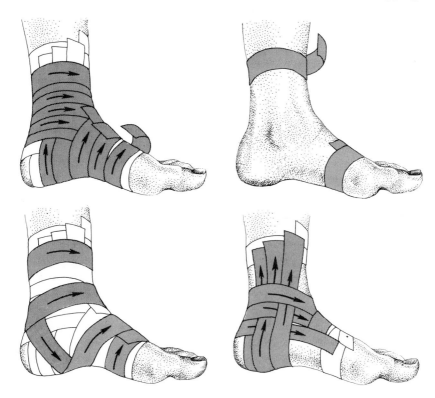

Fig. 11-19. Injured-ankle strapping.

side of the leg, proceeding down around the heel and up the outer surface of the leg, ending on the leg anchor, and finally pulling up firmly as the tape is applied so that the foot is slightly everted.

4. Apply a second leg anchor, overlapping the first one by half its width and bringing it at a slight upward angle.

5. Apply a stirrup strip posterior to the malleolus, carrying it directly downward, around the heel, and up the lateral aspect of the leg, posterior to the malleolus, and attaching it to the upper anchor strip.

6. Beginning immediately under the medial malleolus, apply a horseshoe strip, bringing it around the back of the foot over the Achilles tendon about 1 inch above the bottom of the heel and then carrying it just under the lateral malleolus to the foot-anchor strip.

7. Now apply strips alternately, a stirrup, then a horseshoe, until three of each have been applied, each overlapping the preceding strip by one half its width.

8. Continue just the horseshoe strips up over the ankle and the leg, terminating on the anchor strips.

9. For additional support for the arches apply two or three circular strips around the instep.

10. Apply a lock strip around the heel and another lock strip just below the belly of the gastrocnemius muscle.

ADHESIVE-TAPE REMOVAL

The removal of adhesive tape can be accomplished either manually or through the use of a chemical tape solvent. In manual removal, the tape should first be cut by a tape scissors (blunt ends) or a tape cutter. Now grasp the end of the tape by the fingers of one hand and then gently pull it from the skin, keeping the line of pull low and in line with or parallel to the surface of the skin, meanwhile using the fingers of the other hand to push the skin downward and away from the tape. Never remove tape manually by the use of sudden or excessive force. Should the tape adhere tightly adjacent to the site of a wound, you may need to carefully tease it away, after first cutting the tape completely around the site so as to avoid reinjury.

Should an adhesive residue be left on the skin after the tape has been removed, any of several commercial tape solvents can be used to remove it. After tape removal the area should be carefully bathed with a mild soap and tepid water.

SUGGESTED READINGS

American National Red Cross: First Aid Textbook, ed. 4, New York, 1957, Doubleday & Co., Inc.

Anderson, W. A. D., and Scotti, T. M.: Synopsis of pathology, ed. 9, St. Louis, 1976, The C. V. Mosby Co.

Belilios, A. D., Mulvaney, D. K., and Armstrong, J. F.: A handbook of first aid and bandaging. London, 1962, Baillière, Tindall & Cox, Ltd.

Klafs, C. E., and Arnheim, D. D.: Modern principles of athletic training, ed. 4, St. Louis, 1977, The C. V. Mosby Co.

Ralston, E. L.: Handbook of fractures, St. Louis, 1967, The C. V. Mosby Co.

Stimson, B. B.: A manual of fractures and dislocations, Philadelphia, 1956, Lea & Febiger.

12 □ Emergency medical care

There are occasions in sport when a prompt and proper procedure effectively carried out by the trainer or coach can avert tragedy. Immediate care and management of an acutely ill or injured individual frequently determines the outcome and is a major factor in the determination of residual disability as well; hence it is indeed pertinent for the trainer and the coach to be effectively trained in the various aspects and techniques of emergency care.

The initial evaluation of the injured person is the key to successful emergency care. Such evaluation must be carried out rapidly and accurately so that emergency care can be initiated immediately. As experience is gained, the speed and accuracy of the preliminary examination improves. Although speed is of the essence, nonetheless it is most wise to "make haste slowly" so that the possibility of error is obviated. One must become familiar enough with the various emergency management techniques to proceed quickly and effectively when the preliminary examination has revealed the course to follow. One must, above all, not only remain calm and be capable of making objective decisions but also be able to quiet the patient who not infrequently may be in a state of panic. Delay cannot be tolerated—emergency procedures must be gotten underway immediately.

First attention is always given to the injured person's cardiorespiratory system—is she breathing, does she exhibit a discernible pulse, is she cyanotic? The maintenance of adequate blood supply to the vital organs, especially the brain, is most important. The diagnostic signs and their implications are presented in Table 12-1, which also outlines the steps to be followed in an emergency treatment. The most significant emergency procedures are discussed in detail in the following pages.

Shock

In any injury, shock is a distinct possibility, whereas in severe injuries such as fractures, dislocations, and intense bleeding, shock is always present. Shock is defined as a state of collapse resulting from acute peripheral circulatory failure; severe shock can be fatal. Shock may be delayed or it may be immediate. The characteristic symptoms are often designated as the "five P's"—pallor, perspiration, prostration, pulmonary deficiency, and pulselessness. They vary in intensity, depending on the patient and the injury. Often evidence of injury may not be readily apparent. Thirst and, on occasion, vomiting may be other symptoms. In some situations a state of apathy is apparent. A check of the pulse rate indicates a very rapid and weak pulse. Respiration is shallow and rapid; if the blood pressure is taken, it will usually reveal a systolic reading below 90 mm. Hg. The sequential steps of treatment are as follows:

1. If severe bleeding is present and is one of the causes of shock, it must be brought under immediate control. To avoid further agitation of the patient, keep people away and do not permit her to see the wound.

267

Table 12-1 □ General management of emergency injuries

Category	Type	Symptoms	Treatment	Rehabilitation
Concussion	First degree	Loss of orientation, mental confusion, temporary amnesia, automatism, headache, nausea, tinnitis, vomiting	Put in prone position and make as comfortable as possible; apply cold compresses to head and neck and generally treat as for shock; do not administer fluids or medications; avoid direct questioning; do not leave patient alone; place her immediately in the hands of family or friend to watch	When free of symptoms, may be permitted back in play; advisable to secure medical opinion; best to withhold from sports at least 24 hours
	Second degree	Brief loss of consciousness, retrograde amnesia, tinnitis, disorientation, dizziness, posttraumatic headache, nausea, vomiting nausea, vomiting	Ensure proper breathing, if necessary clear airway; treat as for shock, determine if cervical neck injury is present; if none apparent, awaken patient with ammonia ampule or by application of cold compresses to forehead and back of neck; give oxygen if it is available	Remove from participation and remand to physician; may require 24-hour hospital observation; rest 1 to 2 days; no competition for 1 week
	Third degree	Prolongation and increased severity of symptoms, loss of consciousness (may be intermittent), retrograde amnesia, disorientation; neurological signs may be present—dilated or irregular pupils, blurring of vision, nausea, vomiting, positive Romberg sign	Check for obstructed airway; treat for shock; give oxygen if available; remand to physician as soon as possible	Depending on medical analysis, rest at least 1 week; keep out of sports from 2 weeks to full season; if has had two or more severe concussions with unconscious periods of 1 minute or more, disqualify from sport

Shock		Drop in body temperature, blood pressure, and pulse rate; respiration shallow and rapid; color, ashen gray; cold perspiration; at times, loss of consciousness; if conscious, may be very thirsty; sometimes appears to be drowsy	Control any bleeding; keep trunk and head level, with legs slightly raised; reestablish normal body temperature by covering subject; apply heat if available; if unconscious, turn head to one side so that mucus or saliva can drain out; give oxygen if available; replace fluids, if necessary, with water, salt, or glucose
Hemorrhage	Capillary	Small, fairly slow flow or oozing of blood	Place sterile compress over cleansed wound and apply gentle pressure; hold compress in place with elastic or roller bandage (bleeding stops in a matter of minutes)
	Venous	Steady flow of dark blood; fair volume of bleeding occurs	Apply compress and secure with elastic bandage; elevate injured part (pressure prevents flow and permits clotting)
	Arterial	Bright red blood ejected in spurts corresponding to the heart rate	Delay in controlling bleeding is dangerous and may prove fatal; *prompt action is necessary*; apply firm digital pressure point or compress bandage directly over hemorrhage site; if necessary to use tourniquet, loosen every 10 minutes to prevent gangrene; secure medical aid as quickly as possible; hospitalization may be necessary

Continued.

Table 12-1 □ General management of emergency injuries—cont'd

Category	Type	Symptoms	Treatment	Rehabilitation
Respiratory arrest	Partial airway obstruction	Choking or gasping for breath, snorting or gargling noises, skin suffused and reddish, bulging eyes, vertigo	Apply Heimlich maneuver	May need to be referred to a physician
	Complete airway obstruction	Unconscious, no visible respiration, airflow from lungs undetectable, cyanosis (skin, mucous membranes, lips, nail beds have bluish cast)	Check head position—if neck partially flexed, tongue may have dropped back to cause blockage; look and check for air exchange; apply artificial ventilation: 1. Position victim in supine position 2. Position head by placing one hand under neck, other on forehead, and hyper-extend neck 3. Pull jaw forward 4. Check if mouth and throat are clear—if not, clean out 5. Apply mouth-to-mouth ventilation Continue until victim is able to sustain on her own or paramedical corps take over	Ambulance transport to medical facility
Cardiac arrest	Heart attack, drowning, suffocation	Unconscious, no visible respiration, airflow from lungs may be absent, pupils may be dilated, usually 45 to 60 seconds after circulation ceases no carotid pulse discernible	Initiate CPR immediately—must be started within 4 minutes after heart has stopped 1. Position victim in supine position 2. Position self at side of victim—chest high	Ambulance transport to medical facility

thump, if a witnessed arrest
4. Position head and pull jaw forward
5. Clear mouth and throat if necessary
6. If an unwitnessed arrest, quickly ventilate lungs 4 times
7. Check for carotid pulse
8. Begin compression and ventilation (ratio of 15 compressions to 2 ventilations, 80 times per minute; two rescuers, 5 compressions to 1 ventilation, 60 times per minute)

Continue until victim is able to to sustain on her own or paramedics or mobile coronary unit take over

2. The drop in blood pressure is accompanied by a drop in body temperature. Cover the patient and keep her warm. Try to maintain a body temperature as close to normal as possible through the application of external heat (blankets, hot-water bottles, etc.).
3. The patient should be kept horizontal, with her head turned to one side to facilitate any oral fluid drainage. If she is able to swallow, hot fluids should be administered. If breathing difficulties occur or a cardiac problem is suspected or there is a lower-limb fracture, elevate the head and chest. In a suspected spinal injury of any type, leave the individual in the position in which she was found. Any attempt to move her in such a situation is extremely dangerous. It is best to have paramedics or a physician supervise or direct the moving of the person.
4. Oxygen, if available, can be administered to help nourish the tissues.
5. Restoration of body fluid loss can be done if the patient is fully conscious and able to drink. Either plain water or a salt and water mixture (1 teaspoon of salt to 1 quart of water) may be given. It should be at room temperature, and the patient should be instructed to sip it very slowly in small amounts. Never, under any circumstances, attempt to give fluids by mouth to someone who is semiconscious or unconscious.
6. Pain can be relieved by a sedative administered by the physician. The splinting of injured parts will help in the alleviation of some of the pain.
7. A physician should be called as promptly as possible.

Hemorrhage

Hemorrhage is blood escaping either through blood vessel walls or as the result of a tear or rupture of blood vessels. Hemorrhaging is dangerous and must be controlled quickly when the blood volume loss is considerable. Capillary bleeding (usually identified as an oozing of the blood), which often accompanies the less severe injuries, is easily controlled with the application of an astringent antiseptic such as tincture of benzoin or alcohol and the application of a sterile dressing. Moderate bleeding involving somewhat larger vessels can usually be controlled by either digital pressure or a pressure pad of gauze bandaged over the wound. Severe bleeding, or hemorrhaging, must be controlled promptly; this is best done by applying digital pressure at a pressure point. The trainer-coach must familiarize herself with the general location and direction of the major arteries and veins in the body and the principal pressure points. Such knowledge is priceless when seconds count. In severe bleeding, the type of bleeding may be determined by both the color and action of the blood.

In *arterial* hemorrhage the blood is bright red and it escapes in rhythmic spurts consonant with each heartbeat. This is the more dangerous hemorrhage since the blood is lost in great volume so quickly. Immediate elevation of the injured part and application of a compress over the wound with firm digital pressure to a pressure point between the wound and the heart are the best means of control. When such measures appear to be ineffective, a tourniquet between the wound and the heart should be applied. The tourniquet is *loosened every 10 minutes* to prevent gangrene. A call for a physician or an ambulance should be made concurrently with the first-aid treatment if at all possible. in *venous* hemorrhage a rapid but steady effusion of dark blood issues from the wound. Again, elevation of the injured part and application of firm pressure directly over the area are the best methods of control. The use of a tourniquet is seldom necessary.

Concussion

Head injuries of various types frequently occur in most sports which involve contact. Despite the considerable protection afforded the brain, it is nonetheless subject to trauma as the result of direct or indirect blows to the head. Most traumas can be classified as concussion injuries. The term "concussion" means literally "a violent shaking" and is the term used to describe an impact injury. Cerebral concussion (concussion of the brain) refers to the agitation of the brain that results from either a direct or indirect blow, wherein the force is transmitted to the brain. In an indirect blow, for example, a hard fall impacting the end of the spine will permit the force to be transmitted through the spine to the brain, or a blow to the jaw will also transmit the force to the brain through the articulation of the jaw. Such blows, if severe enough, will result in concussion causing a loss of consciousness, either temporary or prolonged, and produced some mental aberration.

Concussions are separated into first, second, or third degrees.

First-degree cerebral concussion (mild)
1. Loss of orientation or temporary amnesia, or mental confusion.
2. Automatism, wherein normal actions are carried out but with no memory or concept of what is being done.
3. Headache, dizziness, and ringing in the ears (tinnitis) may be present.

Second-degree cerebral concussion (moderate)
1. Loss of consciousness for a short period of time.
2. Retrograde amnesia, wherein there is a loss of memory of the events and situations immediately preceding the traumatic incident.
3. Disorientation, tinnitis.
4. Posttraumatic headache, dizziness.

Third-degree concussion (severe). The symptoms are more severe and prolonged.
1. Loss of consciousness for an extended period of time. The athlete may fluctuate between periods of consciousness and unconsciousness.
2. Disorientation, retrograde amnesia.
3. Neurological signs (dilated or irregular pupils, blurring of vision, and involuntary movements of the eyeball may indicate brain damage).
4. Nausea, vomiting.
5. If there is bleeding and a clear exudate from the ears, a skull fracture may be present.
6. Should paralysis (loss of muscle function) occur, brain damage may be present.

NOTE: the last two symptoms are not necessarily present in all third-degree concussions.

Airway emergencies

On occasion in sports, an athlete may suffer a severe impact or perhaps inadvertently swallow something resulting in an obstruction of the airway. The immediate response is panic, which does not help the situation. In severe concussion when the person has lost consciousness, it sometimes is difficult to identify airway obstruction since cyanosis (darkening of the skin, mucous membranes, the fingernail beds, and the conjunctivas because of oxygen depletion and carbon dioxide build-up) is not always present. Time is critical when airway obstruction is present, since asphyxia for a period of between 5 and 10 minutes will cause death. Immediately get the individual in a supine position—never in a prone, or face-downward, position since such a position may further intensify the blockage. A not infrequent cause of airway obstruction is tongue swallowing. The athlete has received a severe blow or suffered a concussion, and as a result, the tongue has dropped back and down into the throat, thus blocking the airway. The time factor in effecting relief is crucial, since she may suffocate. Relief must be effected in less than 4 minutes.

When the tongue is swallowed, the jaws lock. In most instances of tongue swallowing, if one gets the athlete immediately into a supine position and then tilts her head backward by placing one hand under her neck, the other on her forehead thereby stretching the neck tissues and permitting the tongue to drop away from the posterior pharyngeal wall, it will effect quick relief. However, should this maneuver fail, an oral screw or a bite stick can be used to pry open the jaws. If either of these is unavailable, one should place a number of tongue depressors one upon the other in a staggered position and then use them taped together by placing the bottom depressor between the jaws and then wedging the others in as rapidly as possible until a finger can be inserted to remove the tongue from the airway. It may be necessary when this is done to administer mouth-to-mouth respiration.

Should a foreign body be lodged in back of the pharynx, turn the head to one side (unless a cervical spine injury is suspected), open the mouth, and, using the fingers, sweep out the mouth and pharynx to retrieve the obstruction.

The Heimlich maneuver

If a foreign object, such as a piece of food or chewing gum is the cause of the choking, the Heimlich maneuver can be used effectively. This maneuver can be used in either of two ways depending on whether the individual who is choking is erect or has collapsed and is either too heavy to lift or is unconscious.

When the person is erect, stand directly behind her, placing both arms around her waist, permitting her head and upper trunk to hang forward over your clasped hands. Grasp one fist with the other, placing the thumb side of the grasped fist immediately below the lower tip of the sternum but clear of the rib cage. Sharply and forcefully pull the fist into the abdomen several times, compressing the diaphragm against the air in the lungs, which in turn is forcefully expelled against the blockage, which is usually promptly ejected.

If the athlete is on the ground or the floor, immediately get her onto her back. Straddle her hips, keeping your weight centered over your knees. Place the heel of your left hand against the back of your right hand. Push sharply into the abdomen just above the belt line. If necessary, this can be repeated a number of times to expel the blockage. Avoid extreme force or the application of force to the rib cage to prevent internal organ damage or possible rib fractures.

Cardiopulmonary resuscitation (CPR)

Cardiopulmonary resuscitation is an emergency procedure that opens and maintains a patent airway, provides artificial lung ventilation through the use of rescue breathing, and maintains artificial circulation through external cardiac compression. It is a technique that every individual should know how to use. Emergencies requiring CPR occur most anywhere in daily life and are by no means confined to the sports arena. The trainer and the coach should be familiar with the techniques of CPR in the event that if cardiac or respiratory arrest occurs in an athletic situation, emergency aid can be immediately given. Times is the critical factor, since the difference between life and death may be measured in seconds.

There are three steps, performed sequentially, that provide basic life support. They are easily remembered as A, B, C:

      A   Airway opened
      B   Breathing restored
      C   Circulation restored

Often with the reestablishment of A, B and C tend to resume spontaneously and it may not be necessary to carry them out. On occasion, the restoration of A and B eliminates the necessity for carrying out step C. Bear in mind, THE PRESCRIBED SEQUENCE MUST BE FOLLOWED EXACTLY.

Position of patient. Supine, arms at sides, legs extended.

Position of operator. Kneeling at the side of the patient, at chest level.

A. Airway opened.

    Lift neck with one hand, meanwhile pushing down on the patient's forehead with the other hand. Using the thumbs, open the mouth and thrust the lower jaw forward. Should there be a severe head injury or suspected neck injury, *do not tilt the head back* but displace the jaw only, keeping the head in a fixed neutral position.

    If it is necessary, clear the mouth of any foreign objects, such as the mouthpiece, vomitus, dentures, or dislodged bridgework, but do not waste a great deal of time.

    If the opening of the airway does not cause spontaneous breathing, proceed immediately to step B.

B. Breathing restored.

    Move the hand that was initially placed on the patient's forehead and pinch her nose shut, with the heel of the hand at the back of her neck remaining in place in order to keep her head back. Take a deep breath, place your mouth over the mouth of the patient so as to provide an airtight seal and blow until you see her chest rise. Remove your mouth and listen for the air to escape through passive exhalation. If the patient fails to continue breathing, give four quick breaths and then check the carotid artery for pulse. If a pulse is present, continue with rescue breathing at the rate of 12 times a minute until the patient is able to resume on her own. However, if no pulse is discernible, then proceed to step C to provide artificial circulation through cardiac compression coupled with the rescue breathing.

C. Circulation restored.

    Locate the lowest part of the sternum (xiphoid process). Place the heel of one hand approximately 1½ inches above the xiphoid tip and then place the other hand directly on top of the first hand, all fingers being kept off of the chest. Fingers should be interlocked. Gently rock forward, exerting pressure and keeping the arms straight, and depress the sternum about 1½ to 2 inches. This pressure forces the blood out of the heart. Rock back releasing pressure, but keep the hands in contact with the chest. This procedure is repeated at the rate of 80 times per minute and is interspersed with rescue breathing maintaining a ratio of 15 chest compressions to two quick breaths, thereby alternating B and C.

If two rescuers are available, they are positioned one at each side of the patient. One provides the breathing by interposing a breath after every 5th chest compression done by his partner at the rate of 60 compressions per minute.

When a cardiac arrest is witnessed and ONLY when it is witnessed, a precordial thump may be used as the initial maneuver when pulselessness is present. This is a SINGLE blow delivered over the midportion of the sternum, struck with the fleshy bottom portion of the fist and from a height of no more than 10 inches. Such a blow produces a small electrical stimulus in a heart that is reactive and is effective in restoring a beat. If no immediate response occurs, begin the basic life-support procedures immediately.

Every trainer and every coach should be certified in CPR and should take a refresher examination at least once a year. The ability to initiate and carry out CPR is beyond price.

SUGGESTED READINGS

American Academy of Orthopaedic Surgeons: Emergency care of the sick and injured, Chicago, 1971.

American National Red Cross: Advanced first aid and emergency care, Garden City, N.Y., 1973, Doubleday & Co.

Bakhaus do Carmo, P., and Patterson, A. T.: First aid principles and procedures, Englewood Cliffs, N.J., 1976, Prentice-Hall, Inc.

Byrd, O. E., and Byrd, T. R.: Medical readings on first aid, San Francisco, 1971, Boyd & Fraser Publishing Co.

Ferguson, A. B., Jr., and Bender, J.: The ABC's of athletic injuries and conditioning, Baltimore, 1964, The Williams & Wilkins Co.

Klafs, C. E., and Arnheim, D. D.: Modern principles of athletic training, ed. 4, St. Louis, 1977, The C. V. Mosby Co.

National Academy of Sciences and the American Heart Association: Standards for cardiopulmonary resuscitation (CPR) and emergency cardiac care (ECC). J.A.M.A. **227** (suppl. 7):833, Feb. 18, 1974.

Novich, M. M., and Taylor, B.: Training and conditioning of athletes, Philadelphia, 1970, Lea & Febiger.

O'Donoghue, D. H.: Treatment of injuries to athletes, Philadelphia, 1971, W. B. Saunders Co.

Shires, G. T., and Jones, R. C.: Initial management of the severely injured patient, J.A.M.A. **213**(11):1872, 1970.

Stephenson, H. E., Jr., editor: Immediate care of the acutely ill and injured, St. Louis, 1974, The C. V. Mosby Co.

13 □ Returning to competition

The postinjury period is a critical time, demanding thought and care by the physician, the trainer-coach, and the athlete. The use of graduated physical conditioning activities from the immediate postinjury period until the time the athlete is fit and ready to reenter serious training and competition is well established in medical practice. Unnecessary bed rest or inactivity is extremely debilitating and may be harmful. Results of inactivity include a reduction in circulatory and respiratory efficiency and disuse atrophy, a decrease in the size of the tissues because of the inability of these tissues to function in their normal capacity. Full use of rehabilitation techniques that employ muscle contractions against a resistance are most effective for the prevention of muscle and bone atrophy and should be begun as soon as circumstances allow. Early ambulation will aid in holding the physiological complications to a minimum by invoking substitution reflexes that stimulate pulmonary ventilation and general circulation through the use of the massaging and pumping action of the muscles on the veins. This action increases the delivery of venous blood to the heart and subsequently to the arteries. The phenomenon of cross transfer—exercising of the opposite (contralateral) part— should be employed. It has been established that the systematic exercise of the muscles in a given part of the body produces a definite increment of muscle tonus and strength in other parts of the body.[1-3] Hence a part encased in a cast immobilized by a splint can still receive benefit of exercise by its counterpart, thus maintaining a level of tonus in the injured part that otherwise might atrophy. See Fig. 13-1.

Rehabilitation is a slow process; it cannot be hurried. Patience on the part of all concerned is an absolute necessity. Conscientious adherence to a regularly scheduled and graded program of physical restoration is the prime factor if the athlete is to achieve complete and successful recovery. As soon as feasible after the injury, a program of general body conditioning should be instituted (Fig. 13-2). Exercises that are broad in concept will increase cardiorespiratory response and maintain the general strength and endurance of the body when performed within the current physical limits of the athlete; these should form at least half of the program. Specific exercises for restoring the strength and neuromuscular responses of the injured part, along with exercises utilizing cross transfer, should constitute the balance (Figs. 13-3 and 13-4). The trainer-coach, with the assistance and recommendations of the physician, can establish a suitable program. The references and suggested readings found at the end of this chapter will assist in setting up sound restorative programs. Physical injury is often an unavoidable concomitant of strenuous physical activity. When it does occur, the athlete is usually incapacitated to the extent that she is either not to be permitted or is physically incapable of further participation. Following prescribed care and treatment and upon a physician's advice, a program of physical restoration should be instituted to permit full recovery from the injury and the ability to participate

Fig. 13-1. Nautilus resistance equipment helps to develop strength through a full range of motion.

in the sport again without fear of reinjury. A good physical restoration program should encompass the following principles:

1. Avoid undue haste. Permit ample time to ensure full recovery. The physician should determine when the athlete is able to return to action.
2. A program of total body fitness should be instituted at once and continued throughout the restorative program. Exercises and activities should be such that they contribute to the general fitness without in any way being detrimental to the specific injury under care.
3. Activities and exercises as well as the treatments used should alleviate or reduce the disability and its attendant discomfort as much as possible.
4. Exercise, rest, massage, heat, and strapping should be utilized in a

Fig. 13-2. Light, easy jogging can sometimes assist the athlete in maintaining total body fitness while recuperating.

graduated program culminating in the return of the athlete to full and un-restricted activity. When injury to a lower extremity has occurred, one should institute a program of weight training that will maintain not only the general health of the athlete but will stabilize and improve the strength of her trunk (in particular, the abdomen), the back, and the arms and shoulders. If injury is incurred in a non–weight bearing joint, a jogging program and participation in skills that do not involve the injury should be encouraged. The aim of the rehabilitation program should be to increase the range of motion, improve the strength, and increase the endurance of the affected body part.

5. Many psychological implications often accompany a long and difficult re-covery period. Some athletes are more psychologically sensitive to injury than others. Fear of pain, of sustaining a handicapping injury, and of hav-ing failed her associates are only a few of the factors included. To fully cope

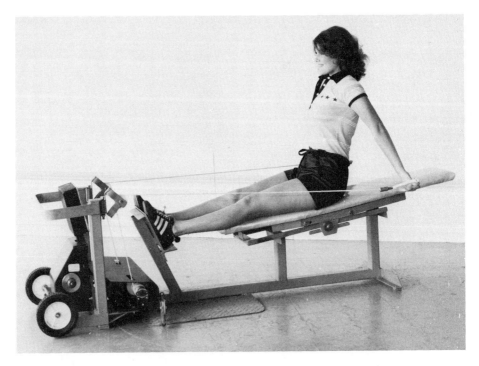

Fig. 13-3. Regaining shoulder strength and range of motion by use of the Mini-Gym.

with the many psychological problems would require the services of a top-level psychologist, and since such services are not generally available, the best single suggestion is for the trainer-coach to approach all injury rehabilitative problems from a positive stance. Stress positive factors rather than the negative ones by, for example, calling attention to how well the patient is improving or by indicating that the conscientious adherence to her rehabilitation program is apparent in her steady improvement.

At best, physical restoration is a slow process calling for considerable patience on the part of both the patient and the trainer-coach. Once it is recognized that healing takes time and patience, time itself will appear to pass more rapidly. The biggest obstacle is impatience. The athlete is in a hurry to get back into full participation and often fails to give herself enough time to permit full recuperation, with the result that the stage is set for early reinjury of the same type. Recurrent injury is not only more difficult and time consuming to heal, but as previously indicated, usually results in a chronic condition that will constantly plague the athlete. Overanxiousness on the part of the player and the coach has no place in the healing period. The advice of the physician must be heeded and the athlete given ample time to return to her preinjury status.

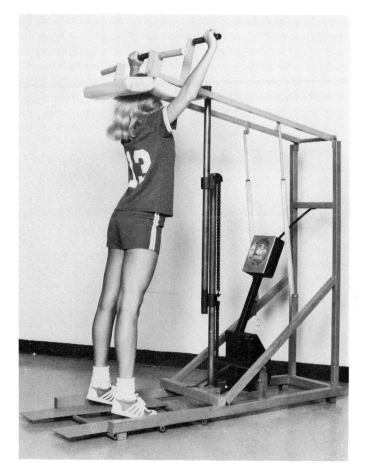

Fig. 13-4. Developing leg, hip, and arm strength with the Mini-Gym.

PRINCIPLES OF EXERCISE PROGRAM

Exercises assigned for therapy can be selected from any one of a number of current texts or from the general physical education program if the trainer-coach is aware of the nature and extent of the injury. She should have some knowledge of the joint or joints and the muscle groups involved so that the selected exercises are of the type that will attain the desired results. The exercises must be carefully selected. There are standard exercises for each joint or specific muscle group. Examples of such exercises are presented later in this chapter.

Bearing in mind the nature of the injury, select exercises that will counteract the effects of the injury in respect to the following:

Strength. Was the injury the result of a lack of strength of the muscles affecting the joint or was it attributable to inequality between opposing muscle groups?

Flexibility. Was tightness of the collagenous tissues the primary of contributory cause of the injury? Would a program of exercises of flexibility prevent recurrence of the injury?

Intensity. Exercises must be progressive, ranging from *mild* during the initial phase to *moderate* and, as recovery is completed, to *vigorous.*

Generality versus specificity. Exercises of a general nature, within the performance capacity of the injured athlete, that contribute to total body fitness should be coupled with exercises specific to the condition under care. In the initial phases of the program, because of the limitations imposed by the injury, general exercises should constitute the bulk of the program. As the patient progresses, a gradual increase in the intensity, duration, and types of exercises specific to the injury should be maintained.

Inherent dangers in the exercises selected. In some instances, exercises of flexibility, unless carefully executed, may tend to overextend a particular joint or greatly increase its range of motion when such is not desirable or a particular exercise for strength development may severely strain another area and so negate, under the circumstances, its desired use in respect to the injury under treatment.

TYPES OF EXERCISES

Therapeutic exercises are generally classified into five categories, based upon how the exercises are administered and performed.

Passive. The patient attempts no voluntary movement but permits the therapist to move the limb or body part.

Active-assistive. The patient attempts voluntary contraction and movement with the assistance of the therapist.

Active. The patient performs the exercise without any assistance or against any resistance.

Resistive. The patient exercises against some type of resistance, either manual or mechanical.

Stretching. Sufficient force is imparted to the limb or body part so as to put specific muscle groups "on stretch." The exercise may be either active or passive. In the rehabilitation period after athletic injury, generally speaking, the active, resistive, and stretching exercises are the types most frequently employed inasmuch as injury is not usually so severe as to employ the first two types to any great degree. Since the athlete can employ the latter three types herself, initial instruction as to the severity and duration of each exercise session can be given initially and then amended as her physical condition improves. Total body fitness must be maintained at all times concomitantly with rehabilitative procedures since muscular debility can occur if the muscles are not exercised. When the athlete has a cast on a limb, isometric exercises for the limb can be initiated on medical prescription, along with a general exercise program. However, care must be taken not to exercise to the point wherein sweating occurs within the cast. This serves to increase the itching as well as create an unhygienic and, on occasion, a malodorous condition.

In devising a reconditioning exercise program, the trainer must be cognizant of the type and extent of the injury as to the following:
1. Muscle groups involved
2. Limitations or impairment of movement
3. Muscular weakness present

4. Amount of ligamentous laxity present
5. Amount of pain that occurs during either stretching or shortening of muscles

On the basis of this information specific exercises can be assigned to meet the requirements of the injury. Depending on the circumstances, both isometric and isotonic exercises may be assigned. Where no joint movement is desired, isometric exercises can be utilized to excellent advantage until such time as joint movement is feasible. When graded resistance is to be used, a balanced program of progressive resistance exercises (PRE) can be employed to advantage (see Chapter 6). Such resistance can be furnished through the use of a partner, weights, or resistance machines. The exercise progression should range through passive, assistive, active, and finally resistive exercises. Where the type and nature of the injury permit, assistive and passive exercises can be dispensed with. The number of repetitions and sets is determined by the type, severity, and limitations of the injury.

When normal strength has returned to the injured part and no pain or tenderness is present when the injured part is contracted or extended and the involved ligaments are firm, the athlete is ready to resume her training or competitive program. In all cases where the initial injury or injuries were moderate or severe the team physician should be the individual who determines when the athlete should be permitted to return to full activity.

The exercise program should be carried out on a daily basis and preferably at the same time each day. In terms of intensity and duration, it should be adapted to the individual's current level of tolerance. As this level increases, the program should also be increased. All exercises should be preceded by a warm-up period, preferably utilizing static stretches. A program of testing should be carried out at intervals to ascertain the individual's progress as well as to serve as motivation. A program of suitable exercises can be established by selection of those pertinent from Table 13-1. Additional exercises, if desired, can be found in Chapter 6 or in the sources listed at the end of this chapter.

RECONDITIONING EXERCISES
Strengthening exercises

1. Toe raises (tibialis anterior)
   Feet in a small stride stance.
   Rock back slightly on the heels, dorsiflexing the feet. Hold the terminal position for 4 to 5 seconds. Return to starting position.
2. Heel raises (gastrocnemius, soleus)
   Feet in small stride stance, heels on a 2-inch riser (a 12-inch section of 2 × 4 inch beam wide side down).
   Slowly rise on toes. Hold terminal position for 4 to 5 seconds. Return to starting position.
3. Plantar flexion and dorsiflexion (tibialis anterior, gastrocnemius, soleus)
   Sitting on a training table or plinth, thigh horizontal, lower leg and ankle at right angles to thigh, hanging free and relaxed.
   Alternately plantar-flex and dorsiflex the foot.

Table 13-1 □ Suggested reconditioning exercises

Affected area	Exercise	Flexibility	With or without assistance	Exercise	Strengthening	With or without assistance
Foot, leg, ankle	1	Plantar flexion and dorsiflexion	w, wo	1	Toe raises	w, wo
				2	Heel raises	w, wo
	2	Foot circling	w, wo	3	Plantar flexion and dorsiflexion	w, wo
	3	Gastrocnemius stretch	w, wo			
				4	Foot curl	wo
Knee, thigh	4	Hamstrings stretch	w, wo	5	Stair climbing	w, wo
	5	Quadriceps stretch	w, wo	6	Knee extension	w, wo
	6	Billig stretch	wo	7	Hamstrings	w, wo
				8	Stationary bicycle riding	wo
Hip complex	4	Hamstrings stretch	w, wo	9	Half squat	w, wo
	6	Billig stretch	wo	10	Quadriceps setting	wo
	7	Hip rotator stretch	w	5	Stair climbing	w, wo
	8	Hip flexor stretch	w	11	Adduction and abduction	w, wo
Hand, wrist, forearm, elbow	9	Wrist rotator stretch	w, wo	12	Hip-joint rotation	w, wo
	10	Wrist joint stretch	w, wo	13	Hip-joint circumduction	w, wo
				14	Hip-joint extension	w, wo
Shoulder complex	11	Shoulder stretch	wo	15	Biceps curls	w, wo
	12	Anterior shoulder stretch	wo	16	Supination and pronation	w, wo
				17	Wrist roll-up	w, wo
	13	Pectoral stretch	w, wo	18	Abduction and adduction	w, wo
				19	Shoulder wheel	w, wo
Trunk	13	Pectoral stretch	w, wo	20	Pectoral strengthener	w, wo
	14	Anterior trunk stretch	w, wo	21	Rhomboid lift	w, wo
	15	Posterior trunk stretch	wo	22	Shoulder shrug	w, wo
	16	Lateral trunk stretch	wo	23	Arm crossover	w, wo
				24	Rowing	wo
				25	Abdominal curls	w, wo
				26	Back raise	wo

4. Foot curl (tibialis posterior, longitudinal arch)

   Sitting on a chair or bench, thigh horizontal, foot placed upon the near end of a towel that has been spread lengthwise away from the patient.

   Grasp the towel with a gripping motion of the toes and, by curling the foot, pull it toward the chair. Repeat the curling-pulling maneuver until the full length of the towel has been bunched to the near end. As foot and ankle strength increases, resistance can be increased if varying weights are placed on the far end of the towel.

5. Stair climbing (foot, ankle, knee, and hip extensors and flexors)

   At the base of a series of steps or bleacher seats.

   Walk slowly up and down a series of steps at a deliberate tempo. Resistance in the form of a weight belt or barbell can be added as progress is made.

6. Knee extension (quadriceps group)

   Sitting on a training table or plinth high enough to keep the feet clear of the floor when the lower leg is at right angles to the thigh.

   The lower leg is slowly raised to extend the knee. The extended position is held for a few seconds and then the leg is slowly lowered to the starting position. As improvement in strength is noted, resistance is added. Any leg press or quadriceps machine may also be used.

7. Hamstrings (hamstring group)

   Prone upon a bench or plinth, lower legs extended beyond the end of the bench. (Keep the knee joint in contact with the bench.)

   Slowly flex the knee joint as far as possible. Hold the terminal position for a few seconds. Return to the starting position. As strength improves, resistance should be added.

8. Stationary bicycle riding (foot, ankle, knee, and hip flexors and extensors)

   Seated upon a stationary bicycle or ergometer.

   Adjust the seat height so that when the leg is fully extended the heel of the foot can rest on the pedal. Initially, set a slow tempo with no resistance. As improvement is noted, increase both pedal speed and resistance to accommodate the ability of the patient.

9. Half squat (quadriceps group—vasti lateralis, intermedius, and medialis; rectus femoris)

   Feet approximately 6 inches apart, heels elevated about 1½ inches on a riser. It may be advisable to place a 20-inch bench behind the buttocks to prevent knee injury by serving as a stop should the patient encounter difficulty in performing the exercise.

   Slowly bend the knees to half-squat position. Hold the terminal position for a few seconds and then return to the starting position.

10. Quad setting (quadriceps group)

    Seated on the floor or on a table, legs extended.

    Forcefully contract the quadriceps muscles isometrically, holding the "set" position from 6 to 10 seconds. Relax the contraction.

11. Adduction and abduction (adductor and abductor muscles of the hip)

    Side-lying position with the affected limb uppermost. The upper part of the body can be supported upon the forearm, if desired.

Slowly abduct the leg, holding the terminal position for a few seconds. Slowly return to the starting position. To obviate the effect of gravity, varying degrees of resistance should be provided by the trainer during the adduction phase of the movement. It can also be applied during abduction.

12. Hip joint rotation (hip joint rotators)
Standing, holding onto the back of a chair or some other object that will provide stability, with the body weight transferred to the nonexercising leg.
Slowly rotate the leg at the hip joint first in one direction and then in the other, continuing alternately. Resistance may be provided through the use of a weight boot.

13. Circumduction of the hip (all muscles involved with hip movement)
Same as in rotation. Swing the straight leg, so that the foot describes a circle of 6 to 12 inches in diameter. Circumduction should be performed in both directions, with and without resistance.

14. Hip extension (gluteus maximus, hamstring group)
Prone on a bench or plinth, the legs and hips off the edge, feet resting on the floor. The legs are straight and the sides of the bench are securely held by the patient.
Slowly raise the affected straight limb backward until complete extension verging on hyperextension of the hip is attained. Hold the terminal position for a few seconds and then slowly lower the straight leg back to the starting position. As strength is regained, resistance may be added in the form of a weight boot or through the use of a resistance machine.

15. Biceps curls (biceps brachii, brachialis)
Standing or sitting, with the affected arm in a position of complete elbow-joint extension.
The forearm is slowly flexed to its maximum limit and then slowly extended to the starting position. Resistance is added as strength is improved.

16. Supination and pronation of the hand and forearm (pronator teres, biceps brachii, supinator, brachioradialis)
Seated or standing, affected arm extended. Alternately pronate and supinate the hand. Resistance such as a pronator-supinator machine or dumbbells may be used as strength is developed.

17. Wrist roll-up (flexor carpi radialis and ulnaris, palmaris longus, flexor sublimis digitorum and profundus digitorum, flexor longus pollicis)
Small stride. A wall wrist roller may be used or a substitute may be constructed consisting of a 12-inch length of broomstick to which a 3- to $3^{1}/_{2}$-foot length of sash cord is fastened to the center. The other end of the cord is attached to a 2-pound weight.
Using flexion of the wrist and fingers only, roll up the length of the cord on the stick. Then slowly unroll and repeat the initial action. Another simple variation is to roll up a towel lengthwise. The towel is grasped with both hands, hands about 2 inches apart. The hands are then rotated in opposite directions, as would be done if one were wringing water out of the towel. The wringing is first done in one direction and then in the other, alternately.

18. Shoulder abduction and (deltoid, supraspinatus, trapezius, rhomboids, pectoralis major, coracobrachialis, teres major, latissimus dorsi)
    Side-lying position upon a plinth or bench.
    Exercises should first be performed without resistance until a level of strength is reached that will permit resistance. The affected arm is raised from a position at the side directly upward and then returned to the position. The terminal raised position should be held for a few seconds before the arm is returned to the starting position.
19. Shoulder-wheel exercises (all muscles of the shoulder complex)
    The shoulder wheel can be used to strengthen the shoulder by regulation of the resistance of the wheel.
    Use the wheel by facing it or by standing with the affected side toward it.
20. Pectoral strengthener (the same muscles are involved in this exercise as in the adduction-abduction exercise)
    Supine on a bench or plinth, arms extended sideward.
    Raise arms to vertical position, holding the terminal position a few seconds and then return to the starting position. After injury, as strength and conditions permit, perform the exercise preferably by holding dumbbells, gradually increasing their weights as strength is gained.
21. Rhomboid lift (rhomboids)
    Supine on a bench or plinth, arms extended sideward.
    Raise arms approximately 6 to 8 inches and return. When conditions permit, weight dumbbells should be used, as indicated in the pectoral strengthener (number 20).
22. Shoulder shrug (trapezius, levator scapulae)
    Small stride, arms at the side.
    The affected shoulder is raised as high as possible and then relaxed and permitted to fall back to its normal position. When permissible, weights should be held in the hand of the affected limb.
23. Arm crossover (triceps, anterior deltoid, pectoralis major)
    Supine on a mat or bench, knees flexed, feet flat (hook-lying), arms extended sideward with or without dumbbells.
    The arms are brought across the chest, with elbows flexed, at shoulder level as far as is possible. Return to the starting position.
24. Rowing (all the muscles of the upper trunk, shoulder complex, and the arms)
    Sitting on a mat or plinth, trunk inclinded forward, arms extended forward, knees bent, feet flat on the floor.
    At shoulder level, pull the arms back as far as possible while bringing the trunk to a position of slight hyperextension. Repeat the exercise in a smooth continuous pattern. Dumbbells should be used when the patient is able to handle them. Wall weights can be used for this exercise.
25. Abdominal curls, with and without a trunk twist (abdominal muscles)
    Supine with the knees bent, feet flat on the floor (hook-lying).
    Hands may be clasped behind the neck or the arms may be folded across the chest. Keeping the feet on the floor, curl the upper trunk as far upward and forward toward the knees as is possible. Return to the starting

position. It may be advisable to anchor the feet under some firm stationary object.

26. Back raise (erector spinae, longissimus dorsi, spinalis dorsi, rhomboids, trapezius)

    Prone on a mat or plinth, hands clasped in the small of the back, legs together.

    Raise the upper trunk and head, hyperextending the spine as much as is possible. Hold the terminal position. Return to starting position. To exercise the spinal rotators, as the trunk is raised, one should rotate them to one side. The next lift should be rotated to the opposite side.

Flexibility exercises

1. Plantar flexion and dorsiflexion of the foot (gastrocnemius, soleus, tibialis posticus, the peroneals)

   Seated legs extended.

   Alternately flex and extend the ankle, proceeding very slowly and holding the terminal position of each phase for 3 to 4 seconds. This exercise may also be done with a partner, providing either assistance or resistance, depending on which is required.

2. Foot circling (gastrocnemius, soleus, tibialis posticus and anticus, extensor longus digitorum, extensor longus hallucis)

   Seated on a bench or plinth, thing of the affected limb at right angle to the lower leg.

   Circle the foot slowly in one direction a number of times and then reverse the direction. Strive to get the maximum range of movement possible.

3. Gastrocnemius stretch (gastrocnemius, soleus, Achilles tendon)

   Standing, arm's length from a wall or other flat vertical surface, weight slightly on balls of feet, which are 3 to 4 inches apart and slightly toed in. The arms are extended, palms flat against the vertical surface, shoulder width apart.

   Keeping the body in a straight line, slowly bend the arms, while keeping the heels firmly on the floor until the elbows are flexed to the maximum. Hold this position at least 10 seconds. Return to starting position. Repeat six times as a minimum. Be certain the knees are kept fully locked in extension.

4. Hamstring stretch (biceps femoris, semimembranosus, semitendinosus)

   Sitting or standing, feet approximately 3 to 4 inches apart and parallel to each other.

   Slowly bend forward from the waist as far as possible. Hold the position for several seconds, with straight arms and the hands resting lightly on the lower limbs. Now slide the hands forward a bit more; if possible, hold the position. Return to starting position. The forward flexion movement is best executed in a series of small flexions, with each successive movement farther advanced than the previous one and each in turn held for 4 to 5 seconds.

5. Quadriceps stretch (vasti lateralis, medius, and intermedius; rectus femoris)

Supine on a table or plinth, partner standing at the side of the affected limb.

The hip and knee joints are slowly flexed. The partner, placing one hand just above the ankle, the other on the knee, continues the flexion movement slowly to the full extent of permissible range of movement, holding the terminal position for 4 to 5 seconds before returning the limb to the starting position. This exercise serves its purpose best if the gradual stretch approach is used, that is, a series of short stretching movements, each slightly greater than the preceding movement with the end position of each movement held for some seconds.

6. Billig stretch (hamstring group, extensors of the lower back, hip rotators, iliotibial band)

Standing, cross the uninjured limb over the affected leg, weight on both feet; place the hand on the side of the crossed leg on the shoulder of the opposite arm, which is placed across the small of the back.

Bend forward from the waist, keeping the crossed leg stabilized by the other leg, with the movement being down and across the crossed leg until tension is felt. Hold the position for 4 to 5 seconds, and then continue the movement as far as the range of motion will allow. Hold the terminal position several seconds, and then return to the starting position. Keep the affected knee straight at all times.

7. Hip-rotator stretch (tensor fasciae latae, gluteus minimus, gluteus maximus, and small outward rotators)

Supine on a floor mat. For better stability the arms may be placed sideward.

Extend the leg to be stretched to an angle of 90 degrees and then slowly let it hang across the body, knee straight, until a pull is felt. Hold for several seconds and then continue the movement slowly to the end of the range of movement, holding the terminal position for several seconds before returning to the starting position. This stretch can also be performed passively if the patient is unable to perform the exercise unaided, progressing to an assistive exercise and then to the active exercise.

8. Hip-flexor stretch (psoas, iliacus, rectus femoris)

Supine on a floor mat or plinth.

Raise the affected limb to the chest, flexing the knee, and grasping just below the knee with both hands. Pull the knee slowly toward the chest until a resistive pull is felt. Hold the terminal position for 4 to 5 seconds. Return to starting position. Vary the exercise, if desired, by bringing both legs to the chest and pulling on both legs, while shifting mat contact principally to the upper trunk. This brings into play the stretching of the lower back extensors as well as of the hip flexors.

9. Wrist-rotator stretch (flexores carpi radialis and carpi ulnaris, palmaris longus, flexores sublimis digitorum and profundus digitorum, flexor longus pollicis)

Seated or standing, elbows flexed at right angles, wrists relaxed.

Circumduct the wrists, describing a cone with the hand, with the wrist as the apex and the fingers as the periphery, stretching the hand as much as possible. The movement should be performed in alternate directions.

10. Wrist-joint stretch (extensores carpi radialis longus, carpi radialis brevis, communis digitorum, and carpi ulnaris; flexores carpi radialis, carpi ulnaris, and sublimis digitorum; palmaris longus)

    Seated or standing.

    Hyperextend the affected wrist slowly as far as it is possible to do unassisted. Now using the opposite hand, apply gentle pressure to the palm until a good stretch is felt. Hold the terminal position for 4 to 5 seconds. Return to the starting position. Now reverse the movement by first flexing the wrist and then applying pressure to the back of the hand. The same procedure can be applied to the wrist if lateral or medial stretching is desired.

11. Shoulder stretch (all the muscles of the shoulder complex)

    Hang from the stall bars, horizontal bar, or other apparatus, feet clear of the floor.

    Relax as much as possible assuming a dead-weight posture in the hang. Maintain the hang position to the point of tolerance.

12. Anterior shoulder stretch (anterior deltoid, pectoralis major)

    A small side-stride stance, fingers hooked together in rear at the buttocks. Slowly raise the extended arms backward and upward as far as possible to the point of tolerance. Hold the terminal position for 4 to 5 seconds. Return to the starting position.

13. Pectoral stretch (pectoralis major and minor)

    A small side-stride stance, arms raised sideward to a position slightly above horizontal, palms upward.

    Slowly and steadily pull the straight arms backward to the point of tolerance. Hold the terminal position for 4 to 5 seconds. Return to starting position.

14. Anterior trunk stretch (rectus abdominis)

    Prone on a body mat or plinth, hands clasped in the small of the back.

    Raise the head and upper trunk upward and backward to the point of tolerance. Hold for 4 to 5 seconds. Return to starting position.

15. Posterior trunk stretch (erector spinae, latissimus dorsi, iliopsoas)

    Kneeling on all fours on a body mat.

    Retract the abdominal muscles and flex the spine by forcing it upward into an arched position while flexing the neck as much as possible. Hold the terminal position for 4 to 5 seconds. Return to starting position.

16. Lateral trunk stretch (serratus anterior, intercostals, erector spinae, rectus abdominis, external and internal obliques)

    Standing, facing stall bars.

    Reach overhead and get a comfortable grasp on a bar, with arms partially flexed. Slowly move the hips laterally as far as possible. Hold the terminal position for 4 to 5 seconds and return to the starting position. Repeat to the alternate side.

REFERENCES

1. de Vries, H. A.: Physiology of exercise for physical education and athletics, ed. 2, Dubuque, Iowa, 1974, William C. Brown Co., Publishers.

2. Hellebrandt, F. A.: Cross education: ipsilateral and contralateral effects of unimanual training, J. Appl. Physiol. **4:**136, 1951.
3. Klein, K. K., and Williams, H. E.: A study of cross transfer of muscular strength gains during reconditioning of knee injuries, J. Assoc. Phys. Ment. Rehab. **8:**52, 1954.

SUGGESTED READINGS

Annarino, A. A.: Developmental conditioning for men and women, ed. 2, St. Louis, 1976, The C. V. Mosby Co.

Arnheim, D. D., Auxter, D., and Crowe, W. C.: Principles and methods of adapted physical education, St. Louis, 1977, The C. V. Mosby Co.

Barney, V. S., Hirst, C. C., and Jensen, C. R.: Conditioning exercises, ed. 3, St. Louis, 1972, The C. V. Mosby Co.

Clarke, H. H., and Clarke, D. H.: Developmental and adapted physical education, Englewood Cliffs, N.J., 1963, Prentice-Hall, Inc.

Klafs, C. E., and Arnheim, D. D.: Modern principles of athletic training, ed. 4, St. Louis, 1977, The C. V. Mosby Co.

Rusk, H. A.: Rehabilitation medicine, ed. 4, St. Louis, 1977, The C. V. Mosby Co.

14 □ Nutrition and athletic performance

OVERVIEW OF NUTRITIONAL PRINCIPLES

The consumption of food serves a person in many ways. Eating has psychological and social significance, but its most important purpose is to provide the body with the nutrients that are essential to life processes.

Nutrients are chemical components that perform one of three roles in the body—supply energy, regulate body processes, or promote the growth and repair of body tissue (Fig. 14-1).[6]

Essential nutrients

Six basic types of nutrients perform these functions: carbohydrates, fats (lipids), proteins, minerals, vitamins, and water. About 45% of the average American diet is comprised of carbohydrates, 45% fats, and 10% proteins.[4]

Carbohydrates. Carbohydrates are compounds composed of carbon, hydrogen, and oxygen, with the ratio of hydrogen to oxygen being two to one. Starches and sugars comprise the carbohydrate foods, which are formed through photosynthesis whereby the sun's radiant energy is converted to chemical form. Simple carbohydrates are classified as monosaccharides, which include glucose, or blood sugar. More common are the disaccharides, composed of two monosaccharide units. Polysaccharides are more complex carbohydrates and are considered starches rather than sugars.

The major function of carbohydrate is to act as a source of energy for the body. One gram of carbohydrate supplies 4 calories of energy. The nerve cells of the body depend entirely on glucose for energy. During the digestive process the complex carbohydrates are broken down to their simple monosaccharide units, enabling them to be absorped into the walls of the small intestine. The absorption time for carbohydrates is faster than that for fats or proteins. After assimilation the monosaccharide units are either converted to glycogen in the liver and stored there or are converted to glucose and carried by the blood to all the tissues of the body for use as energy. Resting levels of blood glucose are approximately 100 mg. of glucose per 100 ml. of blood. During exercise the liver releases additional glucose into the bloodstream to accommodate the increased metabolic needs of the muscle tissue.

Excess carbohydrate is converted into fatty acids by the liver and transported by the bloodstream to adipose tissue cells. These fatty acids then combine with glycerol to form fat.

Fats (lipids). Fats are another group of energy-yielding nutrients and are found in butter, margarine, vegetable oil, meat, egg yolk, milk, nuts, and whole-grain cereals. Food fat is composed of glycerol, a three-carbon compound, to which fatty acids are attached. Prior to being able to enter the blood circulation for transport, fat is broken down chemically into smaller molecules, mainly fatty acids and glycerol. Ingested fat is then utilized in one of three ways: (1) both fatty

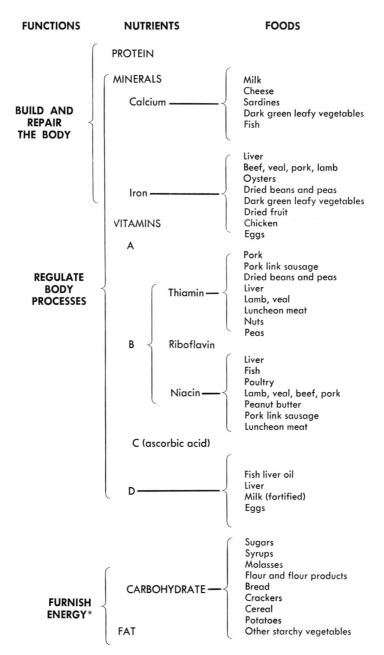

Fig. 14-1. Functions of food in nutrition. (Courtesy National Live Stock and Meat Board, Chicago.)

acids and glycerol are metabolized immediately as a source of energy; (2) glycerol and fatty acids combine to form fat, which is stored as an energy reserve; and (3) glycerol is converted to glucose, which in turn can be used as a source of energy, converted to glycogen, or converted to fat.[4]

Fat is an extremely concentrated source of energy, providing over 2¼ times more calories per gram than either protein or carbohydrate (9 versus 4 calories). Stored fat indicates the amount of excess food being consumed. Most animal foods contain some fat; even a lean steak is approximately 28% fat, which contributes 70% of the steak's calories.[4]

Because of the tendency of fat to leave the stomach slowly (approximately 3½ hours after ingestion), it helps to delay the onset of hunger and promotes a feeling of satiety after eating. Fat also serves an important function as a carrier for four essential fat-soluble vitamins — A, D, E, and K. In addition to serving as the body's "energy-storage depot," fat provides good insulation under the skin (subcutaneous fat), assists in protecting vital organs (kidneys and heart) from physical shock, and performs essential regulatory functions of cell membranes.

Proteins. Proteins are a constituent of every living cell and tissue. Half of the dry matter of an adult is protein. Of this, one third is in muscle, one fifth in bone and cartilage, one tenth in skin, and the remainder in other tissues and fluids. All enzymes are protein, as are many hormones. Proteins are complex substances comprised of many amino acids, which are the structural unit of protein. Twenty different amino acids, which are the structural unit of protein. Twenty different amino acids, all of which contain nitrogen, have been identified as building blocks for body proteins. Eight of these are considered essential amino acids; they cannot be synthesized by the body at a rate sufficient to meet the body's needs for growth and maintenance. Complete proteins are those that contain all of the essential amino acids. Incomplete proteins of poor quality are those that lack one or more of the essential amino acids.

Amino acids perform a variety of essential functions in the body. (1) They are necessary for the growth of new cells and tissues, including replacement of tissue that is constantly being broken down, as well as for normal growth and development. (2) Amino acids also form essential hormones and enzymes that regulate vital physiological functions. Insulin, adrenaline (epinephrine), hemoglobin, and thousands of other enzymes in the body are proteins. (3) The amino acids assist in regulating water balance. (4) They also assist in maintaining optimum acid-base balance by serving as buffers (plasma protein). (5) Antibodies used in combating infection are formed by amino acids.

If caloric intake of protein exceeds the body's needs, certain amino acids are converted to glucose and are either metabolized as such, stored as glycogen in the liver, or stored as fat. Other amino acids are converted to fatty acids and used directly as a source of energy or are converted and stored as fat. The nitrogen residues are converted into urea and excreted by the kidneys, since there is no storage site for such protein.[4]

Minerals. Approximately 4% of the total body weight is comprised of fifteen mineral elements that are essential to good health. Some of their functions are as follows: (1) They maintain the proper acid-base balance essential for the proper functioning of cellular enzymes. (2) They serve as catalysts for many biological reactions by activating the cellular enzymes. (3) Minerals are essential ingredients of many hormones and enzymes (thyroxin, which regulates energy metabolism, requires iodine; insulin, which regulates carbohydrate metabolism, involves zinc; hemoglobin, which is essential in oxygen transport, contains iron). (4) Sodium and potassium are essential for nerve impulse conduction. (5) Calcium, potassium, sodium, and magnesium are intimately involved in the proper functioning of muscle tissue. (6) Calcium and phosphorus are important building constituents of teeth and bone.

Water. Water constitutes 60% of the total body weight and is a constituent of every cell of the body. Its concentration varies in different tissues, comprising 72% of muscle, 20% to 35% of adipose tissue, and 10% of bone and cartilage. The water in the bloodstream serves as a solvent and a transporter for the various nutrients, monosaccharides, amino acids, fats, vitamins, minerals, and hormones. Intercellular fluid bathes all the cells, bringing nutrients to cell membranes and collecting waste products. Within the cell, water is incorporated into the new materials being synthesized and serves as a catalyst and solvent. Obviously optimum amounts of water are essential to nutrition. Studies have indicated that a lack of water is more detrimental to work production than the lack of food.[4] It is also extremely important in the regulation of body temperature, as water evaporation from the body's surface is the most effective means of ridding the body of excess heat.

Vitamins. Vitamins are organic substances needed in very small amounts for normal body functioning.[4] Vitamins are categorized as being either fat soluble or water soluble, with each group having characteristic properties. Daily intake of the fat-soluble vitamins (A, D, E, and K) is not absolutely essential; they are not excreted, and any excess will be stored. Deficiency symptoms are relatively slow to develop. The water-soluble group (C and B complex) should be included in the daily diet; these vitamins cannot be stored but are excreted in the urine. Deficiency problems occur rapidly.

The exact biochemical role of many vitamins is still not clearly known. Those whose functions have been determined serve primarily as coenzymes, which are essential in activating the enzymes themselves. Each cell contains at least 500 different enzymes that serve as catalysts in digestion, in utilization of nutrients, and in the release of energy used in muscle contraction and other basic cellular processes. Without vitamins there would be no coenzymes to ensure the enzymatic action essential to normal cellular metabolism.[4]

Basic food groups

Foods should be selected daily from each of the following groups (Fig. 14-2).

Dairy foods. Milk is a main source of calcium and also contributes proteins and vitamins (A and riboflavin). This group also includes butter, cheese, ice cream, and other milk-made products.

Meat group. This group includes meat, fish, poultry, eggs, and cheese as well as dry beans, peas, nuts, and peanut butter. These foods supply protein, iron, and the B vitamins. The legumes (dried beans, peas) and nuts are also good sources of iron and thiamin.

Vegetables and fruits. Dark green leafy or deep yellow vegetables and yellow

Four Basic Food Groups

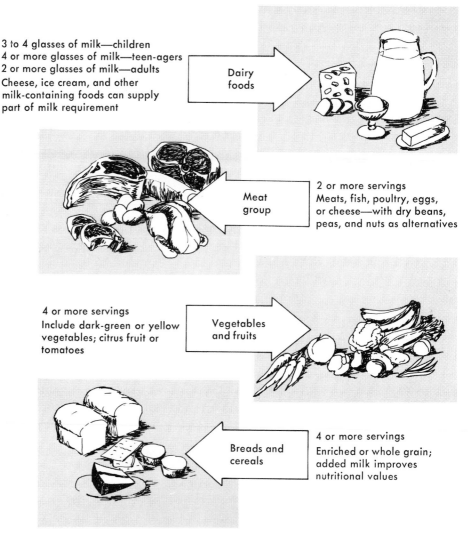

3 to 4 glasses of milk—children
4 or more glasses of milk—teen-agers
2 or more glasses of milk—adults
Cheese, ice cream, and other
milk-containing foods can supply
part of milk requirement

Dairy
foods

Meat
group

2 or more servings
Meats, fish, poultry, eggs,
or cheese—with dry beans,
peas, and nuts as alternatives

4 or more servings
Include dark-green or yellow
vegetables; citrus fruit or
tomatoes

Vegetables
and fruits

Breads and
cereals

4 or more servings
Enriched or whole grain;
added milk improves
nutritional values

Fig. 14-2. The athlete's nutritional needs are similar to those of the nonathlete. (Courtesy National Dairy Council, Chicago.)

fruits should be included for vitamin A; citrus fruits or tomatoes are good sources of vitamin C.

Breads and cereals. Foods in this group supply valuable amounts of protein, iron, several B vitamins, and carbohydrates for energy; these also include rice, spaghetti, macaroni, and noodles.[1]

Individual differences in energy requirements

Every person differs in the amount of energy he needs. For this reason, charts that indicate a recommended daily caloric intake should be considered only a rough estimate and used with caution. At least four factors interact to determine the amount of energy needed by each individual. Basal metabolism refers to the minimum amount of energy needed to maintain basic, vital physiological processes, including respiration, circulation, glandular and hormonal functions, and cellular metabolism. People can differ in their energy requirements for these processes by as much as 20% and still be within the normal range of basal metabolic rate.[7] Body size is another factor contributing to individual differences in energy needs. Obviously a larger person requires more energy to move her body. To perform the same task, the larger person will require approximately 150 calories for every additional 11 pounds of weight. Age also influences caloric needs, since basal metabolic rate (BMR) declines with age, as does physical activity. It is estimated that the total caloric needs decrease by 5% per decade between the ages of 35 and 55 years, 8% per decade from the ages of 55 to 75 years, and 10% every 10 years thereafter.[4] Nutritional experts agree, though, that the main factor influencing energy needs is the amount of physical activity in which the person engages (Table 14-1). Energy expenditure while participating in various sports can exceed sedentary expenditure rates by eight to twelve times. Mayer[9] and other authorities consider inadequate exercise to be the leading cause of overweight and obesity in the United States.

Problem of obesity

To be overweight actually means being overfat, with too high a percentage of the body weight being comprised of adipose tissue. Overweight constitutes a major health problem in this country, with obesity being associated with a higher mortality and an increased risk of coronary heart disease, hypertension, diabetes, and adverse psychological reactions.[11] Many studies have shown that 32% to 39% of adolescent girls are overweight, with fewer boys having this problem. One study on college students classified 29% of the men and 36% of the women as overweight. An investigation of obesity involving 3,508 students at the University of Chicago revealed that 29% of the men and 24% of the women were obese. Twelve percent of adults in their twenties weigh 20% or more above their best weight. The percentage of the population classified as overweight increases with age.

The basic cause of obesity is a positive caloric balance. This results when the average caloric intake exceeds energy expenditure. A surplus intake of only 100 calories per day results in a year's weight gain of approximately 10 pounds! (A

Table 14-1 □ General approximations for daily adult basal and activity energy needs*

Basal energy needs (av. 1 cal./kg./hr.)		Man weighing 70 kg. (70 × 24 = 1,680 cal.)	Woman weighing 58 kg. (58 × 24 = 1,392 cal.)
Activity energy needs			
Very sedentary	+20% basal	1,680 + 336 = 2,016	1,392 + 278 = 1,670
Sedentary	+30% basal	1,680 + 504 = 2,184	1,392 + 418 = 1,810
Moderately active	+40% basal	1,680 + 672 = 2,352	1,392 + 557 = 1,949
Very active	+50% basal	1,680 + 840 = 2,520	1,392 + 696 = 2,088

*From Williams, S. R.: Nutrition and diet therapy, ed. 2, St. Louis, 1973, The C. V. Mosby Co.

pound of fat equals about 3,500 calories.) These surplus calories, whether in the form of fat, carbohydrate, or protein, are converted to fat and stored in the body's energy-storage depots.

The only way in which excess deposits of fat can be eliminated is by establishing a negative caloric balance, which requires the body to utilize its stored fat as a source of energy (Fig. 14-3). A negative caloric balance of 500 calories per day would result in a weight loss of 1 pound per week (Table 14-2). Such a program is

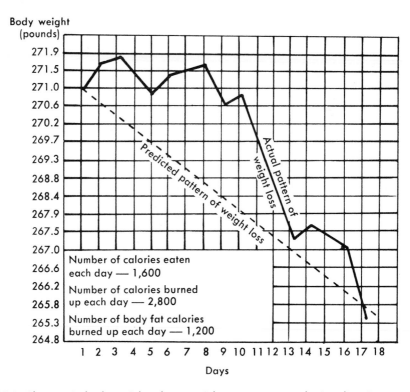

Fig. 14-3. Changes in body weight of overweight person on a reducing diet. Progress chart shows how much body weight can fluctuate as a result of water retention even though daily caloric intake remains constant. This dieter accumulated water for 10 days while losing fat and then showed a rapid weight loss as water was eliminated. (Courtesy Pennwalt, Prescription Products Division, Pennwalt Corp., Rochester, N.Y.)

Table 14-2 □ Calorie adjustment required for weight loss*

To lose 1 pound a week—500 fewer calories daily		
Basis of estimation		
1 lb. body fat	=	454 gm.
1 gm. pure fat	=	9 cal.
1 gm. body fat	=	7.7 cal. (some water in fat cells)
454 gm. × 9 cal./gm.	=	4,086 cal./lb. fat (pure fat)
454 gm. × 7.7 cal./gm.	=	3,496 cal./lb. body fat (or 3,500 cal.)
500 cal. × 7 days	=	3,500 cal. = 1 lb. body fat

*From Williams, S. R.: Nutrition and diet therapy, ed. 2, St. Louis, 1973, The C. V. Mosby Co.

reasonable if the daily intake is decreased slightly and the energy expenditure is increased through regular exercise. As previously mentioned, exercise causes large amounts of energy to be expended above the basal rate. De Vries[3] has shown that the metabolic rate continues to be elevated approximately 6 hours after exercise, resulting in further caloric expenditure. A nutritionally balanced diet should be maintained, but foods that are calorically "expensive" can be minimized.

The use of standard height-weight tables is not recommended for determining the individual's optimum weight, according to Mayer.[10] Looking at oneself in a mirror is often a more reliable guide for estimating obesity than body weight. If a person *looks* fat, she probably *is* fat! The pinch test is another informal method of estimating body fat. Approximately half of the body fat is located subcutaneously between the skin and underlying muscle. At some locations on the body (for example, the back of the upper arm) a fold of skin and fat can be lifted free, using the thumb and forefinger, from the underlying triceps muscle (Fig. 14-4). In general, this pinched double thickness of skin should be 1/2 to 1 inch thick. A triceps fold of skin considerably greater than 1 inch indicates excessive body fatness. A table of triceps skinfold measures indicating obesity has been prepared by Seltzer and Mayer (Table 14-3).

Nutritional needs and habits during adolescence

The teen-age years represent a period during which rapid and noticeable physiological and emotional changes are occurring. The rapid growth of organs and tissues and physiological changes in response to hormonal action make adequate nutrition during these years extremely important. In this phase of the life cycle, the male's nutritional needs are probably the highest in his life, and only during pregnancy and lactation are they higher for a woman.[6]

Analysis of the nutritive adequacy of the diets of young adults between 12 and 18 years of age indicates the diets of boys to be better balanced than that of girls, in part because of the greater quantity of food required to meet the energy needs of boys. (The BMR of women is approximately 5% lower than that of men; in addition, boys tend to be more physically active.) Girls' diets were found to be lacking in calcium, iron, vitamins A and C, and some of the B-complex vitamins. The low calcium and vitamin A levels reflect a general rejection of vegetables. Among the poor dietary habits and factors contributing to the nutritional deficiencies of girls were a tendency to skip meals, smaller quantities of food at meals, lack of milk, eating many unsupervised (poorly balanced) meals, and an overriding fear of obesity.[6]

Great concern has been expressed over the poor diets that are common during adolescence, since the results of nutrient deficits are far reaching, especially for girls. A relationship between unbalanced diet and tuberculosis, the highest incidence of which is during adolescence, has been observed. Emotional instability has accompanied negative nitrogen and calcium balances. Twenty-five percent of mothers bearing their first child are less than 20 years old, and 6% of all deaths among 18- to 19-year-old women result from the complications of pregnancy. Inadequate nutritive intake prior to conception causes the woman to be less able to cope with the added physical and psychological stresses of pregnancy. A higher percentage of babies of teen-agers are born prematurely and have more congenital defects.

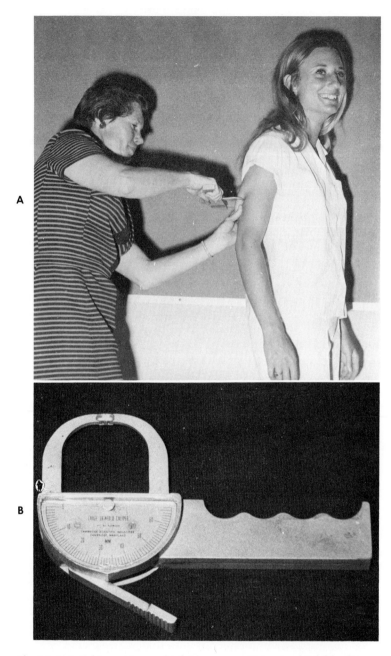

Fig. 14-4. A, Taking a triceps skinfold measure. **B,** Lange skinfold calipers.

Table 14-3 □ Obesity standards for white Americans
(minimum triceps skinfold thickness in millimeters indicating obesity)*

Age (years)	Skinfold measurements†	
	Males	Females
5	12	14
6	12	15
7	13	16
8	14	17
9	15	18
10	16	20
11	17	21
12	18	22
13	18	23
14	17	23
15	16	24
16	15	25
17	14	26
18	15	27
19	15	27
20	16	28
21	17	28
22	18	28
23	18	28
24	19	28
25	20	29
26	20	29
27	21	29
29	22	29
29	23	29
30–50	23	30

*From Seltzer, C. C., and Mayer, J. A.: Postgrad. Med. **38:**A101, 1965; by permission of McGraw-Hill, Inc.

†Figures represent the logarithmic means of the frequency distributions plus 1 standard deviation.

NUTRITIONAL IMPLICATIONS FOR ATHLETIC PERFORMANCE
Influence of diet on work capacity

Although it is true that motivation and neuromuscular coordination are most important to good performance, the dietary program of the athlete influences work capacity in the following ways: (1) by renewing the supply of nutrients that yield the energy necessary for physical work and exercise, (2) by facilitating the biochemical reactions that yield the energy, (3) by modifying the biochemical changes contributing to fatigue, and (4) by maintaining an optimum energy balance and body weight for the athlete.[12]

Energy requirements of exercise

The energy requirements of the athlete are largely dependent on the intensity and duration of her daily workouts as well as the actual competitive situation.

Thus the caloric cost of exercise can vary a great deal between athletes, depending on their particular sport and specialized event—perhaps as much as 2,550 to 5,000 calories per day when the energy expenditure for the activity is superimposed upon that necessary for daily maintenance (BMR) and other light activities.[2] Table 14-1 illustrates how caloric (energy) needs increase as physical activity becomes more strenuous.

Energy sources

Two basic energy sources for exercise are available to the athlete; the fuel source that is utilized will depend on the nature of the activity.

Athletic events of short duration. In events involving intense, maximum effort for short periods of time, such as dashes and swimming sprints, high-energy creatine, phosphate, ATP, and the anaerobic (without oxygen) breakdown of glucose into lactic acid are primarily utilized.

Athletic events of longer, continuous duration. Longer types of athletic events, lasting approximately 2 minutes or more, require a continuous supply of energy that is made available through oxidation processes to replensih the high-energy phosphate. In these activities the availability of oxygen and its efficient use can be the limiting factors in continuous performance. The foods that are oxidized to produce the energy vary considerably in the amounts of energy they yield. One liter of oxygen taken in by the athlete will yield 5 calories in combination with carbohydrate, 4.6 calories with fat, and 4.5 calories with protein. This represents an 8% greater yield of energy from the oxidation of carbohydrates than from fat, which could be an important factor in endurance events.

Various studies have determined that the athlete uses both carbohydrate and fat as energy sources during rest and light work. But as work intensity and duration increases, the greatest energy is derived from the oxidation of available carbohydrate. Studies investigating the effect of diet on performance indicate that endurance in strenuous exercise is impaired by a high-fat diet; subjects on a high-carbohydrate diet showed an 11% greater net muscular efficiency than the high-fat diet group. Evidently better performance efficiency can be maintained by the athlete if the proportion of calories derived from fat is not too high.[2]

For *carbohydrate loading* refer to Chapter 15, in which is discussed the rationale and procedures associated with using carbohydrate loading in endurance events.

Protein, unlike carbohydrate and fat, is not a major source of energy during exercise. Rather, it is important during growth and in tissue repair and replacement. At least one study has shown that a relatively low protein intake had no deleterious effect on performance. Other investigators recommend that protein intake should be increased with regular, prolonged heavy work, but this is not associated with the function of providing energy for muscular activity.[2]

Facilitating energy-yielding reactions

The biochemical reactions necessary for yielding the energy used in exercise depend on the vitamins for their activation. As explained earlier, vitamins serve as coenzymes that acitvate the enzymes, which in turn cause the energy-yielding reactions to occur. The vitamins of the B-complex group are believed to be especially important in this regard.

If one assumes that athlete's diet is well balanced, vitamin and mineral intake will be adequate. The rationale for vitamin supplementation is that some individuals might have borderline deficiencies or that additional vitamin intake might in some way "supercharge" the athletes. However, Van Itallie et al.[12] noted that Keys and co-workers, who made an extensive study of this possibility, were unable to discover any improvement in work capacity attributable to large daily supplementation of vitamins B, C, or E, either taken separately or in combination. Nor is there any evidence to suggest that the requirement for vitamins is appreciably increased during prolonged muscular work.

Recent evidence indicates, however, that a significant percentage of girls and women do not get enough iron in their daily diet and exhibit iron-deficiency anemia. The recommended dietary allowance for girls up to age 9 is 10 mg. per day and from age 10 on through the reproductive years is 18 mg.[13] Dietary surveys of the iron intake of women estimate an average intake of 11 to 12 mg. per day. Over a period of several years, this deficiency causes a depletion in the body's iron stores, eventually resulting in hemoglobin levels below the anemia borderline of 12 gm. per 100 ml. of blood.[8]

It has also been shown that strenuous exercise during the early phases of a conditioning program causes a temporary lowering of hemoglobin and plasma iron levels, probably because of an increased destruction of red blood cells. This condition has been termed "sports anemia."

Iron plays an essential role in the oxygen-transport mechanism of the body and lowered hemoglobin levels appear to affect oxygen-uptake capacity at strenuous workloads.

In view of the fact that many women are borderline anemic and that vigorous conditioning workouts also tend to temporarily increase an anemia, iron supplementation might be advised. For individuals whose dietary intake of iron is already adequate however and who are not anemic, further supplementation would be of no benefit.

Modifying biochemical causes of fatigue

The effect of certain alkalinizing substances on reducing fatigue or hastening recovery has been investigated. It was hypothesized that such agents might help neutralize the lactic acid that is produced during exercise, which is a main cause of fatigue. However, the ingestion of various phosphate and other buffering compounds has not been found to either prolong fatigue or shorten recovery. It is quite possible that these alkalis might have a detrimental effect on performance by interfering with the pH regulatory system of the blood.[2]

Maintaining optimal weight

If an athlete is overweight, a weight-reduction regimen prior to and during training will be to her advantage. Since the energy cost of activity is proportional to body weight in most athletic events, the overweight person expends more energy and burns more of her body reserves to accomplish the same amount of work than she would at her optimal weight.[2] As a consequence, because of this loss of efficiency, she is more prone to fatigue than she otherwise would be. Also, because of her greater mass, she has greater inertia to overcome in initiating and stopping movements. Since her strength is basically the same as it was before the fat gain, she will lose speed, and power because of her greater inertia. A third problem that excessive adiposity creates for the athlete is that it may well predispose her to injury, since she has slightly more difficulty in controlling her body in jumping and landing and in starting and stopping. Subcutaneous skinfold measures are recommended as the best available norms in determining the need to lose weight. Guidelines for weight reduction are discussed earlier in this chapter.

Frequency of eating

Some studies have shown work output to be improved by keeping the caloric intake constant but increasing the number of meals eaten. This finding has not been supported by other investigators; in some cases, improvements in performance were attributed to psychological rather than physiological factors.

Several investigators have found that substituting black coffee for breakfast resulted in the failure of blood glucose levels to rise and was followed by a gradual decrease in glucose (blood sugar) levels during the ensuing 3-hour period. The running times of a group of Muslim athletes were better during religious periods in which three meals were eaten daily, in contrast to another religious period during which they ate only two meals daily.

Generally, findings suggest that athletes should have at least three meals a day and perhaps more frequent lighter meals. This would be particularly true if the training periods are of long duration.[2]

The pre-event meal

Some basic guidelines for selecting the best foods for the pre-event meal as well as deciding when it should be eaten include the following:

1. Digestion should be fairly well completed by game time; the food should have already passed through the stomach and most of the small intestine. In this way the energy that was consumed has been absorbed by the body and is available for use. The circulatory system is not compromised by having to serve the needs of both digestion and strenuous exercise; hence circulation during performance will be more effective. Any tendency that a player might have toward nausea and gastric upset caused by pregame tension is also minimized. Selecting foods that are quickly digestible and eating at least several hours prior to game time help accomplish this goal. Fat intake such as fried and greasy foods should be reduced since this delays gastric emptying. Also, gas-producing foods such as salads, oils, and spices should be avoided. A meal that is high in carbohydrates is easily absorbed and provides the primary and most efficient source of energy when oxidized.

2. Proteins should be avoided because of their residue of fixed acids that can be excreted only through the kidneys. The renal shutdown that occurs during exercise prevents the kidneys from ridding the body of these acid wastes. These, combined with metabolic acidosis of endurance exercise, can contribute to an acid-base imbalance, resulting in fatigue. Consequently, meat, eggs, and fish should be excluded from this meal.[5]

3. Liquids are important in the pre-event meal to replace the anticipated water loss during exercise, but milk and fruit juices should be avoided because of

the fat content. The anticipated salt loss of the body can ordinarily be met by the normal salting of food according to taste.

4. The common practice of tapering off workouts 2 days prior to competition is consistent with pre-event nutritional chemistry. Tapering off workouts allows the body to replenish glycogen stores, which is especially important in endurance events.

Role of coach regarding nutritional practices

The coach is in an excellent position to provide her athletes with a sound understanding of good nutritional practices. Educating athletes about the importance of good nutrition as it relates to health and performance is particularly important in light of the usually poor dietary habits of teen-agers. The coach can also offer sound advice regarding the dubious value of expensive food supplements and other dietary fads.

REFERENCES

 1. A guide to good eating, Chicago, 1964, National Dairy Council.
 2. Bullen, B., Mayer, J., and Stare, F. J.: Athletics and nutrition, Am. J. Surg. **98:**343, 1959.
 3. de Vries, H. A.: Physiology of exercise for physical education and athletics, ed. 2, Dubuque, Iowa, 1974, William C. Brown Co., Publisher.
 4. Food for us all. The yearbook of agriculture, 1969, Washington, D.C., 1969, U.S. Government Printing Office.
 5. Guild, W. R.: Pre-event nutrition, with some implications for endurance athletes. In Exercise and fitness, Chicago, 1960, The Athletic Institute, Merchandise Mart, room 805.
 6. Guthrie, H. A.: Introductory nutrition, ed. 3, St. Louis, 1975, The C. V. Mosby Co.
 7. Gwinup, G.: Energetics, New York, 1970, Bantam Books, Inc.
 8. Haynes, E. M.: Iron deficiency and the active woman, Division for Girls' and Women's Sports Research Reports, vol. II, 1973, American Association for Health, Physical Education and Recreation.
 9. Mayer, J.: Exercise and weight control. In Exercise and fitness, Chicago, 1960, The Athletic Institute, Merchandise Mart, room 805.
10. Mayer, J.: Overweight: causes, cost, and control, Englewood Cliffs, N.J., 1968, Prentice-Hall, Inc.
11. Obesity and health, Washington, D.C., 1966, U.S. Department of Health, Education, and Welfare.
12. Van Itallie, T. B., Sinisterra, L., and Stare, F. J.: Nutrition and athletic performance, J.A.M.A. **162:**1120, 1956.
13. Williams, S. R.: Nutrition and diet therapy, ed. 2, St. Louis, 1973, The C. V. Mosby Co.

15 □ Ergogenic aids—facts and fallacies

Ergogenic aids consist of a variety of substances that purportedly enhance an individual's physical capacities or performance. Over the centuries man has explored the use of literally hundreds of these substances in an attempt to identify those that might increase his physical prowess over his enemies or, in more modern times, afford him an advantage over his opponents in athletic contests. An unfortunate characteristic of contemporary culture is the undue importance placed on winning in competitive sports. To lose is to fail and fail completely, even if the loser has played well. The fact that the athlete may have exerted her best efforts in striving for excellence, and probably excelled her opponent during some moments of the contest, is given little attention by spectators and many coaches as well. It is no wonder that the athlete, too, becomes imbued with the idea that winning is the *only* value to accrue from competition. Under this pressure she is highly tempted to try almost any substance, method, or device that will enable her to surpass her opponents. Consequently, today's athlete is extremely vulnerable to the many claims made in behalf of ergogenic aids, despite the fact that the work-enhancing properties of many have not been substantiated and, indeed, may actually harm the athlete. Some of these ergogenic aids are classified as pharmacological agents, or drugs, whereas others consist of various vitamins and food substances.

PHARMACOLOGICAL AGENTS

Broadly defined, a drug is any chemical agent that affects living protoplasm. In modern medicine, drugs play an extremely important role in the treatment of illness and disease. Over the years a wide variety of drugs have been tried by athletes in an attempt to improve performance by increasing strength or speed, by delaying the onset of fatigue, or by hastening recovery from strenuous exercise.

Drug action

Most agents are highly selective in action, affecting a certain specific type of tissue or cell. For example, some drugs will influence the brain and spinal cord, whereas others might affect only kidney function. Much is still unknown regarding the exact mechanism by which drugs exert their influence. Certain drugs act directly on the target cells by inhibiting specific cellular enzymes. Others act in a more indirect manner. For instance, a substance may stimulate respiration by acting on the carotid chemoreceptors rather than on the medulla. With other drugs, the exact site of action is unknown. In any case, drugs are unable to impart new functions to cells or tissues; they can only act to stimulate or depress regular cellular activity.[8]

Variability. The effect that any drug exerts on its particular target tissues is influenced by a number of factors. Obviously the size of the dosage is important. Optimal dosage concentration can be influenced by the individual's age, weight, and sex, the time of administration (absorption is faster if the stomach is empty), method of administration (oral, injection, etc.), rate of excretion, and the drug's action in combination with other agents that the person may have taken.

Tolerance is another factor influencing drug action. With many drugs, tolerance is acquired from repeated dosages, requiring an increase in dosage to obtain the desired response. Continued usage of these drugs may lead to habituation and eventual addiction.

An individual may exhibit a hypersensitive or allergic reaction to a drug, which may have very serious results. Allergic reactions to penicillin is a common example. Obviously the use of a drug to which a person is hypersensitive would be contraindicated.

If subsequent doses of an agent are taken before previous doses have been inactivated or eliminated, a cumulative action of the drug may occur. Individuals can show considerable variation in response to the same dosage—some people are more sensitive or are allergic; others develop a tolerance more quickly; and cumulative effects can differ. Sex may also be a factor; women appear to be more susceptible to certain drugs.[8]

Problems in research

A number of problems confront the investigator who attempts to determine the effects of a particular drug on performance. A significant problem is that of controlling the dosage for individual subjects, since sensitivity and response to the same concentration of a drug is so variable.

Another problem is related to psychological variables. In some studies, athletes who were given placebos (an inert substance having no significant chemical action) improved their performance as much as those who had been given the actual drug! It would appear that the athlete's psyche influences his performance as much as the ingestion of active chemical agents. Many studies have been conducted without the use of placebos, with half of the subjects being administered the drug and the other half receiving neither drug nor placebo. In these situations, any improvements in performance demonstrated by those who had received the drug might be attributed to psychological influences alone rather than to the action of the drug.

Many investigations have been criticized for using too few subjects, unsound statistical treatment of data, and failure to control important variables. The findings of such investigations must be considered in light of these shortcomings.

Effect of drugs and other agents on performance

Amphetamine. Amphetamine is a sympathomimetic amine that causes physiological responses similar to those elicited by stimulation of adrenergic nerves of the autonomic nervous system. With administration of 10 to 30 mg., its action on the reticular formation results in wakefulness, excitability, euphoria, and a lessened sense of fatigue. Pharmacologists in general agree that the latter effect is purely subjective and attributable to the drug's action on the brain rather than any actual improvement in physiological capacity. Amphetamine has been used extensively in weight-reduction programs because of its ability to cause anorexia (loss of appetite) by its action on the hypothalamus.[16] In common jargon, amphetamines are referred to as "bennies," "dexies," "uppers," "pep pills," etc. and have unfortunately been used to a considerable extent by athletes of all ages and both sexes in an attempt to improve physical performance.

The drug's effect on the cardiovascular system varies. Blood pressure may be elevated or depressed and heart rate decreased, while cardiac output remains unchanged. It is of extreme importance to note that the drug may elicit cardiac arrhythmias, including extra systoles, tachycardia, bradycardia, and partial heart block. Cerebral blood flow and oxygen consumption are decreased.[8]

Individuals vary greatly in their responsiveness to amphetamine. Toxic doses (the concentration that causes undesirable reactions) vary widely, from as little as 30 mg. to as much as 500 mg. for a habitual user who has developed a considerable tolerance.[16] At least five cases of acute amphetamine poisoning, including one death, have been reported among athletes (Italian cyclists)[16] Pathological findings in experimental animals and human beings dying from amphetamine poisoning indicate extensive brain hemorrhage, with convulsions and coma preceding death. A number of deaths have been ascribed to excessive usage when athletes have forced themselves beyond their normal state of exhaustion.[29]

The effectiveness of amphetamine in improving athletic performance has not as yet been substantiated. Studies conducted during World War II indicated that amphetamine was useful in delaying fatigue on prolonged military marches. Some investigators have subsequently reported similar findings; other studies indicate amphetamine to be of little value in prolonging physical work prior to exhaustion.[7,11,24]

Evidence regarding amphetamine's action in improving swimming and running speed is also contradictory. Smith and Beecher[25] found swimming and running times to be improved by 1.16% and 4.39%, respectively. The swimmers' times under actual competitive conditions were also improved. But Karpovich[11] found amphetamine to be of no benefit in treadmill running, in swimming and running time trials, and in actual competition in specified track events. Neither has the use of amphetamines been clearly established in improving muscular strength, muscular endurance, reaction time, nor other basic motor capacities. Lovingood et al.[17] found reaction time to be significantly improved by amphetamine when compared to caffeine. However, Rasch et al.[20] found that neither reaction time nor movement time during a psychomotor task was affected by 20 mg. of amphetamine. It has been observed that athletes on amphetamines have the feeling that they are producing an outstanding physical performance, whereas in reality they are guilty of exercising poor judgment in game situations and are not playing up to their usual performance level.[14,29]

Amphetamine is considered a highly dangerous drug by both medical doctors and pharmacologists alike. The dangers lie in the elimination of warning signs of fatigue, the possibility of addiction with continued use, and undesirable circulatory effects, including collapse. Its use is not recommended unless under strict medical supervision.[8] In view of its doubtful ergogenic value and the obvious health risks attendant with its use, amphetamine should be emphatically rejected by the intelligent sportswoman.

Caffeine. Caffeine belongs to a group of substances known as xanthine derivatives, found in a large number of plants throughout the world, from which coffee, tea, and cocoa are produced. Caffeine is a powerful central nervous system stimulant that exerts its main effects upon the cerebral cortex, medulla, and spinal cord.[8] Even the moderate amounts of caffeine contained in a cup of tea or coffee can lessen the feeling of physical and mental fatigue and reduce drowsiness by its action on the cortex. The exact mechanism by which fatigue is allayed is not clearly understood, but it is generally believed that the individual's perception of fatigue is prevented by caffeine's action on the central nervous system, resulting in an increased capacity for work.

Caffeine acts directly on the heart muscle, increasing the strength of contractions. Increases of 14.8% in cardiac output and 19.1% in stroke volume, without tachycardia, have been reported, along with coronary vasodilatation.[8] It also functions as a diuretic and in large doses causes an increase in the rate and depth of breathing through its action on the medulla. Increases in the basal metabolic rate from 10% to 25% have been observed after ingestion of 0.5 gram of caffeine.

Several studies have shown that caffeine ingestion has increased an individual's work capacity on a bike ergometer and has hastened recovery. Performance in anaerobic sprint events was not affected, however.[13]

Toxic reactions can occur with doses exceeding 1 gram. Symptoms include insomnia, restlessness, muscular tension, increased respiratory rate, and tachycardia. Fortunately, no deaths from caffeine poisoning have been reported.

Tobacco. The many serious health hazards associated with the chronic use of tobacco have been clearly outlined by the Surgeon General's Advisory Committee on Smoking and Health.[27] Although nicotine is the most important pharmacological constituent of tobacco, this agent is rapidly changed in the body to relatively inactive substances of low toxicity. Consequently, the chronic toxicity of nicotine resulting from smoking is very low and probably does not represent an important health hazard. Rather, a group of hydrocarbons that make up the tobacco smoke tars appears to be the carcinogenic agent, and components of the gas phase of smoking have been shown to adversely affect the trachea and bronchi.[27]

Smoking causes changes in a variety of physiological parameters. The nicotine that is inhaled stimulates the secretion of adrenaline (epinephrine) and noradrenaline (norepinephrine), resulting in general vasoconstriction, increased heart rate, and increased respiration. The carbon monoxide content of the blood is much higher in smokers. The greater amount of hemoglobin in combination with carbon monoxide should result in a decreased oxygen-transport capacity, but this has not been substantiated. Smoking has been shown to impair performance on numerous tests of pulmonary function, including total lung capacity, maximum breathing capacity, diffusing capacity, and airway conductance.[15,18,30]

The results of several studies dealing with the effect of smoking on physical performance tests are contradictory. Some investigations have shown nonsmokers to excel smokers in swimming and cross-country running events; smokers scored higher in strength and muscular endurance on nonsmoking days.[4,26,28] On the other hand, Reeves and Morehouse[22] found that smoking appeared to have no deleterious effect on subjects taking a cardiovascular fitness test. In another study, smokers were found to be as equally responsive as nonsmokers to an 8-week endurance training program in swimming. No difference in the time trials was observed between the two groups either before, during, or after the training period.[19]

Apparently individuals differ greatly regarding the degree to which smoking affects their performances. Karpovich and Hale, as cited in Brown and Kenyon,[2] found that over one third of their subjects were tobacco sensitive, experiencing a significant decrease in cycling speed after smoking, whereas the performance of the other subjects was not affected.

In view of the serious health risks associated with smoking and the possibility that smoking may impair the performance of about 35% of the athletic population, girl and women athletes should be discouraged from this habit.

Androgenic anabolic steroids. The androgens, or anabolic steroids, comprise the male sex hormones, including testosterone. These steroids are responsible for the development of the secondary sex characteristics and the rapid growth and muscular development of the adolescent male. Androgens promote protein anabolism (the growth of new tissue, the greater part of which is probably muscle; however, other organs, noticeably the kidney, also gain weight).

Androgens promote skeletal growth by accelerating the growth of the epiphyseal cartilage. These hormones have proved helpful in children whose skeletal growth was retarded. However, dosages that are too high are cause premature closure of the epiphyses, with subsequent termination of bone growth.[8]

The anabolic steroids, for example, methandrostenolone (Dianabol), have enjoyed great popularity among male power-event athletes, including weight lifters, shot-putters, football players, and even middle-distance runners and hurdlers. These athletes wished to gain in size and strength and took steroids ostensibly for that purpose. In some instances, weight gains were achieved, but it is difficult indeed to assess such gains as to their properties—are they water, fat, or muscle? Gains in water or fat would impede performance. Those performance improvements noted have been attributed to psychological variables. However, the relatively few controlled studies dealing with the effects of androgens on physical performance do not provide substantiative evidence of their efficacy. Prolonged usage and excessive dosage may cause infertility, edema, jaundice from impaired liver function, and premature cessation of growth in young male athletes. Neither physicians nor scientists know the potential long-range effects of chronic steroid usage.

With women athletes, androgen therapy can be useful in the treatment of various menstrual disorders, including heavy functional uterine bleeding and dysmenorrhea. Injections of medroxyprogesterone acetate (Depo-Provera) in the early part of the cycle prevents the development of the endometrium and suppresses ovulation. Menstruation can also be delayed in this manner for approximately 4 weeks and possibly longer. The opposite effect, the inducement of menstrual flow, can be achieved by the administration of Norlestrin, an estrogen-progesterone oral contraceptive. Administration of 2.5 mg. of Norlestrin twice daily for 3 days usually induces flow within several days.[1] If an athlete's past records indicate that her performance during the premenstrual and menstrual phases of the cycle to be somewhat below par, as is the case with some individuals, she may wish to alter the timing of her cycle to avoid having a major competitive event coincide with her menstrual period. The athlete, coach, and physician mutually would need to establish careful guidelines to determine if such treatment is warranted.

Androgen will produce masculinization in the female if taken in concentrations generally exceeding 75 mg. per week. Side effects include hirsutism (excessive growth of hair), deepening of the voice, and acne.[8]

Oxygen inhalation. The sports world became extremely interested in oxygen as an ergogenic aid when Japanese swimmers first introduced its use during the 1932 Olympics and subsequently won many events.

The amount of oxygen available to the body for exercise is related to the partial pressure of oxygen in the environmental air. At high altitudes, total atmospheric pressure decreases, along with the partial pressure of oxygen and other gases. The opposite situation exists below sea level or when one is scuba diving. The amount of oxygen entering the capillaries in the lungs is dependent on the partial pressure. Oxygen is transported throughout the body in chemical combination with hemoglobin. At sea level the partial pressure of oxygen causes 97.5% of the hemoglobin to be saturated with oxygen. Consequently, breathing pure oxygen or oxygen-rich mixtures (oxygen with higher partial pressure) can increase oxyhemoglobin transport capacity by only 2.5%. However, the higher partial pressure of oxygen increases the amount of oxygen that goes into *solution* in the blood (not combined with hemoglobin), thereby contributing to an increase in blood oxygen by as much as 11%.[1]

The oxygen-storing capacity of the body is minimal. When an individual is resting, the volume of oxygen in solution or in chemical combination would be depleted in 4 minutes and would be used even faster when one is exercising. A limited amount of work can be performed utilizing anaerobic energy pathways, but the body needs a constant, large supply of oxygen to exercise strenuously over an extended period of time.[16]

Improvements in breath-holding ability and swimming speed have been observed as a result of inhaling oxygen immediately prior to exercise. These improvements have been attributed to a reduction in the carbon dioxide levels (from hyperventilating of the oxygen) rather than to an increase in the oxygen intake or storage.[16]

The benefits of inhaling oxygen *during* endurance exercise are well documented. Bannister and Cunningham reported an increase in running time prior to exhaustion and less respiratory discomfort when oxygen was inspired while exercising was done.[2] Evidently the increased amount of oxygen in the blood in solution results in improved tissue oxygenation, thereby delaying the onset of anaerobic metabolism and minimizing lactic acid production. Also, breathing is easier, and the energy cost of breathing is reduced. Despite the benefits to be obtained from inspiring oxygen during endurance exercise, any practical application of this knowledge to actual competitive sports situations has not been recognized. (The success enjoyed by the Japanese swimmers in 1932 is more likely explained on the basis of improved form and technique rather than the inhalation of oxygen.)

Interestingly enough, the use of oxygen to hasten recovery has not been well substantiated. This fact has not stopped the practice by professional football teams and many other athletes, however.

The fact that the partial pressure of oxygen decreases with atmospheric pressure as one ascends to higher altitudes explains why performance in endurance events (but not sprints or other anaerobic type of events of short duration) will be impaired at high altitudes. As the partial pressure of oxygen drops, less oxygen enters the arterial capillaries, lowering the amount of oxygen available to the tissues. At altitudes above 18,000 feet, mountaineers must begin to make extensive use of oxygen-inhalation equipment for this reason. The athlete's aerobic work capacity, which is essential for endurance activities, also drops with increasing altitude. At an altitude of 7,500 feet (Denver, Colorado, and Mexico City), work capacity, in terms of maximum oxygen intake, is only 90% of that at sea level. At 13,700 feet (backpacking in the California High Sierras), work capacity is reduced by approximately 25%.[16] When a team must compete at an altitude to which it is not acclimated, performance decrements in endurance events must be anticipated. Such was the case in many of the distance events during the Olympic Games in Mexico City for both men and women athletes.

FOODS AND FOOD SUPPLEMENTS

Sugar. It is a common belief that candy, honey, or cane sugar ingested immediately prior to competing provides the athlete with "quick energy," enabling him to perform better. This is a false supposition. Even glucose, which is absorbed into the bloodstream somewhat faster than other sugars, requires approximately 15 minutes after ingestion before it can serve as an active energy source for the athlete. It is generally agreed that anaerobic events of short duration can be supplied by the body's normal glycogen stores. In long-distance marathon events a water or fruit-juice solution with glucose helps replenish the athlete's energy stores during the contest.

Salt. One of the body's mechanisms for maintaining thermal balance and ridding itself of excess body heat generated by strenuous exercise is the evaporation of perspiration. During practice sessions and competition, particularly in a hot environment, considerable water and salt loss will occur as the athlete perspires. It is essential that both substances be replenished to maintain a proper fluid and electrolyte balance. There is no physiological basis for the belief that athletes should not have fluids while practicing or competing; dehydration can be harmful and impair performance. In hot climates, excessive salt loss commonly results in heat cramps. Usually the salting of food to taste at mealtimes provides adequate replacement. If unusually hot weather is encountered, salt supplementation by means of salt tablets or salt solutions is indicated.

Gelatin. The rationale for the consumption of gelatin by athletes is that it could serve as an extra source of energy because of its chemical relationship to creatine. The role of creatine in the energetics of muscle contraction is well established. It was also hypothesized that gelatin (a protein obtained from the collagen derived from skin, connective tissue, and bones of animals) might be a good source of protein for muscle tissue development.

However, gelatin appears to be of little use as an ergogenic aid.[9,12] As a protein source, gelatin lacks several essential amino acids; even if completely utilized, it could not maintain nitrogen balance. Gelatins are receiving extensive clinical use, though, for their effectiveness in maintaining circulating blood volume after hemorrhage and in the treatment of shock.[8]

Vitamin supplementation. The importance of vitamins in the maintenance of health is well recognized. Vitamin deficiencies can induce fatigue, impair work capacity, and cause a variety of serious diseases. But there is general agreement among most authorities that in the absence of any vitamin deficiency the ingestion of vitamins in concentrations above normal metabolic requirements is of negligible ergogenic value. In case of a deficiency, vitamin supplements assist in raising physical performance to normal levels, but not beyond. Several studies cited by Ricci[23] substantiate this finding, as do Rasch et al.[21]

Furthermore, excessive administration of certain vitamins, notably A and D, can be toxic to the individual. An excess intake of vitamin A results in a toxic syndrome known as hypervitaminosis A or chronic vitamin A poisoning. The syndrome is characterized by subcutaneous swellings, usually in the forearms. These lesions are tender and painful, causing hyperirritability and limitation of motion, and are often accompanied by bone lesions as well. Treatment consists of withdrawal of the vitamin; most symptoms disappear within a week.[8]

The chronic administration of excessive amounts of vitamin D leads to a serious disorder of calcium metabolism known as hypervitaminosis D. This condition causes the mobilization of calcium from bone that calcifies in the body's soft tissues, notably the kidneys. Symptoms include weakness, fatigue, headache, nausea, diarrhea, and impaired kidney function. Treatment consists of withdrawal of the vitamin, a low-calcium diet, and generous fluid intake. Several months are ordinarily required for plasma calcium to fall back to normal and the calcium in the soft tissues to be mobilized. Renal function will also improve if kidney damage was not too severe.

Protein supplementation. A question frequently asked is, "Should the sportswoman increase her protein intake during training and competition so as to increase her strength and muscle bulk?" Protein supplementation is a recent sport fad. It has been shown that sports performance is not affected, either favorably or adversely, by protein deprivation or supplementation.[5,14,29] A normal diet provides adequate protein for the sportswoman's needs since protein is used principally for body growth, maintenance, and repair and not as an energy source. It is not metabolized in sufficient amounts during exercise to be of any benefit.

Carbohydrate loading. Recently, some athletes have been using carbohydrate (glycogen) loading through greatly increasing carbohydrate intake some 5 days before competition in the belief that this will provide additional energy that will greatly enhance performance. It has been shown that such loading is of little or no use unless the sustained activity is longer than 30 minutes' duration. Studies on marathon runners have indicated that such loading may be of some advantage in the second half of the race. Taking sweetened liquids during the latter half of the race seems to be of some advantage, but since the physiological evidence is debatable the apparent lift may well be purely psychological.[3,14] In a number of instances carbohydrate loading has resulted in dehydration.[3,10,29]

Blood reinjection. Early in the 1970s researchers indicated that by withdrawing about 500 to 1,200 ml. of blood from an athlete, storing it for a minimum of 3 weeks and then reinfusing either the whole blood, the red blood cells, or the plasma, back into the athlete resulted in a significant improvement in performance. Subsequent studies, however, have shown contradictory results.[6,31] Although such experimentation is interesting and has scientific merit, from the standpoint of sports, nonetheless, it must be considered not only impractical but certainly unethical as well. The attendant dangers of such procedures far outweigh any possible benefits.

MEDICAL-ETHICAL CONSIDERATIONS

It is obvious that many of the so-called ergogenic aids are, in fact, dangerous drugs whose use incurs significant health risks if taken without careful medical supervision. The masking of warning signs of fatigue and the risk of habituation by amphetamine and the possibility of kidney damage in hypervitaminosis D are excellent examples. Consideration of these factors alone would preclude their use. In addition, research thus far shows that most of these substances appear to be of little value in improving an athlete's performance capability.

The competitive situation offers the individual a unique opportunity to test her mental and physical abilities against those of others. Each match provides a multitude of opportunities to experience momentary instances of success and failure as the game unfolds, until the most successful opponent emerges as the ultimate winner of that particular game on that particular day.

But the personal challenge and opportunity to test oneself are lost if the individual resorts to artificial aids for competitive advantage. She is no longer presenting her real self to her opponent; she has lost the opportunity to test her real self, too, and in so doing has forfeited part of the essence and meaning of the competitive experience. She has become a "plastic athlete."

REFERENCES

1. Beatty, G.: Personal correspondence, 1972.
2. Brown, R. C., and Kenyou, G. S.: Classical studies in physical activity, Englewood Cliffs, N.J., 1968, Prentice-Hall, Inc.
3. Costill, D. L.: Innovations in athletic conditioning and sports medicine: nutrition for improved performance, Audiotape, Berkeley, Calif., 1973, University of California Extension Media Center.
4. Cureton, T. K.: Factors governing success in competitive swimming, Swimming Pool Data Ref. Ann. **4:**45, 1936.
5. Durnin, J. V.: The influence of nutrition, Proceedings of the International Symposium on Physical Activities and Cardiovascular Health, Can. Med. Assoc. J. **96:**715, 1967.
6. Ekblom, B., Goldberg, A. N., and Gullbring, B.: Response to exercise after blood loss and reinfusion, J. Appl. Physiol. **33:**175-80, 1972.
7. Golding, L. A., and Barnard, J. R.: The effect of *d*-amphetamine sulfate on physical performance, J. Sports Med. Phys. Fitness **3:**221, 1963.
8. Goodman, L. S., and Gilman, A.: The pharmacological basis of therapeutics, ed. 4, New York, 1971, The Macmillan Co.
9. Hilsendager, D., and Karpovich, P. V.: Ergogenic effect of glycine and niacin separately and in combination, Res. Q. Am. Assoc. Health, Phys. Educ. **35:**389, 1964.
10. Karlsson, J., and Saltin, B.: Diet, muscle glycogen, and endurance performance, J. Appl. Physiol. **31:**203, 1971.
11. Karpovich, P. V.: Effect of amphetamine sulphate on athletic performance, J.A.M.A. **170:**558, 1959.
12. Karpovich, P. V., and Pestrecov, K.: Effect of gelatin upon muscular work in man, Am. J. Physiol. **134:**300, 1941.
13. Karpovich, P. V., and Sinning, W. E.: Physiology of muscular activity, ed. 7, Philadelphia, 1971, W. B. Saunders Co.
14. Klafs, C. E., and Arnheim, D. D.: Modern principles of athletic training, St. Louis, 1977, The C. V. Mosby Co.

15. Krumholz, R. A., Chevalier, R. B., and Ross, J. C.: Cardiopulmonary function in young smokers, Ann. Intern. Med. **60:**603, 1964.
16. Larson, L. A.: Encyclopedia of sport science and medicine, New York, 1971, The Macmillan Co.
17. Lovingood, B. W., Blyth, C. S., Peacock, W. H., et al.: Effects of d-amphetamine sulfate, caffeine, and high temperature on human performance, Res. Q. Am. Assoc. Health Phys. Educ. **38:**64, 1967.
18. Nadel, J. A., and Comroe, J. H.: Acute effects of inhalation of cigarette smoke on airway conductance, J. Appl. Physiol. **16:**713, 1961.
19. Pleasants, F., Jr.: Pretraining and post-training swimming endurance of smokers and nonsmokers, Res. Q. Am. Assoc. Health Phys. Educ. **40:**779, 1969.
20. Rasch, P. J., Pierson, W. R., and Brubaker, M. L.: The effect of amphetamine sulfate and meprobamate on reaction time and movement time, Int. Z. Angew. Physiol. **18:**280, 1960.
21. Rasch, P. J., Klafs, C. E., and Arnheim, D. D.: Effects of vitamin C supplementation on cross country runners, Sportärztl. Praxis **1:**4, 1962.
22. Reeves, W. E., and Morehouse, L. E.: The acute effects of smoking upon the physical performance of habitual smokers, Res. Q. Am. Assoc. Health Phys. Educ. **21:**245, 1950.
23. Ricci, B.: Physiological basis of human performance, Philadelphia, 1970, Lea & Febiger.
24. Seashore, R. H., and Ivy, A. C.: The effects of analeptic drugs in relieving fatigue, Psychol. Monogr. **67:**365, 1953.
25. Smith, G. M., and Beecher, H. K.: Amphetamine sulphate and athletic performance, J.A.M.A. **170:**542, 1959.
26. Steinhaus, A. H., and Grundleman, F.: Tobacco and health, New York, 1948, Association Press (YMCA).
27. U.S. Department of Health, Education, and Welfare: Smoking and health, Washington, D.C., 1964, U.S. Government Printing Office.
28. Willgoose, C. E.: Tobacco smoking, strength, and muscular endurance, Res. Q. Am. Assoc. Health Phys. Educ. **18:**219, 1947.
29. Wilmore, J. H.: Athletic training and physical fitness, Boston, 1977, Allyn & Bacon, Inc.
30. Wilson, R. H., Meador, R. S., Jay, B. E., and Higgins, E.: The pulmonary pathologic physiology of persons who smoke cigarettes, N. Engl. J. Med. **262:**956, 1960.
31. Williams, M. H., Goodwin, A. R., Perkins, R., and Bocrie, J.: Effect of blood reinjection upon endurance capacity and heart rate, Med. Sci. Sports **5:**181, 1973.

Appendixes

A □ Suggested basic equipment for training room

Item	Quantity
Ankle wrap roller	1
Benches (16 or 18 inch)	1-2
Blankets	2-3
Crutches	1 pair
Flashlight (pencil type)	2
Forceps (tweezers)	2
Ice machine	1
Moist heat packs	
Cabinet	1
Packs	4-6
Nail clippers	1
Plinth (training table)	1
Razor (safety type with blades)	1
Reconditioning equipment	
Shoe weights (boots)	2 pairs
Body mats (4 by 6 feet)	4
Pulley weights (triplex)	1
Set of assorted weights	1
Safety pins	200
Scales (balance type preferred)	1
Scalpel	2
Scissors	
All purpose	1
Bandage	2
Surgical	1
Slings (triangular bandages)	3-5
Spine board	1
Splints (pneumatic)	1 set
Stretcher	1
Tape cutters	2
Treatment tables	2
Wheelchair	1
Whirlpool bath	1

B ☐ Training room supplies*

Item	Quantity
Adhesive tape	
½ inch	2 tubes
1 inch	3 tubes
1½ inch	10 tubes
2 inch	10 tubes
Aerosol (12 oz.) (fluoromethane)	5 spray cans
Ammonia ampules (100 to a box)	1 box
Analgesic balm	1 lb.
Ankle wraps (96 inches long)	5
Applicators, cotton-tipped	100
Aspirin tablets	500
Band-Aids (100 to a box; 1 by 3 inch)	1 box
Band-Aids (extra large)	1 box
Calamine lotion (4 oz.)	2 bottles
Cotton	
Nonsterile	4 lb.
Sterile	2 lb.
Elastic bandages	
3 inch	4 rolls
4 inch	4 rolls
Elastic tape (2 inch and 3 inch)	4 tubes ea. size
Felt (36 by 44 by ½ inch)	1 sheet
Flexible collodion (liquid or spray)	1 pint
Fluid electrolytes	—
Foam rubber (assorted)	3 sheets
Gauze	
1 inch	5 rolls
2 inch	5 rolls
3 inch	5 rolls
Germicides	
Alcohol	1 gal.
Hydrogen peroxide	1 pint
Merthiolate	1 pint
Nitrotan	1 pint
Heel and lace pads	5-10 ea.
Instant cold pack	5

*The suggested supplies should be adequate to handle most athletic programs. Experience will dictate increases or decreases in certain items and the addition of other items.

Item	Quantity
Medicated ointments	
Menthol (6 oz.)	1 tube
Zinc oxide (6 oz.)	1 tube
Overwrap	15 rolls
Paper cups	As needed
Petroleum jelly	5 lb.
Rubdown liniment (1 pint)	3 bottles
Salt tablets	500
Skin toughener (12 oz.)	6 aerosol cans
Sponge rubber	
36 by 44 by $1/8$ inch	1 sheet
36 by 44 by $1/4$ inch	1 sheet
Sterile Telfa pads (100 to a box)	1 box
Sterri-strips	1 box
Sun lotion (4 oz.)	4 bottles
Tape adherent (clear spray, 12 oz. cans)	5 cans
Tape remover	1 gal.
Tongue depressors	500
Underwrap (for taping)	15 rolls

C □ Suggested supplies and equipment for a basic training kit

Item	Quantity
Adhesive tape	
½ inch	2 rolls
1 inch	2 rolls
1½ inch	2 rolls
2 inch	2 rolls
Air splint	1
Alcohol (4 oz.)	1 bottle
Ammonia ampules	5
Analgesic balm (4 oz.)	2 tubes
Ankle wraps	2
Antiseptic powder (4 oz.)	1 can
Antiseptic soap (4 oz.)	1 bar
Aspirin tablets	100
Band-Aids (1 by 3 inch)	2 dozen
Butterfly bandages (or Sterri-strips)	
Medium	1 dozen
Small	1 dozen
Cotton, sterile (4 oz.)	1 roll
Cotton-tipped applicators	100
Elastic bandages	
3 inch	1 roll
4 inch	1 roll
6 inch	1 roll
Elastic tape (3 inch)	1 roll
Eyewash and cup (4 oz.)	1 bottle
Felt	
¼ by 6 by 6 inch	1 sheet
½ by 6 by 6 inch	1 sheet
Flexible collodion	1 pint
Foot powder (4 oz.)	1 can
Gauze (2 inch)	1 roll
Germicide (4 oz.)	1 bottle
Instant cold pack	2
Kaopectate	1 bottle
Liniment	1 pint
Maalox tablets	100
Medicated ointment (1 to 3 oz.)	1 tube

Item	Quantity
Moleskin (12 inch)	2 rolls
Ophthalmic irrigating solution	1 bottle
Safety pins (assorted)	1 dozen
Salt tablets	100
Scalpel	2
Skin lubricant	1 tube
Sponge rubber	
⅛ by 6 by 6 inch	1 sheet
¼ by 6 by 6 inch	1 sheet
Sterile Telfa pads (2 by 3 inch)	1 box (12)
Sun lotion (4 oz.)	1 bottle
Surgical scissors	1
Tampons (for bloody nose)	1 box
Tape adherent (12 oz.)	1 can
Tape remover	4 oz.
Tape scissors	1
Thermometer, oral, with case	1
Tongue depressors	50
Triangular bandages	2
Tweezers	1
Underwrap	1 roll
Waterproof tape (1 inch)	1 roll

Glossary

acid-base balance Relationship of acid-forming and base-forming elements of the body.

acute Indicating severe symptoms of brief duration.

adenosine triphosphate (ATP) A high-energy phosphate compound stored in muscle; breakage of the phosphate bond releases energy for muscle contraction and other cellular functions.

adiposity Fat or fatty.

aerobic Requiring the presence of oxygen; prime energy source for endurance events.

amphetamine Sympathomimetic drug that stimulates the central nervous system.

anaerobic Nonoxidative, not requiring free oxygen; opposite of aerobic.

androgen Substance such as testosterone that produces or stimulates male characteristics.

anemia Inadequate amount of red blood cells or hemoglobin, or both.

anorexia Lack or loss of appetite; aversion to food.

antiseptic Method or substance that protects against the growth of pathogens.

astringent Constrictive, contracting, or styptic in nature.

atrophy Wasting or withering of the body or any of its parts.

auscultation Process of listening for sounds in the body to judge or detect an abnormal condition.

Barr body A mass of chromatin located at the periphery of the nucleus that is present in normal females but is not present in normal males; sex chromatin.

basal metabolism (BMR, basal metabolic rate) Energy metabolism, measured 14 to 18 hours after food intake and under conditions of absolute rest; minimum of energy needed to carry on the body processes vital to life.

bradycardia Slow heartbeat, usually 60 beats per minute or less.

buccal Pertaining to the mouth or cheek.

buffering Process by which body seeks to maintain internal homeostasis or balance of its fluids, that is, their degree of acidity and alkalinity.

caffeine An alkaloid found in coffee, tea, cola beverages, and maté; a stimulant to the heart and central nervous system.

calcification Conversion into a bony substance by the deposition of lime salts in the tissues and commonly in bone.

calorie, large The amount of heat required to raise the temperature of 1 kg. of water 1° C.; used as a measure of the energy value of food.

capsule, joint Membranous or ligamentous covering of a joint; it is lined with synovial membrane.

carbohydrate A compound composed of carbon, hydrogen, and oxygen; starches and sugars.

cartilage Touch, elastic connective tissue.

chromatin Substance present in the nucleus of a cell, readily stainable, and considered to be the physical basis of heredity.

chromosome Microscopic rod-shaped body into which the chromatin of the cell nucleus divides during cell division and in which the genes are located.

chronic Continuing over a long period of time; opposite of acute.

chylomicron Small particle of fat found in the blood after digestion and absorption of fat.

coenzyme An enzyme, usually containing a vitamin, that activates or combines with another enzyme to activate a biochemical reaction.

collagenous Referring to connective tissue.

core temperature Internal body temperature, usually measured rectally; about 1° F. higher than oral temperature.

creatinine coefficient Obtained by dividing the total milligrams of creatinine in a day's output of urine by the body weight in kilograms.

crepitus Grating sound produced by the contact of the fractured ends of bones.

débride (débridement) Treating a wound by the removal of all debris and foreign matter and the excision of all devitalized tissue encompassing it. (Pronounced day-*breed*, day-breed-*maw*.)

diastolic Referring to the relaxation phase of ventricles after contraction (systole); in blood pressure readings, the lower figure represents the pressure reading for the diastolic phase.

digestion Process of converting food into substances that the body can assimilate.

dysmenorrhea Painful menstruation.

edema Swelling caused by collection of fluid in the connective tissues.

endurance Ability to sustain vigorous activity for a prolonged period of time prior to the onset of fatigue and to recover rapidly.

enzyme Complex organic substance originating from living cells that acts as a catalyst in certain chemical changes; a digestive enzyme.

epiphysis A secondary ossification center at the end of the long bones (a growth center); bony growth ceases with ossification of the epiphyseal cartilage.

ergometer Apparatus for measuring the work done by an individual or an animal; most common are the treadmill and the bicycle, the latter employing a resistive component, usually friction, against which the subject pedals.

erythrocyte Red blood cell formed in the bone marrow that contains hemoglobin and transports oxygen to all body tissues.

estrogen Hormone produced by the ovarian follicle and other structures that is responsible for the development of secondary sexual characteristics and the cyclic changes in the vaginal epithelium and the uterine endothelium; can also be produced artificially.

extravasation Escape of a fluid from its vessels into the surrounding tissues.

exudate Fluid or matter that penetrates through vessel walls into adjoining tissue; the oozing of serum or pus.

fatigue Temporary diminution of the ability of the body to work.

flexibility Range of motion at the joints; the ability to move the trunk and limbs with ease.

gangrene Death or rotting of tissue caused by circulatory failure from injury, disease, infection, etc.

glucose Dextrose, a monosaccharide; the most important carbohydrate in the body; blood sugar.

glycerol Glycerin; an alcohol consisting of a clear, colorless syrupy liquid having a sweet taste, which can combine with fatty acids to form fat.

glycine Aminoacetic acid; found in abundance in gelatin and other proteins.

glycogen Type of polysaccharide, often called "animal starch"; the form in which carbohydrate is stored in the body for future conversion into sugar and for subsequent use in work or the liberation of heat.

glycolysis Transformation of glycogen to lactic acid during muscle contraction.

hemoglobin Iron-containing protein that is the oxygen-carrying pigment in the red blood cells.

hemopoietic Pertaining to the formation of red blood cells.

hormone Chemical substance produced by an endocrine gland and transported by the blood or other body fluids to its target area; greatly influences the functions of specific organs and of the body as a whole.

hyperextension Extension of a joint beyond straight alignment.

hyperhidrosis Excessive sweating.

hyperventilation Abnormal breathing that is deep and prolonged.

hypervitaminosis Condition in which an excess level of a vitamin in the blood or tissues causes undesirable symptoms.

ingesta Substances that are consumed such as food and drink.

ischemia Lack of blood supply to a part of the body. (Pronounced iss-*kee*-mee-a.)

isometric Pertaining to a contraction wherein the tension of the muscle is altered and heat is produced but the muscle does not shorten.

isotonic Pertaining to a contraction in which the muscle shortens against resistance, thus performing visible work.

lactic acid By-product of muscle contraction that produces fatigue and pain in the muscle; it evolves by glycolysis.

lean body mass Protoplasmic mass of the body, exclusive of the body fat.

lipids A broad term for fats and fatlike substances; characterized by the presence of one or more fatty acids; includes fats, cholesterol, lecithins, phospholipids, and similar substances that do not mix readily with water.

malleolus Rounded process such as the projection on either side of the ankle joint.

menarche Onset of menstruation, usually between the ages of 10 and 17 years.

metabolism All the chemical changes taking place in the body from the time nutrients are absorbed and built into protoplasm (anabolism) or excreted and the release of energy in breaking down protoplasm (catabolism).

metabolites Substances produced by metabolism, usually acidic.

microtrauma Small injuries usually incurred over a considerable span of time that have a cumulative effect resulting in a chronic condition.

morbidity Rate of disease or the proportion of diseased persons in a community.

myositis Inflammation of muscle tissue.

nicotine Alkaloid derived from tobacco.

nutrient Substance that provides nourishment.

obesity Excessive storage of fat attributable to a prolonged positive energy balance.

ossification Formation of bone.

overload Principle involved in attaining improved physical performance whereby the function improves only when the system involved is challenged by a work load greater than that to which it is usually accustomed; any exercise that exceeds in intensity or duration the demands regularly made on the organism.

oxidation Combination with oxygen or the removal of hydrogen.

palpation Examination of the surface of the body using the hands.

parameter A constant whose values determine the operation or characteristics of a system.

periodicity Recurrence of the menses.

periosteum Fibrous sheath surrounding bone.

phenotype Genetic physical appearance or make-up of an individual as developed through environmental influences.

pituitary gland Gland in the lower part of the brain that produces numerous hormones that regulate the growth of body tissues and the action of other endocrine glands, including the thyroid, pancreas, adrenals, and gonads.

placebo Medicine given merely to please the patient; in research, an innocuous pill or capsule given a subject to aid in eliminating psychological variables.

post partum After childbirth.

PRE Progressive resistance exercises.

pronation Turning the hand so that the palm faces downward or backward.

protein Constituent of every living cell; complex substances comprised of many amino acids; necessary for growth of new cells and tissues.

puberty Phase during which an individual becomes physiologically capable of reproduction.

reaction time Speed with which an individual reacts to a stimulus.

RM Repetitions maximum.

satiety Cessation of desire for further food intake,; fullness.

self-realization Full development of one's potential abilities or of one's personality.

shell temperature Temperature of the external surface of the body.

somatotype Body type.

strength Capacity of muscles to exert force or their ability to do work against a resistance.

subcutaneous Beneath the skin.

supination Rotation of the forearm so that the palm is up; rotation of the leg and foot outward.

syndrome Group of symptoms or conditions that characterize a deficiency or a disease.

systolic Pertaining to the heart, particularly the contraction phase of the ventricles; in blood pressure readings the upper figure represents the pressure reading for the systolic phase.

tachycardia Abnormally fast heartbeat.

tonic Pertaining to or characterized by muscular tension.

tonicity Normal tension of muscle fibers at rest.

tonus (tonicity) Constant partial or mild contraction of muscle; *see also* tonic.

torque Force that causes twisting or rotation.

toxicity Quality or quantity of a substance that produces undesirable effects.

trauma Wound or injury; can be physical or psychological in response.

vascularization Blood supply to an area; the development of new blood vessels in a structure or area.

ventilation Alternate intake and expulsion of air by the lungs to oxygenate the blood and remove carbon dioxide and water; breathing.

vitamin Organic food compound occurring in small amounts in many foods; essential for normal functioning of the body.

Index*

A

Abdomen, 16
Abdominal curls, 287-288
Abductors
  hip, 142, 285
  scapular, 139
  shoulder, 135
Abrasions, 233, 234t
Absorption of shock, shoes for, 204
Accident report form, 52-53
Acids, amino, 294
Action of drugs, 306-307
Active exercises, 282
Active-assistive exercises, 282
Activity
  energy for, daily needs of, 297t
  during menstruation, 244
  physical, effect on pregnancy, childbirth, and
      postpartum period, 39-40
Acute injuries, 233-242
Adaptation, heat, 30
Adductors
  hip, 143, 285-186
  hip-thigh, 158
  scapular, 140
  shoulder, 136
Adequate conditioning, role of, 228-229
Adhesive tape
  removal, 266
  strapping, 254-266
Adipose tissue, 29, 30
Adiposity, 17
  excessive, 303-304
Adolescence, nutritional needs and habits during,
    299
Aerobic capacity, 85, *86,* 100
  exercises, 104
    for badminton, 162t
    for diving, 166
    for gymnastics, 168
    for javelin throw, 190
    for shot put, 193
    for softball, 181
    for tennis, 179
    for volleyball, 196
Aerobic components in sports, 99t
Aerobic power, maximum, 28-29
Age, 36
Agility, 85
Aids, ergogenic, 306-315
  medical-ethical considerations of, 314

*Page numbers in italics refer to illustrations; numbers
followed by *t* refer to tables.

328

Airway obstructions, emergency management of,
    270t, 273-274
  use of Heimlich maneuver, 274
Albrecht, Siga, 172, *173,* 175
Allergies, 51-52
Altitude, 37
Amino acids, 294
Amphetamine, 307-308
Anabolic steroids, androgenic, 310-311
Anaerobic capacity, 85, 87, 100
  exercises, 104, 108
    for badminton, 162t-163t
    for shot put, 193
    for volleyball, 196
Anaerobic components in sports, 99t
Anatomic sex differences, 15-19
  implications for performance, 15-19
Anatomy of running shoe, 205
Ancient Greece, 3-5
  games, 4-5
Androgenic anabolic steroids, 310-311
Anemia, sports, 303
Ankle
  and foot spica bandage, 251, *252*
  injuries, 213, 215
  joints, testing, 62
Ankle extensors, 159
Ankle flexors, 160
Ankle wrap, cloth, 253-254
Annual Catalina Classic, 175
Annual Seal Beach Rough Water Swim, 175
Anorexia, 307
Anterior shoulder, 148
  partner's, 146, *147*
  stretch, 290
Anterior trunk stretch, 290
Anthropometric characteristics, 15-23
  relation of injury to, 211-218
Appraisal, fitness, 51-62
Archer, Susan, 168
Arm crossover, 287
Arm
  rotations, 191
  sling
    cervical, 248
    shoulder, 249
  sprints, 126
Arnheim technique of knee strapping, 256-258
Arrhythmias, cardiac, 308
Arterial hemorrhage, 237t
  emergency management, 269t, 272
Arthritis, 211
Asceticism, 5